Apes, Language, and the Human Mind

APES, LANGUAGE, *and the* HUMAN MIND

Sue Savage-Rumbaugh
Stuart G. Shanker
Talbot J. Taylor

New York   Oxford   •   Oxford University Press   1998

Oxford University Press

Oxford New York
Athens Auckland Bangkok Bogota Bombay
Buenos Aires Calcutta Cape Town Dar es Salaam
Delhi Florence Hong Kong Istanbul Karachi
Kuala Lumpur Madras Madrid Melbourne
Mexico City Nairobi Paris Singapore
Taipei Tokyo Toronto Warsaw

and associated companies in

Berlin Ibadan

Published by Oxford University Press, Inc.
198 Madison Avenue, New York, NY 10016

Oxford is a registered trademark of Oxford University Press

Library of Congress Cataloging-in -Publication
Savage-Rumbaugh, E. Sue, 1946–
Apes, language, and the human mind / by Sue Savage-Rumbaugh,
Stuart G. Shanker, Talbot J. Taylor.
p.   cm.
Includes bibliographical references (p.   ) and index.
ISBN 0–19–510986–4
1. Bonobo—Psychology. 2. Kanzi (Bonobo) 3. Human-animal
communication, 4. Language acquisition. 5. Neurolinguistics,
I. Shanker, Stuart. II. Taylor, Talbot J. III. Title.
QL737,P96S254 1998

599.885159'4—dc21   98–14600

1 3 5 7 9 8 6 4 2

Printed in the United States of America
on acid free paper

Preface

For more than twenty years, Sue Savage-Rumbaugh has been studying, and attempting to cultivate, the linguistic and cognitive skills of a number of laboratory-reared primates. Recently, her work with a bonobo (*Pan paniscus*) named Kanzi has been widely acknowledged as having achieved a scientific breakthrough. Kanzi has been shown (Savage-Rumbaugh 1988, 1991; Savage-Rumbaugh et al. 1993) to have acquired linguistic and cognitive skills far beyond those achieved by any other nonhuman animal in previous research. Most notably, Kanzi has proven himself capable of comprehending spoken English utterances of a grammatical and semantic complexity equal to (and in some cases surpassing) that mastered by a normal two-and-a-half-year-old human child.

Not surprisingly, the Kanzi research has led beyond empirical findings to conceptual and theoretical insights as well. Taken together, these insights argue for a radical revision of the philosophical foundations underlying linguistic and cognitive research. The authors' motivation in writing this book lies in our shared belief that the Kanzi research presents a serious and effective challenge not only to scientific thinking about the cognitive and communicational capacities of nonhuman primates, but also to received knowledge concerning the possession of those capacities by humans. At the very least, we feel that the results of this research oblige us to reconsider "what we thought we knew" about the nature of communication and its relation to cognition. What is promised is a complete shift on how communication and cognition are seen—and understood.

Even more significant, and certainly more disorienting, is the light the Kanzi research sheds on the *methods* by which we obtain those facts and express that knowledge. That is, this research raises serious problems for our forms of scientific representation, in that it issues an unavoidable challenge to the methods by which we talk about, represent to ourselves and to others, make sense of, and evaluate abilities and behavior: not only those of primates, but of humans as well. In particular, it questions the *epistemological conception*, the dominant form of representation under which most contemporary theorizing labors. When the implications of the Kanzi research have been fully assimilated, the way we look at, understand, and represent the relationships between language, cognition, and behavior will no longer be the same.

The book is divided into two parts. Although the main goal of this book is to analyze the theoretical and philosophical implications of the Kanzi research, it opens with a detailed, personal narrative, by Savage-Rumbaugh, of Kanzi's infancy and youth (part I). Having read this chronicle, readers previously unfamiliar with these details will be much better placed to understand and evaluate the theoretical and philosophical arguments that follow. At this point, the book shifts from a narrative to an analytical mode. The three analytical chapters of part II then discuss, from a critical perspective, the theoretical, conceptual, and methodological issues raised by the Kanzi research. The topics raised in part II may be grouped under three general headings:

1. The philosophy of mind and language: the challenge presented by the Kanzi research to the Cartesian foundations of modern cognitive science (chapter 2).
2. The methodological rhetoric of cognitive-communicational inquiry: what must be done to place ape and human studies on an unbiased (that is, scientific) footing (chapter 3).
3. New perspectives: the view afforded by a cognitive-communicational inquiry that is free from Cartesian presuppositions and from the rhetorical opposition of "skepticism" and "anthropomorphism" (chapter 4).

Our book is the textual fruit of a three-way conversation that spanned more than three years. Although we have met together a number of times in various locales, much of this long conversation has been pursued, as is now common practice, by e-mail and fax. And, of course, draft after draft of each chapter was passed back and forth between us and was commented on, revised, recommented on, revised yet again, and so on. The end product is a text that we feel is most appropriately characterized as a single multivoiced book. Each of us contributed to the stage-by-stage production of every chapter, and we all stand collectively behind the whole of the book's argument.

However, anyone who knows our previous publications will recognize each chapter's initial author. As Savage-Rumbaugh is the only one to have had the first-hand experience of Kanzi's development from newborn to fully grown adult bonobo, no one will be amazed to hear that it is from her pen (or rather, her computer) that chapter 1 originated. Stuart Shanker is the obvious source of chapter 2, as Talbot Taylor of chapter 3, and Savage-Rumbaugh again of chapter 4. However, for each chapter—with the exception of the first—it would be exceedingly hard, even for us, to determine whose ideas, whose arguments, whose rhetorical strategies, whose forms of expression are whose. Therefore, we offer the book under joint authorship. We do so, further, in order to express our collective conviction that the study of cognition and communication—whether of human or nonhuman primates—*requires* just such a dialogic, interdisciplinary, cooperative methodology. Only in this way can a greater understanding come within our reach.

We hope the chapters that follow will clarify the reasons motivating that conviction and inspire others to do the same.

We would like to express our gratitude to many who, by one means or another, have contributed to our collaboration, to our research, and to the production of this book. At the head of this list, naturally and deservedly, are our spouses—Duane, Virginia, and Rosie. To them we give our most heartfelt thanks for their support, love, encouragement, and . . . indulgence. But one of these, Duane Rumbaugh, has provided even more, for he is the founder and director of the Language Research Center. His intellectual input to the work discussed herein has been central throughout its development. He has, on the one hand, been the ever-present "invisible critic" of this research, as well as a constant stimulus to push deeper into the frontiers of the mind. The staff of the Language Research Center has made the work there possible and contributed in ways that are rich with immediate meaning to all that the apes have shown us. We would like to express our gratitude to Mikel Baron, Karen Brakke, Esambo Botamba, Mary Chapelo, Sherry Elrod, Bill Hopkins, John Kelley, Heidi Lynn, Linda McGarra, Elisabeth Pugh, Dan Rice, Sara Root, and Shelly Williams for their constant care and interaction with the apes and for their important input to the research discussed in these pages.

Many friends and colleagues have assisted us in various ways. We note in particular Elizabeth Bates, Alexandra Bourque, Jerome Bruner, Jack Canfield, Casey Cornelius, Jeff Coulter, Patricia Greenfield, Suzanne MacDonald, Charles Menzel, David Olson, Ed Reed, Michael Tomasello, Nick Toth, Russ Tuttle, Andy Whiten, and Steven Wise. To one colleague in particular, Barbara J. King, at the College of William and Mary, we owe a special expression of thanks; without her expert, enthusiastic, and yet always patient tutelage, two of the authors would never have begun work in this field, and so this book would never have been written. She should know how grateful we are for her guidance and friendship.

We also would like to express our appreciation to the various foundations, institutions, and individuals whose generous support was essential to the completion of our research: the National Institute for Child Health and Development (grant HD 06016), the Social Sciences and Humanities Research Council of Canada, the John S. Guggenheim Memorial Foundation, the National Endowment for the Humanities, the College of Arts and Science of Georgia State University, Atkinson College, York University, the College of William and Mary, and Mrs. Louise G. T. Cooley.

And, of course, we owe much—in the case of the present book, perhaps all—to those whose sympathy and understanding made it all possible: Lana, Sherman, Austin, Mercury, Panzee, Kanzi, Panbanisha, Matata, Mulika, Neema, and Tamuli.

E. S. S-R
S. G. S.
T. J. T
November 1997

Contents

PART I

ENTRY INTO LANGUAGE

CHAPTER 1

Bringing up Kanzi

Kanzi came to the Georgia State University Language Research Center in Atlanta, Georgia, in 1980 with his mother, Matata, when he was just six months old, but his story really starts even before he was born. Matata arrived in Atlanta in 1975, the same year I did. I had elected to come, because I knew bonobos were in Atlanta. Matata came because she was netted, placed in a helicopter, and flown here. I came from Norman, Oklahoma, where I had been studying Washoe, Lucy, Booee, and Bruno—apes who were being taught sign language. Matata came from Zaire (now known as the Congo), the only place in the world where bonobos occur in nature.

In 1975, hardly anyone knew what a bonobo was. Zoos still confused them with chimpanzees, housing both groups together as "racial variants" of the same species. Dr. Kano of Japan was just starting his studies of wild bonobos in Zaire, but he had begun to learn some intriguing things: Bonobo social groups are very stable compared to the fluid and dynamic gatherings of common chimpanzees. Moreover, they are often large and composed of nearly equal numbers of males and females. The males are unusually passive, and in all groups there are close bonds between the sexes.

In contrast, chimpanzee males are domineering and aggressive. Common chimpanzee traveling parties consisted of only a few individuals, and bonds between the sexes are close only for a few days each month when females are sexually receptive.

Bonobo females are nearly always sexually receptive, and they form close friendships with males and with other females. Most surprising is the low level of aggression among bonobos. They prefer making love to making war, and are, by human standards, quite adept and profligate in their sexual endeavors. The all-male war parties and the infanticide that occasionally characterize the social contract of common chimpanzees are absent in the bonobo.

Bonobos hold a special fascination for primatologists because of the way their entire social organization pivots around sexual behavior. If they were a primitive and only recently discovered human society, we would be compelled to say that their groups are held together by love, expressed in a most direct and physical manner, between all individuals, regardless of age or sex. Human sexual behavior, widely touted among the animal kingdom for its variety and its frequent nature, is overshadowed by the bonobo. Unlike ourselves, bonobos do not recognize that sexual behavior is linked to the birth of offspring and all its consequent responsibilities. Therefore, they have no need to define kinship and its attendant duties and regulations. Sexual behavior is something that is freely enjoyed, without consequence, by all group members. Just as we hug each other in happiness and excitement, to make up after an argument, to seal an agreement, or to welcome someone back, so does the bonobo, except their hugs often include sexual contact, as they have no need for clothes and no need to regulate sexual exchanges.

Only in 1929 were bonobos recognized as a distinct species of ape, and even in the 1980s many people considered them to be merely diminutive chimpanzees. Consequently, when the National Academy of Science suggested that bonobos were an indigenous resource that should be protected and cultivated in Congo, some scientists maintained that bonobos were not sufficiently different from chimpanzees to warrant such special treatment. Thus, three animals were captured from the wild, with the permission of the Congolese government, and taken to the Yerkes Regional Primate Center in Atlanta, Georgia, where researchers were to determine whether they, in fact, differed sufficiently from chimpanzees to warrant separate treatment. If so, it was hoped that a special center for their study would be set up in Congo.

It is clear that with regard to their social behavior and group structure, bonobos resemble human beings more than other living apes do. Their mood, temperament, and hesitant but curious nature set them apart from other apes. At times, as I watch them, I seem to be staring into my own distant past and seeing in front of me "quasi persons"—not people, but "near people." The feeling is as though, in an eerie and inexplicable way, I am watching a species that is not the same as me yet is connected to me—is part of me. Even after many years of watching and studying bonobos, I still cannot help but sense that I am in the presence of the emergence of the human mind, the dawn of our peculiarly human perspective and feeling.

Certainly these creatures cannot plan ahead as we do, organize large societies, or produce complex tools, calendars, and religions. Yet for me, there is more to being human than such abstract intelligent actions. There is a kinship I recognize when I interact with young children that does not depend on these abstract skills. It is a kinship of awareness that others share some of my feelings and I theirs. I know, at least in part, how other people feel, and they know how I feel.

With bonobos, I experience a similar two-way understanding. I know how they feel, and they know how I feel. This is possible because of the expressions that emanate from their faces, the way they interpret the feelings of others, the depth of their commitment to one another, and the understanding of one another that they share. Their sharing of emotional perspective is of a peculiarly human sort, and I relate to it, and am bound into their feelings, in a natural human manner, without effort. A human does not need to read a catalogue of bonobo facial expressions or vocalizations to understand the bonobo. When I observe a bonobo, it is as though I am standing at the precipice of the human soul, peering deep into some distant part of myself. This is a perception I cannot shake off or dissuade myself from, no matter how often I try to tell myself that I have no definitive scientific basis for these impressions.

Kanzi's adopted mother, Matata (right), looking toward the older female, Lokelema, with a facial expression that is requesting comfort.

Kanzi's father, Bosondjo, expresses happy and alert interest in events in the adjacent cage, while being groomed by Lokelema.

Lokelema looking up with an expression of concern and hesitancy.

According to our current understanding, bonobos and common chimpanzees went their own evolutionary ways two to three million years ago, some time after our own ancestor split off from the common lineage. We are more distantly related to gorillas and orangutans, as they diverged from the line that led eventually to man some six to eight million years ago. There is no current evidence that suggests that we are more closely related to the bonobo than to the common chimpanzee; yet the bonobo shares with man an emotional capacity for understanding the feelings of others that can only be described as almost human.

The arrival of the three bonobos who had traveled from the depths of Congo to the small, cramped, and dim cage on the end of the Yerkes great ape wing never lead to the establishment of a center for bonobo husbandry and research in Congo as the National Academy of Science had hoped. Many primatologists protested the importation and potential use of a rare and endangered species in any sort of research. Their attention damped international interest in the project; as a result, the people of Congo still, even today, have no understanding of their significant and unique indigenous resource, the bonobos.

As Lokelema, Bosondjo, and Matata grew older, they were joined by several more bonobo females on loan from the Atlanta Zoo. Bonsondjo fathered a number of infants with these females, one of whom was to become the first animal ever to learn language without training, as a child does, and thus the first to truly understand a spoken human language.

Many animals have learned to do tricks in response to spoken commands, but this young bonobo was different. He did not just do what he was told; indeed, he often *refused* to do what he was told even though he understood. This bonobo

Talking with Kanzi about where we might travel in the forest.

came to understand language—how it works and how it may be used. He was able to interpret spoken sentences that he was hearing for the very first time. He also learned to read printed symbols and to use these symbols to talk to people.

His name is Kanzi. In Swahili, Kanzi means "bold and brave." Kanzi certainly is bold and brave as he dares to be the first nonhuman to cross what had been assumed to be an unbridgeable boundary between the world of animals and the world of humanity. Kanzi has shown us that we are not alone among God's creatures to have been blessed with the gift of mind.

Kanzi: The Ape Who Crossed the Line

What is Kanzi like? How humanlike is he? Once you know him well, it often seems as though he is a person who has been stuffed into a fur suit and endowed with superhuman strength, a rather short temper, intense emotions, a desire to dominate all he sees, an impulsive personality, and an extraordinary sensitivity.

I keep having to remind myself that Kanzi is not really a person; at least, he doesn't *look* like a person, and he doesn't sound like a person. But it's hard to think of him any other way when I am with him for long, because he acts so much like a person. He understands my moods, my thoughts, my feelings, and my emotions. Many people say that dogs and other animals have such a skill, but Kanzi is different. It's not an "animal intuition" that characterizes Kanzi; he does not "divine" my thoughts but rather listens with sensitivity and concern when I explain them to him. There is an empathy that human beings share with others for whom they care. Kanzi shares this empathy, for he can read my facial expressions as well as, if not better than, any human being I have ever known.

Kanzi, as an adult, measures up to his name; he is bold and brave; he is also large (165 pounds) and very strong—five times stronger than a 165-pound human male in excellent physical shape. I cannot tell Kanzi what he must do or what he should not do. I can only advise him of the probable consequences of his actions and leave the decision up to him. He listens to me, but he does not always believe me when he cannot understand the reason for what I have said. Kanzi always wants to find out for himself whether I am right or not.

Take, for example, electrical outlets. How does one explain electricity to an ape? I have just tried to tell Kanzi that "shocks" come out of the wall—that the small hole in the wall is dangerous and can hurt him badly. It is clear that he understands something of what I have said to him, because he approaches the outlet with extreme caution, his hair on end. He smells it, he looks at it, he even throws something at it gingerly. The outlet just sits there. Kanzi stares at me with a rather incredulous look on his face—why, he wonders, do I think this thing is dangerous, and why did I lecture him so when he started to stick a screwdriver into it? It appears perfectly harmless to him. As I continue to maintain that this thing on the wall is dangerous, his curiosity becomes fully aroused.

Kanzi had never thought much about those things on the wall, but that day when he was playing with tools he noticed some screws on an outlet and tried to unscrew them. When that did not work, he decided to use the screwdriver to pry the thing off the wall and see what was under it. That was when I presented him with an impassioned explanation of "electricity" and its dangers. Kanzi did not understand the word "electricity," but he did know that I was saying the thing on the wall could hurt him and that I was seriously concerned about this possibility.

At a certain age, Kanzi began to wonder if everything I told him was really true. He had discovered that he could evaluate things for himself, and that many things that I could not do, he could. He could, for example, climb eighty-foot trees without falling or leap between them at heights that scared me just watching him. So naturally he wondered why he could not stick a screwdriver into the electrical outlet.

Waiting until I was not looking, he carefully hid the screwdriver under a blanket. Then, when I was thoroughly occupied with going through a stack of pictures to make a selection for a test of his comprehension, he removed the screwdriver from its hiding place and placed it directly in the outlet. Fortunately it had been insulated with a plastic handle, and Kanzi was not hurt. However, there was no doubt that he experienced a shock. He stood ramrod straight, and his hair rose two inches. He yanked the screwdriver out of the socket and immediately burst into a series of emphatic "Waa" sounds.

This time, Kanzi knew that this harmless-looking thing really was dangerous. He began throwing balls, bowls, blankets, toys, and anything else he could lay his hands on at the electrical outlet. He gestured for me to do the same thing—thinking, I presume, that we needed to attack the thing and get it out of there.

It certainly did not seem reasonable to Kanzi to have such a dangerous thing right there in the room with us. I could understand his point of view. Certainly, when we encountered snakes outdoors, that was exactly my strategy—throw something at them and get them to go away. Quite obviously, however, this strategy would not work with electrical outlets. One simply has to let them, and all the dangers they entail, stay right in one's room.

Kanzi never really doubted me when I explained that snakes were dangerous. Looking at them, he seemed to agree. However, it was not only electrical outlets that he wanted to test but many other things, such as every type of mushroom that grew in the forest, any dog that dared to bark at him, those large funnel-shaped nests that hornets fly in and out of, any tree or large tree branch that appeared a bit too rotten to support his weight, every rooftop that he encountered, the cans of insect repellent we felt compelled to take with us into the forest, and on and on. Like any normal four- or five-year-old boy, Kanzi viewed danger as a challenge to be overcome at the first opportunity. Only unlike a four- or five-year-old human boy, Kanzi had the strength, the agility, and the speed of a super athlete. Moreover, he could use these skills from any position on land or in the trees.

Kanzi was not so brave when, at six months of age, he arrived at the Language Research Center with his mother Matata. Like all ape infants, he stayed with his mother constantly and was carried by her wherever she went. Matata was not Kanzi's biological mother, though she had reared him from the time he was only thirty minutes old, after being permitted to hold him by his natural mother. Matata liked Kanzi so much, however, that she refused to give him back. Because she was nursing her own infant at the time, she was equipped to care for Kanzi. Not knowing any differently, Kanzi elected to stay with Matata.

Bonobo mothers, unlike gorilla, orangutan, or chimpanzee mothers, permit others to carry and fondle their offspring, though generally not until they are a few months old. By that age they are sufficiently bonded to the mother to insist upon returning to her after being held by another. Kanzi's real mother, Lorel, had been raised in a nursery, and Kanzi was her first infant. She apparently did not understand that she should wait awhile before permitting others to hold him. And Kanzi, not having learned who his mother was yet, settled happily into Matata's lap.

By the time Matata and Kanzi arrived at the Language Research Center, when Kanzi was six months old, Matata was willing to allow others to hold him. I had known Matata well for five years and had earned her trust before she had been transferred from the Language Research Center to the Yerkes Field Station where Kanzi was conceived and born. Matata had trusted me ever since I first befriended her, shortly after her unplanned arrival from Congo. I had done my best to ease the transition from the friendly world of free bonobos to that of cold cages and people who wore shiny boots, white coats, and sprayed lots of water. I had wanted Matata to learn not to be scared of all humans and that there were some who cared about how she felt. Matata had come to understand this, and was always gentle with me. Although Matata and I had not seen each other in more than a year, I was not surprised that she was willing to let me care for Kanzi for short periods of time.

What did surprise me was that Kanzi, who before this moment had never touched or smelled a person, was even more eager to meet me than I was to meet him. Without warning, he emitted an electrifying scream and propelled himself from Matata's arms to mine by literally turning in the air as he leapt through space.

Kanzi traveling with Matata in the forest. She has just found a bit of food at a tree marked with a lexigram. Kanzi is taking keen visual note.

He threw both arms and legs around my midsection and looked directly into my eyes with his lips pulled back in a grin that was pasted across his face like that of a clown, all the while screaming at the top of his lungs in the best bonobo fashion that a six-month-old could muster.

My legs and arms began to tremble, for although Matata and I had been friends in the past, we'd hardly had time to say "hello" before her son had jumped onto me. I was scared that somehow she might think I was hurting him because he screamed so loudly and held on so tightly. I feared that at any moment Matata was also going to leap upon me and grab Kanzi away, perhaps not before leaving me with numerous severe gashes from her razor-sharp canines. Female bonobos, although generally gentle, possess the equipment to do serious damage with their surgically sharp canines and lightning-fast reactions. Although Matata had been my friend, I knew that mothers are willing to inflict severe injury on any opponent if they conclude that their infants are in danger. Moreover, I posed no threat at all to Matata. Neither my strength nor my teeth began to match hers, and her infant was in my arms screaming at the top of his lungs. Not knowing what to do, I did nothing. Matata, knowing full well what to do, also did nothing.

As I was later to realize, this was just Kanzi's way of greeting me when he was aroused, and just then he was extremely excited, since I was the first human being to whom he had ever clung.

I later learned that the best way to calm Kanzi down when he was so aroused was to scream back just as loudly myself and pat him firmly on the back to show that I was happy to have him holding onto me. Though I did not realize it at the time, Kanzi was screaming only because he was somewhat frightened of me and fearful that I might not want him to cling to me, even though he had indicated, by his gestures and vocalizations, that he was nearly desperate to meet me. I was amazed and gratified that both Matata and Kanzi accepted me and that Kanzi wanted me to hold him. As soon as we got our messages of interest and acceptance across to each other, Kanzi calmed down and began to show a quiet fascination with my face, my hair, my shirt, my shoes, my pockets, my raised nose—as opposed to the flat bonobo nose—and all the other things that differentiated me from his mother. And so began an infatuation of two species, each for the other, that was to last for all three of our lifetimes and was to extend to Matata's future offspring as well.

Would a Bonobo Learn Language?

Although Kanzi was extremely cute, adorably playful, and as hilariously funny as any young bonobo infant could be, my immediate goal was to teach his mother Matata how to use symbols to communicate her desires and needs. Kanzi, I assumed, was far too young for such instruction. His turn would come much later, when he was two or three years old—old enough to pay attention during training sessions.

I knew all too well how easy it is for apes to become confused when presented with the complex geometric symbols that had been learned by the chimpanzees Lana, Sherman, and Austin, as well as by Tetsuro Matsuzowa's chimpanzee Ai in Japan. Before Kanzi was born, I had been teaching language to common chimpanzees for eight years. I knew that with patient and systematic training it was possible for such apes to learn to read printed symbols. They could also use these symbols to communicate simple things such as the kind of foods and drinks they desired; whether they wanted to go outdoors, be groomed, or play tickle or chase; and if they were frightened. Yet they were also likely to confuse symbols if new ones were introduced too rapidly or if they did not really understand what the symbol represented. Sometimes they would also use any symbol, whether they understood it or not. This meant that one had to be certain that they really understood each symbol they used, rather than assuming that word usage and word understanding go hand in hand, as is typically the case with children.

Matata was much older than the chimpanzees who had learned symbols; and her rearing deep in the forests of Congo had been very different from theirs: and they had all learned to use symbols as infants or juveniles. Nonetheless, Matata appeared to be quite intelligent and, in addition, more naturally communicative than most common chimpanzees. She had many natural means of communicating simple desires. For example, when Matata wanted to be somewhere, but was hesitant to go alone, she would take my hand and lead me with her. If she wanted something that was out of reach and there was no nearby tree, she would position my body just under the desired item so that she could climb on my shoulders to attain her goal. When she heard unusual noises in the forest, she would direct my attention toward them by looking and gesturing in that direction. If she was hungry, she would point to an empty bowl, then hand it to me and push me in the direction of the refrigerator.

Matata clearly possessed the idea of purposeful communication, and I could not escape the impression that she often vocalized to attempt to tell me things—things I did not understand. I know that I certainly vocalized to tell her things that she did not understand. Thus, each of us remained locked into communication systems that worked with our own species but did not work at all between us. I wanted to learn more about her communication system, but she did not know how to teach me. Likewise, she wanted to learn more about my communication system, but I did not know how to teach her. To overcome the barrier between us, I and other scientists had endeavored to employ a visual communication system with apes. By pointing to visual symbols, we could avoid the problems inherent in asking apes to produce speech sounds.

Scientists who have studied the configuration of the ape's vocal tract have concluded that it is impossible for them to speak as we do. The human and ape vocal tracts differ in a number of important dimensions. The human vocal tract curves downward at a 90-degree right angle, just at the point where the oral cavity merges with the pharyngeal cavity. In contrast, the ape vocal tract slopes gently downward. The right angle of the human vocal tract is a necessary extrapolation of our upright posture and the consequent vertical positioning of the head over the spinal column. If our head were tilted forward, as is that of a chimpanzee, we would not be able to maintain our balance easily while walking upon two limbs.

As the hominid head became vertically balanced on the spine, the tongue and the attachments of the larynx at the base of the tongue moved lower into the neck. This reorientation of the vocal-laryngeal tract led to critical differences between the human and ape vocal apparatuses. The lowering of the larynx resulted in the ability to produce lower-pitched, more discriminable vowel sounds. The sharp angularity of the vocal tract and the decrease in the size of the mouth resulted in the ability to completely close off the nasal cavity from the oral cavity (velar closure).

Very young children and apes, as well as persons born with a cleft palate, lack the ability to effect velar closure. Consequently, they can drink liquid and vocalize at the same time—something a slightly older child cannot do without choking. But they cannot speak. Older children and adults, by bringing pressure to bear on the velar palate, can keep water from coming into their nose and lungs, while they are swimming. They also use velar closure to produce nasal sounds such as "m" and "n." Velar closure also permits the vocal tract to implode enough pressure to produce plosive consonants such as "k" and "g." Such consonant sounds are critical to all human languages.

Although languages differ in the specific consonant sounds they employ, no human language is composed strictly of vowels. Therefore, all human speakers must be able to effect velar closure in order to produce language. Consonants are much easier for our ear to discriminate. A language composed only of vowels would have so many that sounded alike that it would be difficult to tell what a person was saying. Consonants solve that problem for us in that they permit us to construct a very large number of minimally different sound units that are easily discriminated by our ears. It is the ability to effect velar closure that makes it possible for us to produce so many discriminable sounds. But the structure of the vocal tract also means that humans, unlike other mammals, cannot breathe and swallow at the same time. We have to stop breathing for anywhere from 0.5 to 4 seconds in order to swallow; if we don't do so, we will choke to death. This situation has necessitated a degree of respiratory control in humans that appears to be absent in other animals. We use this respiratory control, essential to our survival, to engage in highly controlled phonation or sound production.

It is often assumed that a language could be made up of any sort of sounds and that animals could have their own languages made up of their own sounds. However, there are some basic constraints that necessarily operate on any potential vocal structure attempting to produce a language:

1. The sounds must be easily discriminable by the auditory system of the intended recipient.
2. The sounds must be easily and rapidly produced.
3. The sounds that are produced must be recognizably similar in some essential pattern, even though they are produced by animals of different ages and different sizes.

Recent research on the discriminability of sounds has shown that vowel sounds are far more difficult to tell apart at their boundaries than consonants.[1] Vowels seem to have "fuzzy edges." This means that it is difficult to determine the exact point at which, for example, an "ah" sound becomes an "eh" sound, much as it is difficult to say precisely when a red color becomes a pink color. Consonants, in contrast, have "sharp edges." We can easily tell when a "ba" sound turns into a "da" sound, just as we can quickly tell a figure composed only of acute angles from one composed only of curved angles. The topographic maps in our visual cortex are organized to permit precisely the angularity-curvature sorts of boundary distinctions we find easy to make. In contrast, the perception of color is a graded event, produced by the mixing of three different chromatic receptors. There are no receptors uniquely designed to discriminate pink from red; hence, we perceive no sharp boundary between them.

Because consonants are easy to tell apart, we can employ them in our speech to form the perceptual edges around vowels. This permits us to encapsulate units of sound into neat, clear packages that can be readily discriminated by others. The capacity to produce discriminable sound packages that can serve as the building blocks of the open-ended sound-based communication system has permitted the emergence of what we call language.

Surprisingly, it is not only human beings who find consonants highly discriminable. Many other mammals display a similar capacity to discriminate consonants relative to vowels. However, other animals are unable to form consonants in their vocal tracts, even though they can hear and discriminate them. The only sounds that most other mammals can produce are vowellike in quality and consequently are "fuzzy edged."

However, just because apes lack the requisite anatomical equipment to speak, it does not necessarily follow that they also lack the intelligence to use language. In the late 1960s and early 1970s, several separate research groups attempted to

Kanzi traveling with me in the forest. When I supported his weight and carried him in an upright bipedal position, this freed his hands for things other than clinging. He spontaneously began using gestures to show me which direction to take.

get around these anatomical limitations by a number of different means. Some attempted to use gestures. But gestures, like sounds, proved difficult for apes because the anatomy and motor control of the human hand is much superior to that of the ape hand. The ape's hand, like the position of its skull relative to the spine, is that of a quadruped. Apes need their hands for walking, so they develop large calluses on the backs of their knuckles; these calluses severely limit efficient hand and finger movements.

Duane Rumbaugh attempted to circumvent the anatomical limitations of the ape by using the equivalent of written symbols placed on a computer keyboard. As a substitute for vocalizing, they could simply touch a word. This method did not even require that they be able to hear differences between words. Each symbol was visually distinct and became bright whenever it was touched. Touching a symbol was thus intended to be the equivalent of speaking a word.

In order to "talk," apes had to become sufficiently familiar with the visual appearance of the symbols to be able to tell them apart. They also had to remember what each symbol looked like so that they could select it whenever they wished. This visual touch system was first employed with a common chimpanzee named Lana. Lana was raised surrounded by colorful symbols called lexigrams. The lexigrams were arranged on a computer keyboard, and Lana could—by pressing them in the proper sequence—turn on music, watch slides, open a window, cause food and drinks to be dispensed, and invite people into her room to visit and play.

Lana rather quickly learned to discriminate these symbols and to sequence them in simple stock phrases such as "Please machine give M&M," "Please person give piece of bread," "Please machine make window open," "Question person move into room," and so on. She could even recombine these stock phrases together into new ones that she had not been taught, such as "Please person move M&M into room."

The success of this approach led to studies with two additional chimpanzees, Sherman and Austin. These apes were raised in an environment similar to Lana's except that instead of using symbols to activate a machine, they learned to use symbols to communicate with each other. They could ask one another for simple tools that were needed to extract food from especially designed containers; they could tell each other what kinds of foods had been hidden while only one of them was watching; and they could use their symbols to announce simple intentions, such as where they were going, or what they intended to take from the refrigerator or toy cabinet. Unlike Lana, Sherman and Austin used symbols to communicate not only with people but also with each other. To do this, they had to be able not only to talk but also to listen, understand, and cooperate. They had to coordinate their communications, take turns in simple conversations, and coordinate nonverbal gestures with their symbolic messages.

Unlike these common chimpanzees, Matata found lexigram symbols extremely difficult to master. She could not even tell one from the other. Consequently, a task was devised for Matata to get her to pay attention to lexigrams and so to see that each one looked different from the others. One of Matata's favorite foods was bananas, so we placed the "banana" symbol on her keyboard along with some other nonsense-symbols. Each time Matata pressed the banana symbol, she received a piece of banana; then, the banana symbol and the nonsense-symbols all moved to a new location. Whenever Matata wanted another bite of banana, she had to look at the keyboard and find the banana symbol in a new place among the distractors. When she was able to find the banana symbol in this way without error, other food symbols were similarly introduced.

By this time, Kanzi was about one year old and big enough to get in his mother's way. He did not hesitate to take the bananas, apples, or raisins that she had worked so hard to earn, nor did he hesitate to slap any symbol that attracted his attention while his mother was patiently searching for the correct one. Every time Kanzi touched the wrong symbol, Matata's keyboard automatically relocated all the symbols, forcing her to begin her search all over again.

Kanzi also managed to cause problems for Matata by doing gymnastics on her head and shoulders while she tried to locate the symbols, often knocking her hand away from the keyboard just as she was about to touch the correct symbol. Matata, like most other bonobos, was a study in maternal patience. Clearly, she was not happy with the difficulties her son caused and would often scowl at both him and me. However, she never punished Kanzi at this age nor stopped him from taking her food. As he grew older, it became apparent that her extreme tolerance could not last forever—but for the first two and one half years of his life, Kanzi was permitted to do virtually as he pleased, both by his mother and by myself and others who worked with him.

Section of the keyboard showing several lexigram symbols.

Matata seemed to be of the opinion that a youngster Kanzi's age should not be held responsible for the consequences of his actions—consequences he could not yet understand. She also realized that at times Kanzi became upset or distressed for foolish reasons, and on such occasions she had to determine for herself whether there was sufficient cause to be angry. For example, one problem Kanzi repeatedly encountered was getting his hands caught as he put them in places where they did not belong. When this happened, he would panic and try to yank himself free, only making the predicament worse. For example, one day he inspected a chain I was wearing around my neck. While exploring this object, as bonobo infants want to do with every new thing they encounter, Kanzi abruptly twisted it and caught his hand in the resulting loop. When he tried to pull his hand out, he found that he could not. Rather than wait for me to help him get it out, he started screaming at me and tried to scratch and bite my face as though he believed that somehow I was holding onto him on purpose with my necklace and had decided not to let go. He pulled so hard that I could not speak, and I feared that I would soon choke if I did not get him to calm down so that I could free his hand.

While Matata looked at me with great alarm in response to Kanzi's screams, I gesticulated vigorously at my neck to illustrate Kanzi's predicament and that I was not purposefully trying to make him scream. Matata was able to see and understand the situation, so she did not attack me, even though Kanzi was trying to bite me and was calling for her support. Finally, I was able to free his hand by breaking the necklace, but even then he continued to bark at me and remained angry for the rest of the day. Matata tried to console him and show him that I was her friend by grooming me, but Kanzi did not share her opinion and continued to bark and slap at me for the rest of the day every time I reached out to him. Similar events occurred when Kanzi got his hand caught in the hammock, in a coke can, and in the long hair of another person working with him. Each time, Matata evaluated the situation and determined that even though Kanzi thought we were attempting to hurt him, this was not in fact the case.

After two years of effort and more than thirty-thousand trials with the lexigrams "banana," "juice," "raisin," "apple," "pecan," and "orange," Matata's symbol vocabulary skills remained disappointing. Although she had learned to ask for and name each food correctly, she could not select a picture of the food if I pointed to its symbol. She also had difficulty "listening." When I used the keyboard to ask her to give me a specific food, she seemed puzzled. Perhaps she thought I should just take any food that I wanted. Such deficits suggested that she had not yet grasped the representational aspects of these symbols.

All common chimpanzees who had learned to use symbols were considerably more accomplished than Matata. Not only could Sherman and Austin select pictures that corresponded to symbols, they watched when others touched symbols, and they responded appropriately. They used symbols to tell each other about hidden foods and tools, and they sorted symbol-words into categories such as foods, tools, and drinks. They even learned to draw some of their own symbols (see Savage-Rumbaugh 1986). Both Lana and Ai, a chimpanzee raised in Japan and taught to use similar lexigrams, could easily name colors and objects. Ai could count to seven, and Lana could appropriately use the symbols "more" and "less" to answer questions about quantity. Ai was even able to "construct" some symbols from their individual parts with the help of a computer that superimposed the pieces on one another as she touched them.

All the common chimpanzees—Lana, Sherman, Austin, and Ai—attained vocabularies of between fifty and one hundred and fifty symbols, which they employed in rather sophisticated ways. By these standards, Matata was quite backward. In fact, her progress was so dismal we were fearful that it would be difficult to justify continued inclusion of bonobos in our research program.

The overarching goal of the research program undertaken by our center had been the development of technologies and teaching strategies designed to facilitate the learning of language by persons with mental retardation. Funds for this work had been made available by the National Institute for Child Health and Development (NICHD) since the early 1970s, when the project had begun with Lana and a very small keyboard. At that time, no one knew whether or not chimpanzees could use complex visual symbols in even the simplest fashion. But Lana rapidly learned to use them to request foods and drinks from vending devices that were linked to a small computer-controlled keyboard in her room.

Research studies with Lana, and later Sherman and Austin, provided a strong foundation of basic knowledge about language acquisition. Through this work, we began to define the fundamental building blocks or units of language. We also began to apply these principles to the language instruction of mentally retarded children.

We found that while it was easy to get chimps to use symbols in a way that looked like language, it was much more difficult to get them to understand and use symbols in a manner that was truly equivalent to that of young children. To do this, apes would have to develop the capacity to comprehend words, to attend to others, to take turns speaking, and to recall their symbols completely—whether the referent is present or not. They would have to learn to separate symbol use from reward or immediate gratification so that their speech could function to convey information. For all these abilities precede the formation of grammatically complex sentences (see chapter 2).

It had been our hope that by studying a different ape, the bonobo, additional insights into the mysteries of language would be achieved. Because bonobos employed more elaborate gestures in the field, it seemed possible that they had evolved a greater capacity for language than chimpanzees. It was even possible that they utilized a simple language in the wild that no one had been able to recognize. I had been optimistic that Matata would outpace all of the chimpanzees who had learned symbols. She was a willing student who worked very hard, but after two and one half years of effort, we were forced to conclude that she was not going to fulfill our expectations. Even more disconcerting, as far as funding prospects were concerned, nothing really new about language acquisition had been learned from Matata's failures.

Mother and Child

Even though I was disappointed with Matata's halting linguistic progress, I was nonetheless fascinated by the complexity of the relationship that was evolving between mother and son. It was characterized by tolerance and understanding. In fact, during the first four to five years of his life, the only form of discipline I ever observed Matata impose on Kanzi was to encourage him to settle down at night-time. Every evening, she began a solemn ritual of building the perfect nest. Since she was not in the forest and lacked access to the tree branches that would normally serve as bedding material, we provided her with five to seven large, rugged blankets made of heavy carpet.

Matata had very definite ideas as to how these blankets should be arranged before sleeping. Each one was taken to a high location, where she carefully straightened it and laid it down. Then, while seated on it, she artfully pulled its edges into a half-circle around herself. She repeated the process with each blanket, assiduously intertwining their edges until she had formed a nest with high cushy sides, something like a large inner tube with a soft center. Next, she reclined in this structure to test it out, and made any adjustments or repairs that were needed. Finally, she groomed herself and Kanzi before dozing off to sleep.

Kanzi, like many children, was never ready to go to bed when Matata was. He always wanted to stay up and play, and he would try to pull Matata's blankets into his own "play nest"—where the blankets ended up on top of his head as often as underneath him. He would also flop on Matata with a full play face, smiling and laughing while waiting for Matata to play bite and tickle him. After being so indulged for fifteen to twenty minutes, Kanzi usually nursed and then went to sleep as Matata groomed him. As he grew older, however, he wanted to continue playing even after he had nursed. He also wanted more of Matata's blankets for his playnesting activities, which became ever more vigorous, though never serious. He would begin twirling, pirouetting, and brandishing his blankets about right next to Matata as she was attempting to quietly and perfectly arrange her nest.

By two years of age, Kanzi was large enough that these nightly nest antics seriously began to bother Matata. Often I would stay as she settled down for the evening. On these nights, she always invited me to sit in her nest once it was properly constructed and groom with her. While we groomed, Kanzi would display his acrobatics, which were always punctuated by flinging himself with great abandon either onto my head and shoulders or into my lap.

Every time I began to groom Matata, Kanzi became more desirous of attracting my attention, so he would increase the number and vigor of the flips, flops, turns, and spins designed to do so. When Matata could bear the distraction no longer, she would take Kanzi's hand or foot into her mouth and, using her teeth, slowly begin to increase her pressure until Kanzi looked at her and realized that she was serious. This would cause him to quiet down for awhile as he puzzled over what it was that had so irritated his mother. Eventually, however, he would begin twirling and spinning again until Matata reminded him, with unquestionable firmness from the pressure of her teeth, that she was not happy with this behavior. Finally, Kanzi would figure out that Matata was not going to tolerate anything but quiet behavior in the evening nest and then he would become quiet and allow himself to be groomed. When Matata finished her evening grooming, she would tuck Kanzi into her inner tube–shaped nest and repair the sides, using the blankets from Kanzi's play nest. She would then give me a little hug followed by a gentle shove and stare directly at the door to indicate that it was time for me to go.

A common frustration in attempting to teach symbols to Matata while Kanzi was around was her insistence that, in most endeavors, Kanzi be permitted to have his way. Matata did not mind when I intervened to reprimand Kanzi for something she also thought he should not do, such as disturb our evening grooming session. However, she made it perfectly clear that I was not permitted to make any decisions regarding how Kanzi was otherwise allowed to behave.

Thus, if Kanzi jumped in the middle of a large bowl of food that I was preparing—something Matata herself would never do—that was all right, as Kanzi was simply playing and did not intend to spill things all over the floor. Or, if I was attempting to arrange some toys or test objects, it was okay for Kanzi to flail about in the midst of these materials until he had scattered them all around the room, or to steal my pen and paper and run away. Again, Matata herself never thought of misbehaving in such a fashion, for she was well aware that such things bothered me. Yet, from her perspective, Kanzi was not really attempting to challenge me with such actions, he was just carrying them out in jest.

Nonetheless, Kanzi was quick to recognize when I was irritated and to solicit Matata's support if I tried to take back my pen or insist that he pick up the things he had just scattered all over the floor. He felt compelled to explore with considerable elan all dimensions of behaviors that were "okay" with Matata but frustrating to me. This exploration of behavioral options as interpreted by me versus Matata often became Kanzi's raison d'etre for an entire morning or afternoon. Whenever I grew exasperated and raised my voice to insist that he pick up something he had just thrown on the floor, he would yell for Matata to come. She would then lumber over with a suspicious look on her face and attempt to determine what was going on between me and Kanzi. He would vocalize to try and convince her that I was requiring him to do a dastardly thing, while I would attempt to show her the mess that Kanzi had made and proceed to insist that he rectify the situation. Matata would then watch me cautiously, allowing me to continue only as long as Kanzi did not become too upset or run to her. Since his goal was to test me, he usually did not run to Matata, nor did he get really upset—he only got just upset enough to cause his mother to stay there and keep her eagle eye on us both.

Potty training proceeded in much this manner. Potty training an ape is much like potty training a child. One simply picks them up and takes them to the potty at what appears to be an appropriate time. The trick is to watch closely and select the times wisely. Matata had not been potty trained, as she was far too large to pick up and carry to the potty, so she saw relatively little need for me to potty train Kanzi. Moreover, the one thing young Kanzi liked least of all was to be asked to sit quietly in a single location. He was quite content to be carried to the potty but unwilling to stay long enough to calmly accomplish what I intended. Matata sympathized with him, apparently assuming that sitting on the potty was an unusual form of punishment that I had invented for her son. So Kanzi would stay on the potty only for as long as I could cajole and entertain him. Our progress in this endeavor alternated between exceptionally slow and none at all as long as Kanzi remained with Matata. As with many other things that I had tried to teach Kanzi while Matata was there, he understood what I wanted him to do, but saw no reason to do so; therefore, he frequently elected not to use the potty.

When Kanzi was almost two and one half years old, the Yerkes Center decided that Matata should be bred with Kanzi's father Bonsondjo and become pregnant. Like the females of common chimpanzees, bonobo females experience a swelling of their genital tissues when they are sexually receptive. The timing of their sexual cycles is similar to that of the human female, but differs in that it is visually advertised to all by the engorgement of genital tissue. After they give birth and while they are lactating, bonobo females do not experience these swellings, nor are they able to conceive. (Like human females, however, and unlike all other nonhuman primates, bonobo females continue to engage in sexual interactions during this time.)

Since it was important that Matata be separated from Kanzi for as brief a period as possible, she was given a medication that caused her to slowly stop lactating before being sent to join Bosondjo. It was hoped that this medication would aid her quick return to sexual cyclicity and that when she joined him at the field station she could conceive quickly and return to Kanzi.

Fortunately, for several months before Matata was to leave to join Bosondjo, Kanzi had begun to permit us to carry him out of her sight. In fact, he even allowed us to leave Matata on what we called the "chimp side" of our research center and traveled with us to the "childside" where work was in progress to teach children with retardation a language using a keyboard similar to Matata's. Of course, Kanzi could not play with any of these children, but he much enjoyed watching them play from a distance, just as children like to go to the zoo and observe apes from a distance. Matata objected vociferously when Kanzi left to go on these short visits, but to my complete amazement he paid her no mind and went anyway. He seemed to trust me to take him back to his mother when he asked and was quite willing to go almost anywhere with me.

When the time came to sedate Matata and take her away in a small cage, we did not want Kanzi to have to watch; so we arranged a visit to the childside, and while Kanzi was out of eyesight and earshot, Matata was tranquilized and whisked away. When Kanzi returned from his visit to the childside, he seemed to think that Matata must be hiding somewhere. He did not vocalize or cry out in distress at all, but he asked to be carried to every room in the laboratory over and over. In each room he looked in the cabinets, under the furniture, behind curtains, on shelves, under the blankets, out the window, and so on, as if he was bound to find Matata at any moment. He evidenced emotional distress only once, when I stepped out and left him with another caretaker to go home and get some food. He became so upset at my departure that I remained with him day and night for the next three days. By that time, Kanzi seemed to have given up looking for Matata and had decided that the milk we offered, while not as good as Matata's, was acceptable. I was then able to leave him for brief periods of time with Liz and Kelly, two of Matata's other teachers and friends whom he had known since he was six months old.

Kanzi Had Been Keeping a Secret

Even though Kanzi was preoccupied with his search for Matata on the day of her disappearance, he still managed to use the keyboard a great deal. To everyone's astonishment, on the first day of Matata's absence, Kanzi produced 120 separate utterances using twelve different symbols ("banana," "juice," "raisin," "peanuts," "chase," "bite," "tickle," "orange," "outdoors," "swing," "cherry," "sweet potato," and "ball"). Prior to Matata's absence, we had been encouraging Kanzi to use the keyboard and, consequently, had added lexigrams such as "ball" and "chase" that might prove of interest to him. However, his usage of symbols had been rather sporadic, and we were not certain how many symbols, if any, he really comprehended. For example, the day before Matata left, Kanzi used the keyboard only twenty-one times to ask for just three different foods. That day, Kelly, one of Matata's teachers, made the following observations of Kanzi's keyboard usage:

> Kanzi is playing with a ball—I initiate an interaction with him saying "ball" and begin to slap the ball. When I stop he wants me to continue. I wait for him to request this at the keyboard but he has difficulty finding the symbol. I touch "ball" while he watches, then he touches "ball" and we play again. He then says "orange" and gestures for me to take him to the cooler. I get an orange out for him, but he calls it "banana" when we return to the keyboard.

The following day, when his mother was gone, we saw a very different Kanzi at the keyboard. Not only did he use many single symbols appropriately to tell us what he wanted to eat or do, he formed the combinations "raisin peanut" when he wanted both foods, "sweet potato tickle" when he wanted both to eat sweet potatoes and be tickled, and "melon go" when he wanted to go outdoors with some melon. He even touched "juice" simply to comment on how happy he was that I had given him a very large glass of grape juice, his favorite drink—carefully holding it so that it would not spill while walking all the way across the room to make this comment at the keyboard.

Kanzi had been keeping a secret. He had been learning these words all along, but had never used them in a reliable manner. We thought he did not know how to talk with the keyboard, but he did.

Simultaneously with this abrupt appearance of competent language skills, a similar thing happened with regard to Kanzi's use of the potty. Whereas he had previously appeared to have a great deal of difficulty remembering to use the potty, upon Matata's departure we suddenly had a well-trained young bonobo. I mention this not because it is significant that a bonobo could learn to use the potty, but because the sudden appearance of this behavior was, like his ability to talk, a clear indication that his previous performance had been a reflection not of his knowledge but of his motivation.

Kanzi diligently searches for just the lexigrams that he wants.

Matata's sudden absence caused Kanzi to become extremely attentive to the kind of things that I and his other teachers had been attempting to show him. With Matata gone, we were suddenly the most important individuals in his life, and his desire to please us increased commensurately. No longer did he have to choose between his mother's view of potty training and ours or between her attitude toward using symbols and ours. Our "human perspective" prevailed because it lacked competition from Matata. It became increasingly clear that Kanzi had learned a great deal more about how we did things than he had bothered to demonstrate in the past. Now, with Matata gone, all of what he had learned, but rarely if ever displayed, came pouring out of him.

I had originally intended to use the time during Matata's sojourn to begin systematic instruction with Kanzi, making certain that he could both use and understand symbols. I had hoped to expand his vocabulary, make certain he could select pictures to go with symbols, and enable him to take so-called "blind tests" so that any statements I wished to make regarding what he had learned would be acceptable to other scientists. Lana, Sherman, and Austin had previously achieved each of these milestones, and Kanzi needed to do so too, I believed, if we were to make additional progress in our understanding of the process of language learning.

Blind tests are essential because apes, like people, sometimes select the right answers for the wrong reasons. The person giving such a test either does not know the answers or is not visible to the ape when questions are presented, and thus cannot inadvertently help the ape answer the questions.

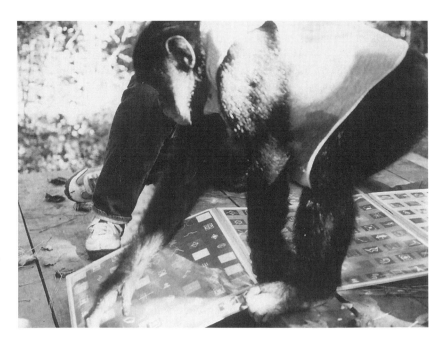

After locating the lexigrams that he wishes to use, Kanzi places the keyboard on the ground and walks across it as he forms the compound utterance "grab-chase."

Scientists have paid a great deal of attention to this issue because of a concern that very slight movements, such as a twitch of the eyebrow or a nearly imperceptible nod of the head, can cause the ape to get the right answer without really knowing the symbol. Given simple and highly practiced tasks, such covert cues can be effective, and therefore misleading. However, in order to cue a subject when many different words or answers to a question could occur, the experimenter would need to develop a specific subtle movement to be associated with each symbol. To present many different subtle cues reliably, one would have to be purposely intending to cue the ape at just the right time and do so throughout a test of many trials. Only if the scientist intended to cheat or defraud his colleagues would subtle cuing be possible when long tests with many different alternatives were presented.

Apes, like humans, are astute observers of direction of gaze, and when the experimenter looks directly at an answer, if the answers are far enough apart, sometimes the ape can determine the answer by noting where the experimenter is looking. Of course, it is easy to tell if the ape is depending on your gaze. If you look intentionally at the wrong answer and consequently the ape makes an error, he has probably used your gaze as a cue.

My goals for Kanzi were ambitious, and I would have been gratified had he made only partial progress toward taking such tests during Matata's absence. Realistically, I was also prepared for him to go through a traumatic period of adjustment to being without his mother, during which time I assumed he probably would not be able to learn anything. When he began, instead, on the very first day of Matata's absence, to use the keyboard far more frequently than he ever had, to form combinations of symbols, and to tell me not only what he wanted me to do for him but what he *planned* to do next, I was in a state of disbelief. It was several weeks before I and others working with Kanzi began to accept the fact that he had really learned to talk even though we had not been attempting to teach him. As this realization grew, I concluded that I had to strive to rearrange the entirety of my thinking as to what language was, what animals were, and what it was I should be attempting to learn from Kanzi.

Here was an ape who was really "talking" to me. It was not just that I had successfully taught him how to use symbols to stand for things so that he could convey his desires effectively, as I had done with Sherman and Austin. I had not intentionally taught Kanzi anything, nor had I been able to teach his mother what he had somehow learned, even though I had been trying daily to do so for two years. What was happening?

I searched back through all of the notes that I, and others, had made during the past two years, looking for any hint that somehow Kanzi had been learning language all along. How could I explain to skeptics what I had done to foster Kanzi's language learning when I did not even know it was happening? Not only had I not documented anything *I did* to facilitate Kanzi's accomplishment, I had no real record of what *he had done*. One always hears stories of children who do not talk until they are three years of age or older, then suddenly begin to speak in complete sentences, never passing through the stages of babbling, baby talk, single-word utterances, and ungrammatical sentences that characterize the early stages of language learning in other children. Well, now I had a similar story to tell, only it was not about a child, it was about an ape. And the ape was not speaking but was using printed symbols—the equivalent of learning to read and speak at the same time. From the moment the enormity of what Kanzi had done became clear to me, I knew that I would not be believed.

Kanzi was an animal, and animals were not supposed to be able to just grow up like children, learning whatever the people who raise them expose them to. Unlike people, who possess a sense of self-consciousness, a morality, and presumably an innate capacity for language and rational thought, animals are supposed to be different. While some of them are thought to be "clever" and quick learners, it is not assumed that they can really decide for themselves what to learn and how to learn it.

If helped along by psychologists who reinforce the right behaviors, it is known that some animals can be made to appear intelligent. Pigeons, for example, can be taught to play a simplified version of basketball. But language is not a game of basketball, and Kanzi's utterances had not been carefully programmed into his repertoire of behavior. Indeed, they had not even been practiced. We could not have reinforced Kanzi's actions, nor selected certain bits of his behavior to amplify, because his learning was not taking place in the form of visible actions. It had been occurring covertly; Kanzi had been watching, looking, listening, and learning just as though he were a young child. And when, because of his mother's absence, it became propitious to utilize what he had learned, he elected to do so.

In spite of his abilities, Kanzi was not ready to take a blind test. Indeed, he was not ready to take any test at all, blind or otherwise. He was happy enough to use the keyboard to talk, but he had never previously been required to sit still and answer a lot of questions that, from his perspective, were meaningless, in order to earn a morsel of food. When I tried to encourage him to participate in such a test, he evidenced no willingness at all to answer any questions. Like any normal two-year-old child, he wanted to do what attracted him at the moment. Moreover, anything that I insisted he do became precisely the thing he would refuse to do.

Short of starving Kanzi, there was no way to get him to agree to participate in a formal test of his skills at this point. Certainly, we were not going to withhold food, as our utmost concern just then was to get him to eat well even though he was concerned about Matata's absence. We could not risk traumatizing him or fostering the onset of depression by asking him to do without food in addition to being without his mother. Consequently, it seemed better to focus on ways of fostering his language development rather than rush to "verify" what he could do. Certainly, if he was as competent as I believed him to be, there would be ample time in the future to document his capacity.

Not knowing what I had done to permit Kanzi to learn what he had, I knew even less about what to do for the future. One thing was clear: Since we had not taught Kanzi symbols, but he had learned many of them anyway, we did not need to focus on explicit instructional attempts in the future. Indeed, such attempts could inhibit progress rather than facilitate it. Only Kanzi knew what he was ready to learn and what he wanted to learn. We could do little more than guess. Thus, I decided to abandon all instruction and focus my attention instead on what was *said to Kanzi* rather than on what we could teach him to say.

I, along with Kanzi's other caretakers—Rose, Kelly, Liz, and Jeannine—tried very hard to help him understand everything that was said to him. We also left whatever he chose to say completely up to him. In a sense, then, we provided a linguistic framework for Kanzi. Yet the keyboard had so few symbols that spoken words really comprised most of this linguistic framework. Because Kanzi was not able to produce the consonants and vowels that comprise speech, however, we accompanied our words by pointing to any appropriate symbols that were on the keyboard when we talked to him.

On the first day Matata was gone, Kanzi had used all twelve symbols on the keyboard; therefore, it seemed important rapidly to increase the number of symbols available to him. I wanted to add words that I knew we would want to say to him, as well as those he might wish to say to us. But what would a young bonobo elect to talk about? Since I was going to teach him not symbols now, but rather a language model and look at what he learned, I could not just select a symbol and proceed to make certain that he differentiated it appropriately from the others. It would be up to him whether he bothered to learn it at all. How was I to know what he would bother to learn? The only clue I had to follow was the knowledge that field researchers had gathered regarding the behavior of apes in the wild.

Morning Exploits

Kanzi's day typically started whenever he awoke. Jeannine was usually the first to arrive; after relieving whomever had spent the night with Kanzi, she would begin straightening up the group room while waiting for Kanzi (who was still asleep in the bedroom) to awaken. Kanzi often announced that he was awake by using his keyboard to say something to Jeannine. On one typical morning, for example, Jeannine heard "peaches" and then "hug" and knew what Kanzi wanted. She prepared him a bowl of peaches, took them into the bedroom, and gave Kanzi a big hug while he happily consumed them.

After finishing his peaches, he invited Jeannine to play "keep-away" with the rubber band by making the sign for "grab" (touching his knuckles to his wrist) and lighting the "rubber band" symbol on the keyboard. Kanzi was so good at keep-away games that he nearly always won. He would give the other party plenty of chances by pretending to drop the item near them or pretending that he had forgotten the game and that he had laid the item down while attending to something else. But the second you reached for the item, Kanzi was there to grab it from under your very nose. Anything could suffice as the item to be "kept away"— from the most desirable food or toy to the most insignificant little stick or rock— since the point of the game for Kanzi was not really to keep something away, but just to play the game—that is, to demonstrate just how good he was at keeping things from us. Kanzi invented numerous variations on the basic keep-away theme, from hiding the item to pretending to swallow it in the midst of the game. Keep-away games with food items were his favorite, because he could actually make the item disappear bit by bit. The game was not over until the food had completely vanished; depending on how much Kanzi was enjoying the game, this could happen quickly or very slowly.

When Kanzi finally tired of the keep-away game, he asked Jeannine to take him to the group room by first pointing to the keys in her pocket, then to the lock on the bedroom door, and then toward the group room. Many of Kanzi's complex communications entailed the use of multiple gestures such as these. He invented simple gestures that he needed on the spot to get his message across, often combining such gestures with vocalizations and lexigrams as well.

Kanzi began employing gestures when he was less than one year old. His first gesture was used to indicate to whomever was holding him that he wanted to go somewhere. This gesture consisted of extending his arm in the desired direction of travel while being carried. The development of this "go" gesture was facilitated by the fact that Kanzi wished to be carried much of the time by human companions rather than his mother. We walked bipedally and supported Kanzi's weight with our arms. This left him free to use his hands for whatever he desired rather than clinging, as he had to do when Matata carried him. Not only did Kanzi experience this unusual early opportunity to learn to use his hands for something other than clinging (early, that is, for a bonobo infant), but also any gesture which he

Kanzi plays a game of "stick-keep-away" with an experimenter who is lying on the ground to the left. The experimenter is trying to get Kanzi's big stick with his little stick.

Kanzi was later joined in this travels in the forest by a younger sibling Mulika. Here, Mulika at one year of age, is learning lexical symbols. Like Kanzi, she insisted in riding on our shoulders as we traveled in the forest.

did make was responded to by human companions who wanted to encourage the development of his communicative skills.

When Kanzi grew old enough to ride on Matata's back, he often used his "go" gesture to ask Matata to travel down an outdoor trail by extending his arm in front of her face as he rode on her back; or if she paused to rest when he wanted to continue traveling, he would communicate this to Matata by gesturing "go." Of course, Matata had a mind of her own, too, and she would not always comply with his requests. Certainly, she must have been the only ape mother in the world who had an infant who attempted to give her travel advice.

Most of the day, wild apes travel about the forest in search of food. Little is known about how, if at all, they plan their travels or whether they communicate any such plans to one another. However, they are able to make good use of the forest's resources and seem to have an intimate knowledge of plants and their fruiting seasons. Therefore, I decided to try and build Kanzi's vocabulary around the activities of traveling and locating food in the forest. We were fortunate to have available fifty acres of primary forest adjacent to our laboratory. Within this tract of land were many small mammals, such as raccoons and rabbits, and small reptiles, such as lizards, snakes, and turtles. A river bounded the forest on one side, a golf course on another, and undeveloped land on the remaining sides. Edible plants such as muscadines, blackberries, strawberries, and onions grew wild. Because Atlanta lies in a temperate zone, all the vegetation in the forest was seasonal, and during a number of months each year it was too cold for an ape to be outdoors for more than ten or fifteen minutes. However, in the spring and summer months, the forest was somewhat similar to that of the tropics.

A series of trails were laid out in the forest. In place of fruiting trees, I established locations where coolers were placed containing one or more foods; the foods found at each location did not vary, since in the wild, a tree growing in a particular place always produces the same type of fruit. Small structures, each unique, were built at these natural stopping points along the trails. Some structures afforded minimal protection from heavy rains. Each location was given a name and a lexigram symbol. The coolers were freshly stocked each day with the appropriate food, and we began to travel about the forest with Kanzi, just as if we were a small group of bonobos searching for food in the wild.

During our wanderings, Kanzi not only gestured in the direction that he wished to travel, but when he rode on anyone's shoulders he also turned the person's head forcefully to cause him or her to look in the direction he was pointing. If this was not sufficient to change the person's course of travel, he would lean his entire body in the direction he wished to go. With Kanzi on one's shoulders, it was difficult to maintain a course in a direction that was not to his liking. Thus, people usually ended up either going where Kanzi wanted to or putting him down. At times, I felt like a horse being broken and trained by an adamant, indefatigable rider.

Instead of people using gestures to cue apes, what we had in this situation was an ape using gestures to cue people. Kanzi did not mind being subtle about his cues as long as the message got across. If not, he was also quite happy to be very blatant.

On that typical morning, when Jeannine opened the door to the group room, Kanzi raced in and began checking on everything that he had not seen in there the night before: Jeannine's bag, a load of groceries she had bought, a new toy she had laid out for him. No new object or change in location of an old object was minor enough to escape Kanzi's attention; he took in every detail of the rooms in which he ate, slept, and played. While exploring the group room, Kanzi noticed an umbrella lying on the cabinet—it had been raining that morning. He immediately picked it up and threw it across the room. The umbrella had done nothing to Kanzi to solicit such an act, but Matata was very fearful of umbrellas, and Kanzi must have recalled her fear, even though she was no longer present. Matata did not understand how they worked and seemed to think of them as strange sticks that suddenly metamorphosed into large canopies. It seemed that she simply did not like them in principle—as far as I knew she was never harmed by an umbrella. Perhaps, however, the men who captured her carried umbrellas or used nets that shot out of sticks as umbrellas do. In any case, although Matata had rarely seen umbrellas while Kanzi was small, apparently she had transferred her concerns about these unusual sticks to him.

Jeannine, noting Kanzi's action, decided to put the umbrella away in the 'T-room' and used the keyboard to announce her intention to Kanzi. He watched as Jeannine carried the umbrella into the 'T-room' and then requested to be taken to the keyboard, where he said "umbrella" and gestured toward the 'T-room.' When Jeannine took Kanzi into the 'T-room', he proceeded to look into every cabinet until he located the one holding the umbrella. He then pushed Jeannine's hand toward the umbrella, wanting her to pick it up. Jeannine retrieved the umbrella and then put Kanzi down. Kanzi said "hide" and pointed to the umbrella, so Jeannine "hid" the umbrella again. Once it was out of sight, Kanzi said "umbrella" and gestured for Jeannine to carry him from place to place again until he found the umbrella. Kanzi played this hide-umbrella game with Jeannine several more times before he finally tired of it and asked to go back into the bedroom. During this self-initiated game, he seemed to overcome his initial fear of the umbrella. Perhaps the ability to have it put out of sight and then to find it again convinced Kanzi that the umbrella object behaved like all others in that it stayed where it was put until retrieved. It never jumped out at him or Jeannine, nor did it pop open of its own accord; thus, it appeared to be a rather trustworthy, if unusual, item.

Back in his bedroom, Kanzi lay down on the bed and said "tickle," then pointed to the flashlight to ask Jeannine to tickle him with it. Just as Kanzi liked to play "keep-away" with different objects, so he also enjoyed playing "tickle" and another game, "tag-chase," with a variety of objects. Jeannine tickled him all over his body by pressing and twisting the flashlight in various joints, while Kanzi smiled and laughed and pretended to try and stop her from tickling each new spot. Bonobos, like all apes, are much stronger than human beings and their muscles are quite dense. Thus, something that might feel a bit painful to us can bring forth loud peals of laughter from them.

Matata often tickled Kanzi by placing her mouth gently over a joint in his back, his neck, his knee, or his elbow. She then pressed down with her teeth and rubbed them back and forth, just as we do with our fingers when tickling. Kanzi loved this sort of play, and the flashlight, as Jeannine used it to tickle him, surely felt much the same as Matata's teeth. At one point, Jeannine dropped the flashlight and began tickling Kanzi with her fingers. Kanzi stopped laughing, sat up, and began to look around. Jeannine asked him if he was looking for the flashlight. Kanzi answered by saying "flashlight" at the keyboard and then began searching under the covers till he found it. He picked it up and handed it to Jeannine and again requested "tickle." Jeannine resumed her "flashlight tickles."

When they were done playing, Kanzi pointed to the door of the group room to indicate that he was ready to go outdoors. As he already knew how to get to all of the different locations outdoors but had not yet learned the symbols for many of them, Jeannine laid out an array of pictures of the various locations in front of Kanzi and asked him which one he wanted to visit. Kanzi selected the picture of the childside, on the other side of the building, then climbed on Jeannine's shoulders and gestured toward the childside. Even though he loved to travel to the new locations that were in the woods, he also liked to visit the childside where he could observe people coming and going and perhaps catch a brief glimpse of some of the children as they entered the building.

A cooler filled with apples had been located on the childside, so that if Kanzi became hungry, he could munch on apples while he watched the people go by. As Jeannine headed toward the childside, Kanzi gestured to the keyboard to indicate that he wanted to talk. Jeannine stopped and, with Kanzi still on her shoulders, held the keyboard up above her head so that Kanzi could speak without having to get down. Kanzi commented "apple," indicating that he recalled the type of food that he had found on the childside during earlier visits and that he hoped to have some more of it. Jeannine agreed and carried Kanzi to the apple cooler, where Kanzi helped himself as he watched the people passing by—a serviceman who was there to fix the air conditioning, the mailman, a student dropping by to ask about a job, and two mothers coming to learn how to use keyboards with their children. Only the serviceman noticed Kanzi, and he seemed to think that Kanzi was just an exotic pet Jeannine was showing off.

Since it is against the policy of the research center to allow anyone other than employees to approach apes, Jeannine waved the serviceman on when he began to come closer to look at Kanzi. Kanzi was very interested in the serviceman because he wore a lot of tools around his waist and because he kept going in and out of the "mechanical room." (This is a small room located on the outside of the building that contains all the control panels for the ventilation and electrical systems of the buildings, as well as the master fire-alarm panel.) Kanzi had always been told that this room was dangerous and that no one was allowed to go in it—which was true. However, he now observed this man casually walking in and out and taking great interest in some big boxes that Kanzi could glimpse whenever the serviceman came out and left the door open. Even more fascinating was the fact that this man climbed up a ladder right through a hole in the roof of this room and came out on top of the building!

Kanzi had been gravely cautioned not to go on top of the building—which he could easily have done—for two reasons. First, none of us could readily climb up there to follow him and make certain that he was okay. Second, all the heating and air-conditioning facilities were on top of the building, and we did not want him exploring this equipment. Since it was impossible to convince Kanzi that he should not explore interesting-looking boxes, we had told him that a scary monster lived on top of the building and so it was a very dangerous place. Kanzi had believed us, and he avoided the top of the building. Now a calm, happy serviceman was walking around on the top of the building who did not seem afraid at all. Moreover, it must have puzzled Kanzi that Jeannine did not seem to be concerned that this man was on the roof, nor was she warning him about the monsters. Even more interesting was the fact that there were no monsters jumping out at this man. Needless to say, Kanzi was most intrigued by this state of affairs.

I had just seen Kanzi and Jeannine walk past my office window and realized that Kanzi was up and ready to begin his day's exploration, so I strolled out to join them. When I noted Kanzi's fascination with the man on top of the building, I became worried that Kanzi would begin to think that this was a place that he too needed to explore, in spite of what we had told him. Thus, I decided to try and say something that would indicate to Kanzi that this fellow was indeed in danger. I cupped my hand over my mouth and yelled up to the serviceman, "You better be careful, don't you know that monsters sometimes come up there on the roof," in a tone of voice that indicated I was not totally serious. And then I winked and pointed to Kanzi. I was trying to say, "Play along with our game and pretend that you are being careful and watching out for those monsters."

Such indirect techniques of indicating pretence are often used between adults in the presence of children who are old enough to understand if one adult simply asked another adult to "act like you see monsters." I feared that Kanzi would have understood if I had I said to the man on the roof, "Please *act* as though you see monsters up there." So I attempted to use this indirect means of conveying the pretend game. The serviceman on the roof looked down at me as though I was surely a crazy person. He could not understand at all what I was doing. Either I really thought there were monsters on the roof, or I was a complete fool running around with a monkey and acting as though there were monsters on the roof, when I knew perfectly well that this was not the case. Of course, I should have realized that my ploy would backfire, but I always made this sort of mistake because it was hard for me to remember that Kanzi did not look at all like a child to most other people.

The workman looked down at me, Kanzi, and Jeannine and just shook his head and went on about his job. That fascinated Kanzi even more. From Kanzi's perspective, I had actually told the serviceman to watch out for the monsters, yet he did not seem at all frightened. Perhaps I was wrong: perhaps there were no monsters on top of the building after all. It also seemed that Kanzi understood that my tone of voice somehow signaled less concern than the situation would have merited had there really been monsters on the roof. Kanzi seemed to be beginning to make judgments not only of what I said, but about *how* I said it, and when there was a dissonance between these two states of affairs, it aroused his suspicion of my veracity.

My heart sank, as I knew that in the not-too-distant future we would see young Kanzi determined to carefully explore the top of the building to find out whether there were really monsters up there or not. A perfectly good and reliable means of keeping Kanzi out of mischief on the roof was spoiled because the world as we portrayed it to Kanzi and the world as it really was were not the same. I suppose it is inevitable that someday a person will go up on the roof and no monster will appear.

It was not that I had wanted to lie to Kanzi, only that I could not explain to him—in a way that he could understand—*why* boxes loaded with air-conditioning and heating equipment were dangerous or why he should not go someplace that I could not readily follow. Kanzi was not thinking about testing the roof today, however, as he was a little scared of the serviceman himself. Thus, I took note of the incident and tried to figure out a plan for the future. I could, of course, always put Kanzi on a lead, but I wanted to avoid doing so for as long as possible, since the more freedom Kanzi had, the more he encountered and elected to talk about at the keyboard.

Once the workman had finished the repairs, packed all of his tools in his truck, and left, Kanzi decided that it was time to go somewhere else. He turned and tugged at the keyboard which Jeannine was carrying to let her know that he had something to say. When she opened the keyboard and placed it on the ground in front of him, he carefully touched the symbol "Austin" and then directed his "go" gesture toward the area where Sherman and Austin lived.

Sherman and Austin were now adolescent male chimpanzees. Since we had no adult male bonobos, Sherman and Austin were Kanzi's role models, and he admired them greatly. He loved to play chase and keep-away with them; he was especially friendly with Austin, and often asked to go and visit him. Sherman sometimes played a little rough with Kanzi, but Austin was always patient and calm. Kanzi even allowed Austin to carry him around on his back. That very first night after Matata's departure to the field station, Kanzi had even elected to sleep with Austin rather than in his new bed with me. He left me, clung to Austin, and waited for Austin to make a large nest like his mother did and then to settle down and groom. Austin, however, was not interested in making a large nest, preferring to sleep instead on a single blanket spread out on the floor. Austin also was not interested in grooming Kanzi, though he did not hesitate to share his nest and he generally entertained Kanzi by playing with him.

It seemed that Kanzi felt a need for a hairy body to snuggle up to, and although Austin did not behave much like a bonobo mother, he certainly looked more like Matata than I did. But after about an hour of trying to go to sleep with Austin, Kanzi apparently decided that something just was not right and decided to rejoin me. Even though I did not look much like Matata, I behaved more like her than Austin did. From then on, he always preferred sleeping in a bed with me or one of the other caretakers.

Taking note of Kanzi's request, Jeannine agreed to visit Austin, and Kanzi climbed onto her shoulders to be carried there. As they neared Austin's playyard, Kanzi again tugged on the keyboard, and when Jeannine opened it for him, he said "orange." Oranges were the food typically found in the cooler placed near Sherman and Austin's playyard. By asking for them before the cooler was even opened, Kanzi revealed that he remembered the food typically found there. Jeannine opened the cooler and gave Kanzi an orange, which he spontaneously decided to share with his friend Austin. He tried to push the orange through the wire to Austin, but it would not fit, so he bit it open and passed half of the orange through to a very grateful Austin.

Kanzi seemed to enjoy sharing food with Austin. He also liked to share food with me, with other people, and with the dogs that lived at the laboratory. In return, he expected us to share food with him. He wanted a bite of everything he saw someone eat, especially if they appeared to be enjoying their food. Only Kanzi was not content with a separate piece of their food, he wanted some of the food that was actually in their mouth. Sharing food, mouth-to-mouth, was something that his mother had taught him.

In the wild, young bonobos learn which foods to eat and which not to eat by tasting the food as their mother consumes it. Since they obtain food directly from their mother's mouth, they cannot make a mistake and accidentally ingest a poisonous food. However, many people who worked with Kanzi did not wish to give him food from their mouths or to take food from his mouth; they were concerned about the possibility of passing germs back and forth.

"Germs"—this was another one of those concepts (like electricity) that one struggles with mightily to explain in some reasonable manner to a doubting ape. You could tell Kanzi that you don't want a bite of that smushed banana he is dangling on his lower lip toward you—because it has little invisible things on it that might make you sick. He can't see any little things on the banana, but he can understand that you are hesitant to eat it. Therefore, he wonders why *he* should eat it. If you tell him that the banana is perfectly good but you don't want to eat it, he assumes that if the banana is okay to eat, then you must be rejecting him, not the banana. Until he was nearly seven years old, Kanzi continued to behave as though his feelings had been deeply bruised whenever someone he liked refused to take some of the food he offered from his mouth or would not let him have some of theirs.

Austin, having no germ fears, was happy to take half of Kanzi's orange. Kanzi then gestured "chase" by clapping his hands together, and Austin chased him up and down along the fence. In the midst of the chase game, Kanzi abruptly stopped and started looking at himself in the mirror just outside Austin's yard. He then began making funny faces in the mirror. First, he inverted his lower lip until it covered his chin (something only apes can do), then he sucked in his cheeks until his face looked like a large raisin. Next, he jumped up and down on all fours, simultaneously shaking his head back and forth; then he held various parts of his body up to the mirror for a close inspection—his face, his stomach, his penis, and finally his buttocks. Finally, with a big smile on his face, he began to do a bonobo "dance," which consisted of trying to shake both his hands and both his feet at the same time without falling down.

Austin watched all of this with great amusement, for he also loved to look at himself in the mirror. Austin's use of mirrors, though, had become far more sophisticated than Kanzi's little dance. Austin used mirrors to apply makeup to his face and to try out fur shawls to make himself look even larger and more intimidating than he already was. He also had figured out how to use a small mirror to redirect beams of light. When slides were projected into his room, he would cause them to bounce around from wall to wall by holding up a mirror in front of the projector and redirecting the light.

Austin enjoyed many other forms of visual play as well. When watching super-8 movies of wild chimpanzees, he would interpose his body between the projector and the screen so that his own reflection cast a chimp shadow onto the movie picture; he would then make this shadow chase the chimpanzees in the movies. He also liked to watch his shadow outdoors and would practice moving in unusual ways to change the pattern it cast. Most of all, Austin liked to watch himself on live television. When the camera was turned on him and he was given a monitor, he would begin to play the movie "ham." Two of his favorite routines were to eat imaginary food, scooping large bites of nothing out of bowls while pretending to swallow them with great gusto, and to try and shine a flashlight down his throat while directing his large gaping mouth toward the cameras. Sometimes it even appeared that he was purposely wiggling the soft palate in the back of his throat. I never understood why Austin was so fascinated with his own throat—perhaps he was simply trying to figure out why he could not speak.

When he had finished contemplating his reflection, Kanzi again asked Austin to "chase" by using the handclapping gesture. Although the primary mode of communication was visual symbols, all of the apes at the lab used many spontaneous gestures as well. They often learned these from one another. Kanzi had learned the chase gesture from Austin when he was quite young. Fortunately, Kelly had been there to see this happen. She noticed that one weekend Kanzi seemed especially intrigued by watching Sherman and Austin play chase with one another. They frequently used the handclapping chase gesture as they did so, and Kanzi seemed to want to join in; however, these large adolescent males were having such a great time with each other that they completely ignored the young bonobo male on the other side of the wire. Kanzi sat and looked at them wistfully. The very next day, Kelly saw Kanzi attempting to make the handclapping gesture. As she described it:

> Learning to clap his hands was quite a feat for Kanzi. I remember one Saturday morning sitting in the cage with both Kanzi and Matata when Kanzi was about a year and a half old. Matata and I were in her nest grooming, while Kanzi sat about ten feet away from us. I could see he was concentrating on something very intently, yet could not see exactly what he was doing since his back was turned. When he later turned to face me it appeared as if he was trying to transfer something from one hand to the other. Then I realized he had nothing in his hands and was simply trying to make his two hands meet. He held one hand close to his body with the palm up while holding his other hand high over his head with the palm down. Slowly and carefully, he tried to bring both hands towards each other, working on this task with an expression of utmost concentration on his face. However, he could not quite coordinate both hands at the same time and ended up clapping only air instead of his hands! It was really funny to watch him do this because he was so serious about it, yet his hands kept missing each other! But he practiced very diligently on this new task, sometimes up to twenty or thirty minutes at a stretch. By the end of the day he had improved to the point where he occasionally was able to get both hands to make contact, but not on every attempt. He continued to practice on and off all throughout the day Sunday. By the time I left Sunday evening, I saw that his perseverance had paid off as Kanzi was clapping his hands with regular success.

Travels in the Forest

After chasing with Austin, Kanzi grew hungry. He climbed onto Jeannine's shoulders and gestured toward the woods. Jeannine held up the keyboard, and Kanzi said "juice." Jeannine commented that juice was found at the Treehouse, then she sat Kanzi down and placed five pictures from her bag in front of him to see if he knew where he was going. Kanzi quickly selected the Treehouse photo and climbed back onto Jeannine's shoulders while carrying the Treehouse picture with him. As Jeannine and I walked to the Treehouse, we commented at the keyboard on things that we saw along the way, such as the turtle that crossed our path, the ball that Kanzi had left at the trailer the previous day, and the car that passed us on the road just before we turned into the woods. Kanzi quietly noted everything we said but continued to hold onto his Treehouse picture as we walked. At one point, he gestured toward me, indicating that he would like to ride on my shoulders a while, so I obliged by standing close to Jeannine and letting him climb onto me.

Just before we reached the Treehouse, I felt Kanzi's body begin to stiffen, and I noticed that the hair on his legs, which was all I could see of him when he was astride my shoulders, was beginning to become erect. Kanzi made a soft "Whuh" sound and gestured to the side of the trail. There, a short distance from my foot, was coiled a very large snake. I screamed and jumped back several feet, almost falling as Kanzi grabbed hold of my head to hang on. Kanzi's keen eyes had enabled him to give a last-minute warning that had come just in time. I returned Kanzi to Jeannine, found a very long, sturdy stick, and proceeded to prod the snake until it moved into the bushes and disappeared. As soon as I moved toward the snake with the stick, Kanzi produced extremely loud "Waaa" calls, as though to warn me that what I was about to do was dangerous. Each time I actually struck the snake with the stick, Kanzi felt it necessary to "Waaa" yet again. Pretty soon Jeannine and I were "Waaaing" ourselves. "Waaa" seemed to be a pretty good word for "snake," and when it was uttered with the gusto that Kanzi mustered, the ferocity of the sound itself was almost effective enough to scare the snake away. I soon became so accustomed to giving "Waaa" barks to alert Kanzi whenever I saw a snake in the woods that I began to find myself "Waaaing" even when I was walking home alone and came across a snake.

Having cleared the snake from the trail, Jeannine, Kanzi, and I proceeded on to the Treehouse. As soon as we arrived, Kanzi leapt from my shoulders and rushed to the cooler. Each cooler was tied with a strap and held tight with a plastic squeeze lock. Kanzi was fascinated by these locks and wanted to learn how to open and close them on his own, so he tried to open every cooler by himself, whether he was interested in eating the food or not. I held the keyboard up to Kanzi and asked him to stop trying to open the cooler and answer a question for me if he could: "What is in the cooler?" Did Kanzi recall the foods typically found in the Treehouse cooler even though he could not see them? Kanzi quickly answered "juice-banana," then shoved the keyboard aside and again set to work on the lock.

Kanzi's answer was correct, and although simple for him, it reflected the astounding mental mapping of the forest sites he had achieved in a relatively short period of time. Within the first five months after Matata left, Kanzi had come to recognize sixteen different locations in the woods, and he knew the foods that were typically found at each location. He could select a photograph of the location, or of the food, to indicate a desire to travel to any of the different places. For some places, such as the A-frame, he had already learned the lexigram symbol as well. When he asked to go to a certain place by choosing a picture of that location from a group of photos, he always knew the kind of food that would be in the cooler even before it was opened, and if you asked him to tell you, he was happy to do so, either by selecting a photo or by pointing to the name of that food on the keyboard.

Kanzi seemed to have a map of the entire forest in his head and could easily travel to any spot he desired. When visitors came to the lab, he took great delight in showing off his forest by climbing onto their shoulders and announcing a list of places to visit. At first, we would tell them how to get to where Kanzi wished to go, since they knew nothing about the forest. We soon found that Kanzi was even better at this than we were and that he could guide them directly to any location he had selected, either by gesturing in the correct direction every time they came to a fork in the trail or by hopping down from their shoulders, taking them by the hand, and leading them down the proper trail. In fact, Kanzi mastered the forest more quickly than most of the lab workers who were his companions on these forest rambles. Some of them still carried maps in their backpacks and

Kanzi uses gestures and glances to show the experimenter that he would like to have the experimenter climb the vine next to the tree that he himself is planning to climb. Youngsters often climb vines and dangle from them to play side-by-side in the air in the wild.

checked from time to time to see if they were on the yellow trail, the blue trail, or the white trail, as each was marked on the map. Kanzi certainly had no need to check the map. He not only knew the trails but the relative locations of each food site. If we agreed to go off the trail at any point, Kanzi could make a beeline straight through the woods to the location he had selected, even though he had never traveled that route before.

Kanzi's companions preferred to stick to the trails because they were cleared and easier to traverse. Kanzi, however, could easily pass through the densest of underbrush and never lose his bearing or take an unnecessary sidetrack, regardless of whether he had ever been in that part of the forest before or not. It seems rather trite to say that, in the woods, Kanzi seemed intimately at home and extraordinarily well prepared to handle almost any situation he encountered. His anatomy made it possible to negotiate high trees, muddy swamps, and dense thorny underbrush, seemingly without a care and certainly without a scratch.

Mosquitos landed on him but did not bite because their proboscises could not quite reach his skin as they stood on the layer of coarse hair that covered his body. (Apes do not have fur but have bodily hair that is no more dense than our own. It simply appears to be fur because it is longer.) When Kanzi headed off the trail into the swamp, we sometimes went along in the beginning, swatting at the mosquitos, tripping over fallen logs, and sinking into the mud. We were inevitably frustrated as we could climb only the sturdiest of small trees, and even then we were unable to swing about with Kanzi's cavalier grace. We cursed the thorns on the underbrush while we crawled along on our knees, vowing never to let Kanzi lead us this way again.

Kanzi seemed quite puzzled by all our difficulties, our slow pace, and what he must have viewed as an irrational fear of trees. He always wanted people to climb trees with him and indicated this by taking their hands and placing them directly on the tree while looking up at it and then back at the person. If that did not work, Kanzi would climb a short distance up the tree, then turn and gesture "come." Some of us would attempt to climb a tree on occasion, while others absolutely refused. If one dared to do so, it was important to be careful, for as soon as you were in the tree, Kanzi would approach and want to play by dangling from your feet or arms. He seemed to think that we could easily support his weight and that he needn't worry about falling—we would catch him. However, catching thirty to thirty-five pounds as it hangs beside one in a tree is a difficult job, and it was easy to be caught off-balance by Kanzi. Thus, my first rule whenever Kanzi and I were in the same tree was to hold on as tightly as I possibly could at all times. I never knew when Kanzi might decide to use my leg or my arm as a vine and suddenly hang on it with all of his weight.

After I gave Kanzi the bananas and the juice from the cooler, he climbed on top of the Treehouse, where he reclined to eat slowly and savor each bite while surveying the forest. As at all the other locations, he had come not only to expect the food that had been placed there but to feel especially like eating that food at that location. That is, Kanzi behaved as though bananas and juice tasted *particularly* good when he was at the Treehouse, peaches and strawberries were just delicious when he was at Lookout Point, the raisins at Midway were exceptional, and so on.

Many times, as we went into the woods, I carried a little food in the backpack to make certain that Kanzi had enough to eat in case the coolers had not been filled properly or had, as sometimes happened, been visited by one of the industrious raccoons that inhabited the forest. (The raccoons were so adept at getting coolers open no matter how we secured them that occasionally I wondered if we shouldn't be studying their problem-solving skills as well as Kanzi's.) Whenever I carried food along, it always seemed that Kanzi never felt like eating bananas till we happened near the Treehouse, or never felt like eating strawberries till we approached Lookout Point. Suddenly, once we were at Lookout Point, a great craving for strawberries would set in. Perhaps apes in the field utilize this location-triggered "craving" to help them recall where to find certain fruiting trees in the vicinity.

It would be wrong, however, to convey the impression that Kanzi always had to eat M&Ms at Flatrock or peaches at Lookout Point. Many times, he was not even hungry and would simply go to a location and play without showing any interest in the food at all. If I opened the cooler and offered him some food, he would turn it down. But when he was hungry, he seemed to have a certain fondness for the foods that were associated with that location. Having learned these food-location associations with amazing alacrity, he also possessed a rather uncanny memory for any new foods that he happened to have at other places. For example, one day, late in the fall, I let him visit my house, which was only about two hundred yards from the laboratory. While he was there, he found some very tasty jelly in the refrigerator. He did not return to my house again until the following year, as it grew too cold to travel outdoors. However, when he returned, he at once used the keyboard to ask for some "jelly" and pointed to my refrigerator, though I had forgotten that he had eaten jelly there before.

I had originally begun the practice of carrying photos as a way to remind Kanzi of our destinations when we first began to introduce him to the woods. Since Kanzi initially did not understand the names of the locations, when I announced my intent to travel to Flatrock, for example, I would also show him a picture of M&Ms and of Flatrock, hoping that if the words and symbols were meaningless to him, at least the pictures might help him understand that I was attempting to convey a plan of future action. Then as we traveled I would occasionally draw his attention to the photo to try to remind him of our destination as we came across other locations in the forest, hoping that he would begin to understand that my intent to travel to a faraway location such as Flatrock, even though expressed thirty to forty-five minutes earlier, nonetheless remained intact.

Kanzi quickly caught on to this use of the photographs and would ask to look at them frequently as we traveled toward our predetermined goal. Soon it began to seem superfluous to carry the pictures and constantly remind Kanzi of what it was that we intended to do, and we often forgot to take the pictures out of the bag. Kanzi knew all the locations and how to get to them and had begun to initiate most of the travel decisions himself. He also occasionally decided to make up for our forgetfulness with regard to the photographs, by finding them in the bag and carrying them himself. At times, he would stop along the way, point to a photograph, and look at us, apparently asking, "Do you know that this is where I am headed?" We would always agree, reaffirming for him that the location or food in the photograph was our goal also.

Later, we attempted a similar study with a nine-month-old child. We introduced her to the keyboard and to the use of photographs and let her choose a desired location of travel, even though she was not old enough to talk. Like Kanzi, she quickly realized that she could express her desires by selecting photographs; also like Kanzi, she often wanted to carry the picture with her and point to it as she traveled toward her goal. Neither could speak, and both were just learning to communicate with others about events that were going to happen sometime in the future. The pictures permitted them to gain some reaffirmation that indeed the intended actions of the group were still in accord with what had been agreed to at an earlier time.

Along the trail to Flatrock and M&Ms, we passed CrissCross Corners, but Kanzi did not seem to notice. As we approached the division in the trail just beyond CrissCross Corners, Kanzi reminded me to turn to the right by gesturing and leaning in this direction. Shortly after the trail turned to the right, we came to the foot-bridge that traverses the swampy area between the inner loop of food sites and the outer loop, both of which are on higher ground than the low area in the middle. Kanzi hopped off my shoulders and began to skip along the footbridge. Even when he wanted to be carried in other parts of the forest, he seemed to always enjoy walking on the footbridge. The swamp area was large; the footbridge ran for nearly two hundred yards and was often very slippery if it had rained recently. I was always very grateful when Kanzi decided to walk as we came to the bridge, be-cause it was very narrow and tricky to negotiate even without an extra forty-five to fifty pounds of wiggling weight on my shoulders.

Along either side of the bridge lay the densest ground cover of the forest; a variety of stiff privet bushes, which grew well in the low muddy area, made it virtually impossible to make your way through the forest off the trail except by crawling through the mud on your hands and knees, and in some places even on your stomach. So I stayed on the bridge. Kanzi, however, seemed made to traverse low, swampy, muddy areas. He was totally at ease in these bushes, as though he had encountered his natural element. Since no one really wanted to follow Kanzi on his short forays off the bridge and into the privet bushes, the bridge became Kanzi's favorite place to play hide. Sometimes he gave us the benefit of using the keyboard to announce that this was what he was going to do; other times, I would be following him as he tripped happily along the bridge in front of me only to round a corner behind and suddenly—*no Kanzi*. He seemed to delight in his abil-ity to vanish without a trace when no one was looking. Moreover, he could move through the dense privet bushes without a sound once he elected to fade into them.

I had read the field reports about how bonobos in Zaire eluded researchers by simply fading into the brush without a sound. Fieldworkers sometimes reported that they felt literally surrounded by bonobos, as if being watched by the entire group, yet they could see not a one. As Kanzi vanished into the privet bushes, I knew distinctly how they felt. Of course, I always worried that something might happen to him while he was out of sight. What if he found an unusual mushroom and popped it into his mouth and it turned out to be poisonous later on? Did he know better than to do that? What if he came across a copperhead or water moc-casin—would he see it in time, and if so, would he be inclined to avoid it? What if he just decided to walk so far away into the privet bushes that he eventually came to the river that ran alongside the forest. Would he jump in the river? Would he drown? Of course, he never did any of these things, and I had no real reason to believe that he would, yet it was difficult not to worry while he was out of sight. For his part, he thought the whole affair great fun, for he could always peek out and see me whenever he wanted as he knew I would be standing on the bridge. He never went very far, maybe fifty or seventy-five feet, but the bushes were so dense that it did not matter. Even though he was nearby, he could not be seen.

When Kanzi vanished from the bridge on the way to Flatrock, I did not show my concern for his safety but continued to act calm and do my best to play my role in the game—which was to search for him. Jeannine and I moved apart and began looking under the bushes close to the bridge, calling out "Kanzi, Kanzi, where are you," which was what he loved to hear. I crawled a little way into the privet bushes but of course could see nothing. Jeannine walked ahead on the trail and then back down the direction we had come from and announced that she had seen nothing. When we could not find Kanzi, I decided to engage in another strategy that had, on past occasions, successfully pulled Kanzi out of the privet bushes. I sat down and began to look through the contents of my backpack, commenting to Jeannine on things that I knew were of particular interest to Kanzi. I mentioned the pictures, the towel, the can opener, the bowl, the wipees—all with no response. Then I noticed some balloons, one of Kanzi's favorite toys, and said loudly, "Oh, Jeannine, look, I found a red balloon in the backpack." From out of the woods only a few feet away we heard the little "Eehhh" sound Kanzi makes when something catches his interest—but still no Kanzi. So I continued to look in my backpack, mentioning the soap bubbles and the hat; and then in the very bottom, I found a small candy surprise. I had hardly gotten the words out of my mouth when suddenly Kanzi was sitting on the bridge right in front of me, staring into the backpack. He found the surprise, then picked up the M&M picture, which he had dropped on the bridge when he disappeared into the bushes, and announced that he was ready to proceed by climbing back onto my shoulders and gesturing in the direction of Flatrock.

As we proceeded on down the bridge we came to Midway, where there were raisins hanging in a bag over our head. Thinking that Kanzi might want some raisins, even though he had not mentioned them, I held the keyboard up and asked, "raisin?"—trying to determine if he wanted to stop to get the raisins. Kanzi, who had not yet learned the "no" symbol, responded by placing his hand on my head and turning it sharply in the direction of Flatrock. Once he had me looking in the proper direction, he gestured "go" to let me know that he was not interested in stopping for raisins, but only in proceeding on to M&Ms. Shortly past Midway the footbridge ended, and we were back on higher ground and out of the privet bushes. Kanzi climbed down from my shoulders and tugged on the keyboard to indicate that he wanted to say something. I placed the keyboard on the ground, and he commented "kiwi ball."

Balls are Kanzi's favorite toy, and he often carried one with him during our walks in the woods. Equally often, he left them somewhere in the woods, apparently on purpose. He would seem to tire of dragging the ball along constantly, so he would stop, look around, and then place the ball near some bush or tree. When he first began to leave his ball in the woods, we did not think much about it. Yet we soon noticed that he seemed to be able to recall where he had left it days or even weeks later.

When Kanzi said "kiwi ball," I wondered if he had just remembered that he had left a ball near Log Cabin, where we usually find kiwis in the cooler, or whether he was simply trying to tell me that he wanted both a ball and some kiwi. I did not recall him leaving a ball there, but he often went in the forest with Kelly and Rose when I was not with him. When we arrived at Log Cabin, I saw no ball. Kanzi dropped his M&M photo and pointed to the cooler to indicate that he was ready to have some kiwi. While he was eating, I made notes on the things we had done so far that day. When I looked up, Kanzi was gone again. I asked Jeannine where he had gone, and she said that he had just gone behind Log Cabin. A moment later he popped out with his ball in hand. Not only had he left his ball at Log Cabin, just as he said, but he had hidden it in the bushes; only he knew where it had been left.

After playing with the ball, Kanzi then showed me the M&M picture, tapped the M&M symbol on the keyboard, and headed off toward Flatrock with his ball. At Flatrock, he inhaled the M&Ms, as was his habit. I tried to dissuade Kanzi from eating too much candy, so M&Ms was one of the furthest locations from the lab, and I limited the number of M&Ms that were placed there. Kanzi loved M&Ms and tended to eat them as fast as he possibly could. The only way I could slow him down was to scatter them on the ground after I retrieved them from the cooler, so that he had to look through the leaves of the forest floor and find each one before he ate it. He was aware of my trick, however, and today he came up behind me and grabbed the bag out of my hand before I had a chance to scatter even a few M&Ms on the ground. All the M&Ms went into his mouth at one time.

After Kanzi ate the M&Ms, he began to look tired. It was getting to be midday, the time at which both Kanzi and bonobos in the wild usually take a nap. Kanzi settled down in my lap, looked over toward the keyboard, and commented "bedroom." It was a long way back to the bedroom, at least a forty-minute walk, and Kanzi looked too sleepy to make the trip, so I suggested that he take his nap at Flatrock. Kelly and Rose would soon come to relieve Jeannine and me. Jeannine had been with Kanzi since seven o'clock that morning, and it was now two o'clock. It was difficult for any of us to keep up with Kanzi for more than seven or eight hours without a break. If they did not find us napping in the bedroom, I knew they would come and look for us in the forest. As Kanzi dropped off to sleep, I continued making notes about what he had done that day.

Suddenly, the wind picked up and we began to hear rumblings in the distance. I looked up to see storm clouds moving rapidly above the trees and realized that we were about to be caught in a summer thunderstorm. I woke Kanzi up and told him "rain come" and that we had to "chase [to] Hilltop." Hilltop was the closest place where we could find shelter from the rain. It was only a small plastic tarp thrown around some poles in tepee fashion, but it was certainly better than nothing at all.

We grabbed our backpacks and rushed up the hill as fast as we could. Kanzi clung tightly to Jeannine's stomach, gripping her shirt with his hands and feet, just as he would have held onto Matata. It was already sprinkling, and we had carried no umbrellas with us. We reached the tepee just before the sky decided to literally pour water, and all three of us scrunched inside together—only to find that we were not alone. A family of wasps had decided to make their home in the very top of the tepee, and they did not appreciate our intrusion. I realized they were there only when I heard Jeannine scream as she was stung. Shortly thereafter, Kanzi let out an equally loud yell as an angry one landed on him. In a matter of seconds, all three of us were outside the tent, drenched by the rain, with Kanzi still clinging tightly to Jeannine.

Luckily, I had not been stung. I grabbed the first large stick I could find, carefully reentered the tepee, and knocked down the nest. It fell on the wooden floor, and I backed quickly out of the tepee. Luckily, the wasps did not follow and attack me. Instead, they became somewhat disoriented as they flew out into the rain. In a few seconds I knocked the nest completely out of the tepee, and we sought shelter again, this time thoroughly drenched. We all sat there miserably wet and waited for it to stop raining. Kanzi scrunched up his eyes and tried to resume his nap, but somehow it just wasn't the same. The rain lasted another thirty minutes, then the sun came out again. Rose and Kelly appeared shortly thereafter, carrying umbrellas and dry towels and fresh backpacks. All of us were glad to see them. Jeannine and I left Kanzi in their care and headed back to the lab.

Evening Tours

During his evening trips, Kanzi was always very quiet and subdued. One night Kelly and I tried to camp out with him, thinking that he might enjoy such an experience. The later it became, the more concern he evidenced. He repeatedly told us that he wanted to go back to the group room, and when we refused, he pouted and fussed. When we tried to convince him to crawl under the covers and sleep, he resisted and simply sat in the door of the tent and gestured toward the laboratory. I ended up walking back through the woods in the dark at two o'clock in the morning with a very scared Kanzi holding onto me as tightly as possible.

Ever since Matata had left, someone had stayed each night with Kanzi. He had become accustomed to sleeping in a bed and watching television before he dozed off. Moreover, with his keyboard, he could order late-night snacks of all his favorite foods while watching television. He had become accustomed to a material world that was far richer and more entertaining than the world his mother could provide, and like many people who travel from primitive rural villages to the highly industrialized cities of the world, he elected not to trade the amenities of modern life for the simpler existence of yesteryear.

Kelly was in the bedroom, getting things ready for Kanzi. As I left him with her, I noticed that he told Kelly he wanted to watch "Austin [on] TV." He also asked for his "ball" and some "cereal." Shortly after Matata left, he had become attached to his ball in much the same way that some children become attached to a special blanket. He always wanted to make sure his ball was in bed with him at night and often sat in the middle of the bed with the ball on his lap watching television until he went to sleep.

Kelly put on a tape of "Austin" for Kanzi to watch and went out to find his ball and prepare his cereal for him. As Kanzi waited for Kelly to return, he began to arrange and rearrange the blankets in a big circular nest around himself. Once his nest was finished, he began to pay more attention to the television. He liked to watch many things on TV, among them *Tarzan*, *The Iceman*, *Quest for Fire*, and *My Pet Monster*. He also liked to watch tapes of Sherman and Austin, as he knew them from firsthand visits. Although they were now adult males, he often enjoyed seeing tapes made when they were much younger, closer to his own age. On these tapes, he could see them using their keyboard to talk with me, as well as games of chase, grab, and tickle being played with me and other people that he knew.

We had made many hundreds of hours of such tapes for documentary purposes while Sherman and Austin were growing up: consequently, Kanzi had a great variety of such tapes for entertainment. Kanzi began to ask for these tapes by saying "Austin TV" and sometimes commented on things he saw while watching them such as, for example, the 'scary monster' that suddenly appeared.

He would ask for other favorite tapes by saying "Fire TV" when he wanted to watch the movie *Quest for Fire*, "Ice TV" when he wanted to watch the movie *Iceman*, "childside TV" to see tape of things that were happening on the childside, and "gorilla TV" or "bunny TV" to ask to watch a tape we had made for him of the "gorilla" and the "bunny" who visited our lab from time to time, Kanzi's version of something like Sesame Street characters. From time to time one of the persons at the lab donned the gorilla or the bunny costume and made an appearance doing something that caught Kanzi's attention, such as playing with one of his balls or hiding in the forest. We often taped these appearances, and Kanzi loved these tapes best of all.

Kanzi combined other words on his keyboard to indicate a desire to see specific things, but there were no names on his keyboard for many of the videotapes he liked to watch. To help him, photographs of the contents of these videotapes were pasted on the tape cartridges themselves, so that he could select the one he wanted.

Kanzi had quickly become a sophisticated television viewer. When he watched tapes of events that had taken place in the forest or near the lab, he could reliably discern where he had seen someone hide a ball or surprise and then travel to that place to recover the coveted item. If he saw a gorilla on television near the lab one evening, the next day he would approach the precise location where the television had depicted the gorilla. With hair puffed out, he would cautiously approach, while sniffing various items that he had seen the gorilla touch while watching the videotape.

Once Kanzi has seen a tape, he is able to anticipate when especially exciting segments are about to appear if he views the same tape again. For example, in one tape, a gorilla (that is, a person dressed in a gorilla suit) hides in a van, and Rose gets in, ostensibly without seeing the gorilla, who continues to hide behind the seat as she drives off. Upon Kanzi's second viewing, as the tape approached the segment in which the gorilla was about to jump out and scare Rose, Kanzi produced loud "Waaa" calls even *before* this happened, revealing that he recalled what was about to occur from the previous occasion on which he saw the videotape.

After Kelly came back with his cereal, he snuggled up next to her and commented "Coke," as he saw Sherman and Austin drinking some Coke on the TV. A bit later, he also commented "M&Ms" when he saw me give Sherman and Austin some M&Ms on the TV. Kanzi then grew tired and lay down in his nest and began to gently tickle with Kelly. Kanzi is generally extremely happy in the evening, and this evening was no exception. He demonstrated his good humor by chortling away with a wide range of sounds, much as a young child might babble to itself before falling off to sleep, but somewhat louder. I dropped in to tell Kanzi good night, and he responded with a whole medley of vocalizations. The next day, Kelly described his evening soundfest in our daily record of Kanzi's activities:

> Kanzi got into what I refer to as his "conversational mode," in which he vocalizes continuously in much the same way a small child will babble. He "talks" in this manner when other people are talking, especially if they are talking to each other rather than to him. It is as if he feels the need to be part of the conversation. He makes a lot of these vocalizations at night when he is ready for bed. Something about the night turns him into a motor mouth and I frequently get headaches when I put him to bed from his incessant chattering! As he drinks his nightly glass of water, stretched out on his back, he also feels an obligation to continue his conversation. With a large mouthful of water he looks just like a little fountain, bubbling over, as he tries to talk and drink at the same time. Even as he slows down and can barely even move due to fatigue, he still deems it necessary to answer each of my questions with some sort of verbal comment. When he is that tired it seems to take all his strength to utter any sound as he scrunches up the little muscles in his face and tries to talk. It is obvious that it is quite an effort for him and often he will open his mouth to speak, yet three or four seconds may elapse until he is finally able to get a sound to come out.

Living with Kanzi

Kanzi's days continued to be filled with treks in the woods, campfires, visits to Sherman and Austin, time with Matata, and special videotapes made just for him and, later, his two younger sisters, Panbanisha and Tamuli. As he grew older, the number of words he could understand steadily increased. We added symbols to his keyboard until it began to seem unwieldy at 256. Although Kanzi understood many more than 256 words, it was difficult to find just the word one wanted when one had to search a display of 256 words. Fortunately, however, Kanzi is not limited to lexigrams—he employs vocalizations and gestures as well. In fact, he typically combines several of these modes to make a more complex request, thus expanding what he can say beyond the limits of the keyboard itself.

For example, one of Kanzi's favorite games in the summertime is to have someone fill his or her mouth with water and chase him while trying to drench him with the water. Kanzi also likes to fill a balloon with water and play keep-away until the balloon bursts. When he wanted to play such games with the water hose, and there was no symbol for "hose" on his keyboard, he conveyed his intent by saying "water chase," then pointing to the hose. He would indicate that he wanted to play the water chase game by saying "water balloon" and then gesturing toward the hose. To be certain of Kanzi's intent, I would generally rephrase it aloud in English for him. If I had correctly discerned what Kanzi wanted me to do, he would respond with loud, happy vocalizations. For example, if he wanted me to fill the balloon full of water so that we could play keep-away, I could say, "Oh, I think you want me to make a water balloon and play chase?" If this were the case, Kanzi would respond with happy vocalizations that sounded as though he were attempting to say "un-huh." If not, he would studiously ignore me.

Kanzi also produces a vocalization that sounds a lot like the whining noise young children make when they want something quite badly that they do not have. Kanzi uses this sound in many different circumstances, but they all seem to have in common his desire to have something that someone is withholding. For example, one day, after several bouts of chasing with the hose, the balloon, and a number of other objects, I noticed that Kanzi was tapping my foot and vocalizing "Annngh" as though he wanted something. I looked down to find that I was standing on his collapsed water balloon—he was trying to show me that I needed to lift up my foot so that he could retrieve his balloon.

Kanzi has invented a number of gestures that are more specific than the pointing or indicative gestures he frequently uses when there is no symbol on his keyboard for a certain object. For example, to ask that someone open something for him, such as a bottle, he makes a twisting motion with his hand (as if twisting off a lid), sometimes on the bottle, or just above the bottle. Another gesture he has developed is a rapid handshaking motion, typically directed toward a particular object. The contexts in which Kanzi uses this gesture have led us to interpret it as meaning "do something" or "act upon something." For example, one morning Kanzi discovered some sweet potatoes cooking on the stove. Seeing the steam rise, he began making his "do something" gesture while pushing my hand toward the boiling pot. I did various things to the potatoes—stuck them with a knife, spun them around, and so on—which Kanzi enjoyed watching. Each time I stopped, Kanzi would gesture, by shaking his arms, for me to continue performing some type of action on the potatoes. Another example occurred when he discovered a turtle outside. He was not sure he was brave enough to approach the turtle by himself, yet felt it had to be dealt with in some way. So he pushed my hand toward it, then made his "do something" gesture. He has similarly used this gesture when encountering other animals or strange objects, in an attempt to elicit some action toward those objects by others.

Kanzi manifests great pleasure in participating in social games; however, unlike many other animals who play similar games with human beings, Kanzi thoroughly enjoys watching people play with each other. Just as we go to sporting events and watch people catch, throw, chase, and battle over balls, Kanzi delights in watching people at the laboratory play physical games. He can be relied on at any social gathering to initiate games between people by saying "chase," then taking someone's hand, for example mine, and pushing it toward another person, such as Kelly. I interpret this as a request for me to chase Kelly and, if Kelly agrees, I will chase her until I tag her. As soon as Kelly is tagged, Kanzi will ask us to invert our roles by pushing Kelly's hand toward me, and again saying "chase." Kanzi initiates not only chase games between other people, but also games of tickle, grab, hide, and keep-away.

When three or four people are with Kanzi, he usually tries all combinations. For example, Rose will be asked to chase Kelly, as will Liz; Liz will be asked to chase me; I will be asked to chase her; and so forth. Kanzi even requests three-way chase games, by pushing both my hand and Liz's toward Kelly, for example. Often during such games, Kanzi will lounge in a tree or on the ground and watch

Kanzi uses the keyboard to suggest a game of "chase-keep-away" to his younger sister Mulika.

Mulika trys to keep away from Kanzi as he chases her around the car.

with an expression of amusement on his face. He particularly prefers instances in which people try their hardest to outmaneuver one another, and he always requests repeat performances from participants who do a particularly entertaining job from his perspective. Kanzi's interest in watching us play chase, hide, and keep-away is far greater than our physical stamina for these games. Also, I must admit that at times we feel silly playing spectator sports for a crowd of one, especially when that individual is an ape. Consequently, these games always end much too soon from Kanzi's perspective.

Kanzi's interest in asking one person to chase, grab, or tickle another is significant from both a social and a linguistic perspective. It means that he is communicating not only about things that should happen directly to him but about things that he wants to see others do around him. He displays a keen awareness that different sorts of social relationships exist between different people, and he wants to observe how people relate to one another when they play. He is particularly curious to see what happens when roles are reversed in games like chase, grab, or slap. From a linguistic standpoint, requests designed to ask one person to chase another are complex, in that they require Kanzi to specify the chaser and the chasee, as well as the game itself. Unlike Kanzi, Sherman and Austin always included themselves in these games, and generally they elected to be the chasee. Thus they had no need for a grammatical rule that would mark the different roles of two players. They needed only to specify who should play chase with them and then to run toward, or away from, that person. However, since Kanzi elected to observe the chasing activity rather than participate, he needed a grammatical means of indicating who was to be the agent and who was to be the recipient. Because the names of individuals involved in such games all belong to the class of "agents," without some means of specifying how the two agent terms are to be related, vis-à-vis the verb, the meaning of a sentence is unclear. Kanzi adopted the order of his gestures as a device to get his messages across clearly, presumably because the language he was learning was English, and English relies on ordering rules for such things. Had Kanzi been exposed to another language, and had his listeners been speakers of a language that used another means of indicating grammatical relationships, Kanzi probably would have adopted a different grammatical device.

It is interesting that the kind of combinations that clearly require Kanzi to employ a syntactic rule in order to be correctly understood are those in which the speaker (in this case, Kanzi) is neither the agent nor the recipient of the action. This suggests that syntactic constructions may have coevolved with the ability to ask party A to act on party B, independently from the actions of the speaker. That is, the ability to divorce one's own perspective from the communications one is producing would inevitably lead to the need for linguistic constructions that are dependent on rules to specify relationships between words of a similar class.

However, many of Kanzi's combinations did not require grammatical rules for effective communication. For example, although Kanzi followed English word order when he said "food childside" to indicate that he wanted to look for food in the cooler on the childside, he could just as well have said "childside food" and still have been understood. Similarly, when he said "childside orange" to ask to take his orange to the childside, he again followed English word order; but had he used the inversion of this order, his meaning would nonetheless have been clear, because he was holding an orange at the time, and oranges are not generally found on the childside. It is important to note that when words of different classes are used, syntactic rules are almost never required for clear communications as long as the sentences are only three or four words long.

In addition to employing simple syntactic devices, Kanzi also takes an interest in saying the same thing in several different ways and noting the relationships between symbols, photographs, and objects. For example, when someone makes a vocal comment about, say, a ball Kanzi is playing with, he will often touch the ball lexigram on the keyboard, point to a photograph of a ball if any are around, and then gesture toward his real ball, as though denoting that all of these items are equivalent in some manner. Sometimes, he will even take a toy or a food and place it directly on top of the lexigram that stands for that object. When several keyboards are available, Kanzi frequently uses all of them, sometimes repeating his statements on multiple keyboards, other times using different keyboards for different utterances.

Kanzi also talks to himself, particularly at nap time or other quiet periods of the day. He does this by picking up the keyboard, moving a short distance away from the rest of the group and turning his back. He then scans the board and touches particular lexigrams. If I try to look over his shoulder to see what he is saying, he

Kanzi wants to be alone. He first picks up the keyboard and wraps it around himself.

He then decides that this is not sufficient, so he stands up with the keyboard still wrapped about himself and carries it about thirty yards away.

He then sits down and begins talking to himself. On such occasions, he did not seem to want us to know what he was saying. If we approached, he either turned his back or moved away. Here he is pointing to the symbol for his favorite object, "ball."

generally picks up the keyboard and moves further away. At times, he touches symbols, then glances over his shoulder to look at me, as though he wants me to see that he is talking, but does not want me to see what he is saying. Occasionally, I can catch glimpses of his comments, but if I try to talk about it with him, or make a comment on what he is saying, he seems to find this disturbing, and he will either quit talking to himself or move completely out of sight. When I do catch a glimpse of his monologues, I frequently see him pointing to the lexigrams "good" and "bad." He also talks about his "ball," his favorite foods, places he likes to go, and about tickling, chasing, grabbing, and biting.

When the lexigrams "good" and "bad" were first placed on Kanzi's keyboard, I did not think he would use them frequently, or with intent. I put them on so that everyone would have a clear way of indicating to Kanzi when we felt that he was being good or bad. To my surprise, Kanzi was intrigued with these lexigrams and soon began using them to indicate his intent to be good or bad, as well as to comment on his previous actions as "good" or "bad." When he was about to do things that he knew we did not want him to do, he started saying "bad, bad, bad" before he did them, as though threatening to do something he was not supposed to do. He would, for example, announce his intent to be bad before biting a hole in his ball, tearing up the telephone, or taking an object away from someone.

One day, when Kanzi was supposed to be taking a nap with Liz, who was exhausted and went to sleep, Kanzi refused to lie down. After she had been asleep about fifteen minutes, she suddenly realized that the blanket she was using as a pillow had been rudely jerked out from under her head. She sat up to look over at Kanzi who commented on his action, saying "bad surprise." Another time, when he was supposed to take a nap, he did not want to do so. He asked to play "chase water" instead, and when told that he could not do so, he commented "bad water" and proceeded to take the hot water hose and spray it all over things.

Kanzi knew that taking blankets away from someone, particularly if they were sleeping or sitting on them, was not acceptable. Indeed, this was one of the few behaviors that even Matata would not tolerate. One day, when Kanzi was nearly six years old, I noticed that he had a very fresh injury on his hand and he appeared to be unusually subdued, almost depressed. When I asked Kanzi how he had gotten hurt, he responded, "Matata bite" and then gestured to his hand with a plaintive expression. I later learned that this was indeed the case. His assertive, rambunctious attitude had become too much for Matata, who was preoccupied with Kanzi's new sister, Mulika, and did not want to play with Kanzi. He tried to gain his mother's attention by stealing some blankets from her nest, an act she did not appreciate. When he refused to give the blankets back, Matata bit his hand hard enough to actually break the skin. Kanzi appeared to be shocked and subdued. Never before had Matata done such a thing, no matter how rude he was toward her. Even bonobo mothers have limits to their patience.

Kanzi not only shows concern over his own injuries, but also over the injuries of others. For example, on one occasion, while attempting to open a can of cherries by throwing it, he accidentally smashed the can into Kelly's knee. She screamed in pain and grabbed her knee with her hand. Kanzi did not realize that the can had landed on Kelly, so when she held her hand tightly on her knee, Kanzi assumed that it was her hand which had been hurt. He approached and looked at Kelly's hand intently, but saw only a small scab from an old cut. Seeing nothing else wrong with her, Kanzi assumed that this must have been the cause of her distress. Wanting to help her feel better in some way, he gently pushed Kelly's hand toward a canteen of water which Rose was holding. Rose asked Kanzi what he wanted, and he replied by pointing to the canteen and then to Kelly's cut, to indicate that Rose should pour some water on Kelly's wound. When Rose complied, Kanzi gently tried to clean the cut. Of course, it was not Kelly's hand that had caused her to scream, but she was so intrigued by the thoughtfulness Kanzi was showing for her that she completely forgot about the pain in her knee.

The ability to empathize with another party suggests that Kanzi can understand that different people experience the world in different ways. He recognizes that he himself can feel quite well while another person is in pain, and that he can be in pain while another person feels fine. Kanzi not only recognized that Kelly was in pain but wanted to do something to help.

When Kanzi is in pain, he will point to the location that hurts and show it to me. He will even show a sore limb or sore throat to the veterinarian. He seems to understand in some limited sense that we are attempting to help him, and he has been willing to cooperate with having his temperature taken and even receiving frequent injections when necessary. Though many apes are hesitant to take medication, Kanzi is always extremely cooperative in this regard, even though he may not like the taste of the medicine he is receiving. His cooperative attitude with regard to unpleasant medication and injections suggests some understanding that these activities reflect our attempts to help him feel better.

Matata, in contrast, refuses all injections and is highly suspicious of any food that contains even the slightest trace or lingering odor of a drug. Indeed, she is so sensitive to the possibility that drugs may be placed in her food that she occasionally refuses to accept food that is prepared in a manner that differs in any way from what she is accustomed to.

Kanzi suffered through a number of illnesses and injuries as he grew up, but the most serious was an infection of the air sac tissue below his chin. Unlike humans, apes have pouches under their throat that can be filled with air and that may help resonate the sound produced by their vocal cords. When this tissue becomes infected, it must be repeatedly drained, and high doses of antibiotics must be injected every four hours. Although Kanzi was quite willing to accept the frequent injections his illness required, the veterinary staff did not believe that he would continue to do so on a daily basis for several weeks. Thus, it was determined that he should be taken to another facility and placed in a small squeeze cage that barely gave him room to sit and certainly no room to stand. The front of this cage was attached to rollers and, by a system of levers, could be cranked forward until it nearly reached the back wall of the small enclosure, trapping the animal within a vise. Such cages are used routinely with apes that refuse to accept injections. They confine the ape so rigidly that it cannot get away from the needle or knock it out of the veterinarian's hand.

Kanzi had never experienced any sort of confinement, so he was terrified when he awoke from sedation and found himself in a completely strange place in this small cage. He heard around him the screams of strange chimpanzees, whom he could not see, and he was as frightened by their cries as by his own predicament. Had he been able to get out of the small cage, he certainly would not have left the tiny room that held it, because of the awful noises outside the door. Everyone at the Language Research Center was concerned about the traumatic effect of this experience on Kanzi, and we took turns staying with him day and night so that he was never alone. He continued to permit us to give him injections through the bars of his small cage, and it was never necessary to squeeze the walls together to force him to accept them.

We attempted to reduce the fear generated by the screams around him by letting Kanzi watch us take a video camera out of the door. Since we regularly made tapes at the lab, Kanzi understood that a video camera could show him pictures of areas he could not see for himself. We taped the chimps in their long rows of cages outside Kanzi's isolation room. I hoped that he would be able to see that the chimps outside his room were all right, even if they were unhappy. However, the tape was so frightening to Kanzi that he would not even watch it. He turned his head away and asked for tapes of the bunny, Matata, and other things from the Language Center that were comforting and familiar to him.

In spite of his extreme confinement, Kanzi did not become depressed, but generally maintained a good humor, though he was certainly bored. I could never have endured the long confinement in that room as well as Kanzi. I stayed with him in eight-hour stretches before someone would come to relieve me, and even these periods were almost unbearable. Strangers in white lab coats regularly walked by, day and night, and stared at us through the small window in the door. Water leaked onto the floor from pipes in the ceiling. The light was either a harsh yellow glare from the single fluorescent fixture in the ceiling or total darkness. Kanzi endured all of this, in addition to frequent injections and periodic sedations, with a stoic fortitude that would become most people.

His air sac infection finally abated, and he was permitted to return to the Language Center. This was perhaps his day of purest joy. He was extremely grateful to be back and showered everyone, apes and humans alike, with affection. Once back at the Language Center, Kanzi became fascinated with the tapes of the other apes around him that we had made while he was in confinement. He wanted to watch these over and over now that he was no longer there but was safe instead. It was as though he could now deal with the fears that these noises had caused him before, since he knew that they were no longer coming from directly outside his door.

Theory of Mind

The cognitive ability to grasp that someone else may see and think about the world differently from you is characterized by scientists in terms of the possession of a "theory of mind." Many cognitive scientists believe that, unlike us humans, apes and other animals are incapable of recognizing that their perspective of the world may differ from that of those around them. Hence, they are said not to recognize that other individuals "think" and so are incapable of attributing intent or premeditation to the acts of others or of holding them at fault for any undesirable actions. Dogs, for example, might not like a master who treats them unkindly, but they are not said to "blame" him for this, only to avoid him. Presumably, they do not recognize that the master is deciding to do this, only that it happens. However, because we humans supposedly do possess a theory of mind, when someone mistreats one of us, we apparently form beliefs about the miscreant's state of mind— determining, for instance, that his action was intentional and calculated to cause us harm.

The use of language for the purpose of communication can be thought of as resting on the assumption that the point of language is to tell others things we assume they do not know. Scientists who study the behavior of animals disagree about whether or not animals are doing the same sort of thing when they make noise. Dogs may bark, for example, because they are excited. Other dogs, hearing excited barks, may also become excited and bark themselves. The dog who barked first may have only been expressing his own mood, much as we do when we laugh or cry spontaneously. Can he have intended to tell some other dog that he was excited? Since we cannot ask other animals—or, for that matter, very young children—if they make sounds with a particular purpose in mind, scientists typically disagree about the justification of attributing purposive behavior or communicational intentions to them. What is clear is that we have not yet developed a reliable method for addressing such questions.

Nevertheless, there can be no doubt that Kanzi attributes intentions and feelings to others and that he recognizes the need to communicate things about his own mental state to others. From his early gestural communications, like asking me to make his own mother permit him to nurse, to his present ability to tell me where his ball is hidden or that he has a sore throat, Kanzi's communications are inevitably characterized by a desire on his part to get an intentional message across. If one method does not work, he recognizes this failure and attempts to alter what is said in order to clarify his intent.

Neither I nor others taught Kanzi how to engage in purposeful communication— it was an ability he developed on his own. Moreover, this ability first began to emerge when he was about nine to eleven months old. For example, when Kanzi was seven months old, I knew he wanted to play because he would approach me with a happy face and begin playing. As I sat in Matata's large nest grooming her, Kanzi enjoyed having me tickle his neck, pull on his toes, and slap him gently on his lower back. He liked to bat my face with his hands, kick my head with his feet, and tug on my hair. We would play in this way for twenty to thirty minutes at a time.

Kanzi's sister Mulika demonstrates how she feels about "man's best friend." When he was young, Kanzi often tried to use the keyboard to ask the dogs to play chase and tickle with him. However, as he grew older, he seemed to realize that they did not understand lexigrams and this behavior ceased, though he continued to vocalize and gesture to the dogs to make his wishes known.

The experimenter has just shown Kanzi some food in the cooler and Kanzi is about to touch "fire lighter" to indicate that he wants to make a fire and cook the food.

Then, at around nine months, he began to give me signals of his intent to play. For example, instead of just climbing about me and dangling his feet on my head, he would climb above me, hold one foot out in my direction, and wiggle it suggestively while monitoring my face and eyes. If I pretended not to see, he would position himself squarely in front of my eyes and again shake his foot to invite me to play. He not only gesturally signaled his intent to play, but also his intent to be carried, his intent that I assist him in retrieving objects out of his reach, his intent to give me a hug, his desire to leave Matata, and indeed, anything that he wanted me to do for him. Later, he began to use the keyboard to signal similar things, but in a more specific way; his use of symbols occurred as a natural outgrowth and elaboration of these earlier gestural indications of intent.

In addition, with the keyboard, Kanzi can express intentions that are difficult to convey by gesture alone. For example, he can tell us where in the forest he plans to travel. Here it is easy to determine whether or not Kanzi means what he said—we need only look to see whether or not he goes to the place he named. Kanzi also often specifies the travel route. For example, if he is headed for Midway, where raisins are found, he may say "A-frame raisins" or "juice raisins" to indicate which trail he intends to take to Midway—the one that runs past the Treehouse (where he can find juice) or the one that runs past the A-frame. Kanzi similarly tells us whether he wants to play tickle, chase, bite, grab, slap, or hide, and if we agree to play, we have only to note the game he initiates to see that his expressed intentions coincide with his behavior.

Kanzi has gathered some sticks, some pine needles and a plastic bag in a pile and is lighting them with a cigarette lighter. When he was young, he held the lighter in one hand and flipped the switch with the other. As he became an adult, he began to use the lighter as we do, by holding it in one hand and flicking the switch with his thumb.

Skeptics suggest that somehow people are able to surreptitiously help Kanzi make his actions and words agree. They suggest that although Kanzi appears to use language to express his intentions, this may not be the case as long as people are present, because people are a source of subtle cues. If these critics could only experience how difficult it is to get Kanzi to play a game he does not want to play, or go to a location that is not to his liking, they would not be so concerned. It is not only impossible to covertly signal to Kanzi to do something he does not wish to do, it also seems that the larger he becomes, the more difficult it is to find any means whatsoever to get him to do anything other than what it is he has his mind set on.

(*top, left*) *The items in front of Kanzi as he listened to the sentence "Can you knife the sweet potatoes?"*

(*top, right*) *Kanzi's expression as he hears the sentence.*

(*bottom, left*) *Kanzi picks up the knife between the bowls of water and raisins.*

(*bottom, right*) *Kanzi inserts the knife into the sweet potatoes.*

Kanzi, like many children, also reveals an understanding of the difference between what is and what we may believe to be the case by engaging in games of pretend. His favorite pretend game centers around imaginary food. He pretends to eat food that is not really there, to feed others imaginary food, to hide such food, to find it, to take it from other individuals, to give it back to them, and to play chase and keep-away with an imaginary morsel. He will even put a piece of imaginary food on the floor and act as if he does not notice it until someone else begins to reach for it, then grab it before they can get it.

Just as with a real object, Kanzi will remember the location of the imaginary invisible object, and the fact that he has placed it in a specific location on the floor, for five to ten minutes or more. During that time, I will also pretend not to notice where he put the food, so I can catch him off guard and grab it when he is not looking. However, even if I engage him in a completely different activity, when I try to grab the imaginary object, Kanzi will attempt to stop me and get it for himself. Often such games will be started by noting a picture of food on some object. Kanzi then pretends to grab the food off the picture and eat it, while sharing some with me. He also will pretend to grab some food off the TV screen and give me a bite of it.

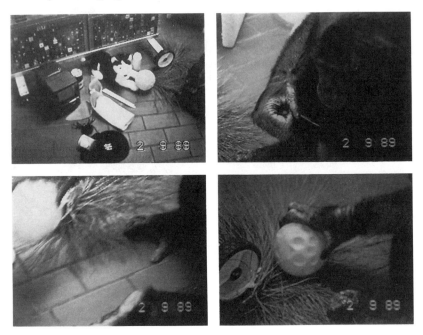

(*top, left*) *The array in front of Kanzi as he listens to the sentence "Can you put the ball on the pine needles?"*

(*top, right*) *Kanzi's expression as he hears the sentence.*

(*bottom, left*) *Kanzi picks up the ball.*

(*bottom, right*) *Kanzi places the ball on the pine needles.*

Interestingly, Georgia is known as the Peach State, and on car license plates, the state has recently placed a drawing of a peach. Kanzi often grabs a bite of such peaches as he passes by the license plates on cars. Such games are something like the bonobo version of a child's tea party. Kanzi similarly enjoys feeding a toy dog imaginary food and engages in imaginary games with toy dogs and chimpanzees, as children play with dolls. Kanzi's imaginary food games lack the more elaborate structure and utensils of a child's tea party, but they retain the key elements of playing with imaginary food and doing all the things with it that one might do with the real item.

Kanzi also engages in pretend games that have to do with danger. For example, he may pretend that a toy dog or toy gorilla is biting him or is chasing and biting a person. He also likes to put scary monster masks with large teeth over his head and then pretend to chase and bite someone. He may also ask me to pretend to be such a monster and to chase and bite him. Occasionally, as I chase him, he will even scream, as though he is pretending to be afraid of me. When I stop in response to such screams to see if he is really afraid, he seems puzzled as to why I have stopped the game and gives no evidence of real fear at all.

Like many other apes, Kanzi also pretends that toy chimpanzees are younger companions to carry about, tickle, hug, play bite, and share food with. However, he tires rather quickly of this companion who does not really play but must be carried about all the time. In contrast, his younger sister Tamuli will constantly carry such a doll with her and cry loudly if it is taken away. One day Kanzi killed a squirrel that had strayed too far into his playyard, and afterward he allowed Tamuli to have it. Tamuli carried the squirrel about as if it were a baby, making certain to position its head upright and to pull its little feet around her waist as though it were clinging to her. She groomed it carefully and pretended to nurse it, just as she saw Matata do with her younger sister Neema, who was only a few months old. Tamuli was extremely proud of her "baby" and showed it off to everyone. She knew, of course, that she had a squirrel, not a real bonobo infant; from time to time she would put it down while she got interested in something else, and then she would run back to play with it. While pretending that the squirrel was her baby, she would follow Matata around doing everything to the squirrel that she saw her mother do with her new younger sister Neema. It was necessary to

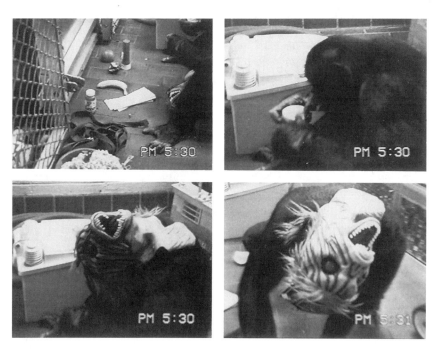

(*top, left*) *The array in front of Kanzi as he hears the sentence "Can you go scare Matata with the mask?"*

(*top, right*) *Kanzi eating food as he listens to the sentence.*

(*bottom, left*) *Kanzi puts the mask on his head and sits still for a second.*

(*bottom, right*) *Kanzi heads toward the colony room where his mother is located.*

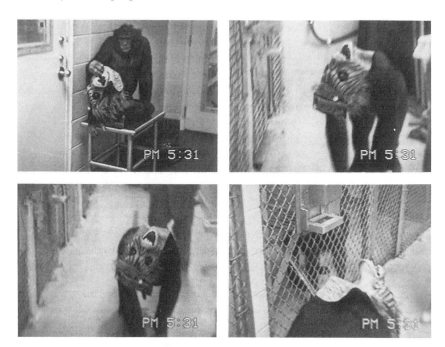

(*top, left*) *Kanzi takes off his mask and waits by the colony room door for some-one to open it as he does not have a key.*

(*top, right; bottom, left and right*) *After the door is opened Kanzi puts his mask back on and parades up and down in front of Matata's cage.*

take the squirrel away, because a dead animal posed a health risk to the bonobo group, and Tamuli was very sad when I made her give it up and behaved as though she were somewhat depressed the rest of that day.

As Kanzi grew older and the variety and complexity of his communications increased he began to put symbols together to express ideas that were his own. More important, many of these ideas could not be expressed by a single symbol alone, or by selecting multiple symbols independently—they could only be conveyed by combining symbols.

For example, Kanzi frequently initiated games of tag. Sometimes we simply tagged him with our hands; other times, the goal was to tag him with a particular object. He began to indicate which version of tag he wanted to play with combinations such as "chase ball," "chase pine cone," "chase water," "chase you," and so on. When he uttered these words in combination, we knew he wanted to play tag with a particular object or person; if he had simply said "pine cone" or "ball," we would not have understood what he wanted to do.

Similarly, Kanzi also began to indicate where he wanted to be carried, using combinations such as "Austin carry" and "childside carry" to say that he wanted to be carried to see Austin or to the "childside." If Kanzi had said only "Austin" or "childside" as we walked about in the woods, we would have changed the course of travel and gone where he requested but we might not have thought to carry him since we were attempting to encourage him to travel on his own, though in other situations when he asked to be carried we often complied with his request. So if Kanzi wanted to be carried to the "childside," he needed to combine symbols to make this wish known.

Not all Kanzi's combinations involved a verb. Sometimes he formed simple sentences such as "backpack lighter" to ask for the backpack so he could get out the lighter when he wanted to make a fire. He said "trailer ball" to indicate that he wanted to go to the trailer and look for a ball that he had left there. He commented "hot water there" to indicate that he wanted to make a cooking fire by the river, and "childside food surprise" to say that he wanted to go to the childside and get a food surprise. Kanzi often made combinations that were quite different from any that he had ever heard others employ, revealing that he recognized the power of combining words to convey his own ideas and thoughts. For example, if someone became upset over some misbehavior on his part, he often requested a "milk hug" to indicate that he wanted to be held and coddled with milk, while making up. Combinations such as these enabled Kanzi to convey very specific things that single words could not convey, yet they depended less on grammatical rules than on the knowledge of the context for proper interpretation.

Although Kanzi's utterances did not usually require grammatical rules in order to be properly interpreted, by five years of age he was producing symbol combinations with sufficient frequency to permit a systematic analysis of the way in which he ordered words. It was important to look for evidence of grammatical rules in Kanzi's utterances because many linguistic scholars have argued that the utterances of apes should not be characterized as truly linguistic in nature unless it can be shown that they employ grammatical rules similar to those found in human languages. These scholars have also maintained that only human beings are endowed with the ability to organize things according to the categorical relationships between them, and that it is this special ability that makes language possible.

This seemed to me an extreme position. After all, Kanzi had learned to comprehend and use printed symbols on his own without special training. He had also learned to understand many spoken words, even though he himself could not speak. He knew that words could be used to communicate about things he wanted or intended to do, even though those actions were not happening at the time of the communication. He could also purposefully combine symbols to tell us something (for example, something that had happened earlier in the day, when we were not present) we would have had no way of knowing otherwise. He recognized that two symbols could be combined to form meanings that neither symbol in isolation could ever convey. He used this skill to communicate completely novel ideas that were his own and had never been talked about with him. Consequently, whether or not he could be shown to possess a formal grammar, the conclusion remained inescapable that Kanzi had a simple language.

Nonetheless, many scientists continued to insist that until the use of grammatical rules could be shown in his language, the rest of what Kanzi had done was of little interest. Such an extreme view is taken, I believe, because many scientists are hesitant to conclude that apes are capable of rational thought, foresight, or purposeful communication—behaviors formerly held to be exclusively human. If we allow that apes such as Kanzi are indeed attempting to tell us what is on their minds, and that their minds are shaped by their experiences just as the minds of young children are, we lose our claim to being drastically different from all other creatures on the planet. We also thereby bring ourselves to confront the question of our relationship to other animals. We cannot hold animals fully responsible for their actions, just as we cannot do so with children. Still, we grant children certain rights and responsibilities that are commensurate with their level of intelligence and understanding. We do not consume children as food, operate on them for practice, confine them for public display, or hunt them for recreation.

If we accept that human behavior shares important commonalities with that of the ape, then what should our obligations to apes be? Can we continue to employ them as biological preparations in medical studies? Can we continue to strike down their forest homes with wanton disregard for their survival? These become troubling questions once apes are perceived as creatures who think and feel much as we do. However, if we maintain the comfortable illusion that apes are merely clever imitations of ourselves, with no real understanding of the world they inhabit, then our present treatment of them may seem more palatable. Doubtless there is a strong motivation in current thinking to justify and maintain the perception of apes as mindless caricatures of man.

I realized that I needed to determine whether or not Kanzi was beginning to use any grammatical rules if I was going to convince the scientific community that he was using language creatively. To address this question I looked at a large group of his utterances with the help of Patricia Greenfield, an expert on language development in children. We found that Kanzi was utilizing word order in many of his combinations. Interestingly, sometimes this order followed English word order and sometimes it seemed to be his own. For example, when Kanzi produced action-object combinations such as "hide peanut" or "grab head," he tended to follow the typical English word order of action first, object second. However, when he specified the relationship between an agent and an action, he tended to put the action first and the agent second, for example, "chase you," "grab you."

Standard English, in contrast, places the agent first and the object second. However, when he formed such combinations, Kanzi usually indicated the agents by pointing to them, something that is not characteristic of spoken English. When Kanzi used a proper name, for which he could only use a lexigram, in combinations like "Liz hide" or "Matata bite," he tended to follow English word order. Thus, it is interesting that Kanzi's deviations from English word order occurred mostly when there were also deviations in the mode of expression—that is, they occurred when Kanzi used a gesture rather than a lexical symbol.

Kanzi also made many combinations in which he specified a place that he wanted to visit or an object that he wished to have. In these combinations, Kanzi placed his goal (object or location) first and his action (go, chase, carry, etc.) last. Again, his word order differed from that of spoken English, and again, many of these action words, such as "go" and "chase," were conveyed by gestures. Thus, we found that whenever Kanzi combined a symbol with a gesture, he tended to place the gesture after the symbol. This was a rule of Kanzi's own making and one that only Kanzi typically followed.

Our analysis suggested that Kanzi had developed some simple grammatical strategies that were indeed based on his recognition of the role that words serve in different communications. Not only did he tend to adopt English word order when he combined symbols, he devised his own rules for combinations of gestures and symbols. Kanzi's communications strongly challenged the assumption that humans alone are able to perform the thought process of manipulating truly arbitrary symbols according to grammatical conventions.

Even though Kanzi's combinations caused a number of linguists to raise their eyebrows in disbelief, the real key to his intelligence was not in what he said but in what he understood. The keyboard provided a vehicle for Kanzi to make his thoughts known, but it was also a limited system. Often the words he wanted to use to form a particular sentence were not on the keyboard, and even though he tried to compensate for this problem, it was not always possible for him to express his ideas, particularly the more complex ones.

More words could be added to the keyboard, but the search time for any given word increased geometrically as the number of available words went up. The more effort Kanzi (or any of us) had to put into searching for a needed word, the less attention could be devoted to planning a complex utterance. Therefore, keyboard utterances, even those of Kanzi's human companions, were rarely longer than two to three words. Forming even short combinations with rapidity in the midst of a communicative act required not only an intimate familiarity with the keyboard but also practice.

New researchers coming to the laboratory often took a year or more to become as sophisticated as Kanzi in the use of the keyboard. If one were to measure the communicative ability of adult humans by their conversational facility with the keyboard, one would severely underestimate their intelligence because of the inherent limitations of a keyboard system. Similarly, we were likely to underestimate Kanzi's capacity. We knew that the communicative skills of human adults went far beyond what we saw them say at the keyboard, because they also spoke. Unfortunately, Kanzi could not speak, so we could not use this skill as an independent measure of his true intellectual capacity.

Syntax Grasped

Kanzi's throat and larynx are not constructed in a manner that permits him to speak clearly, but there is nothing wrong with his ears. He can hear everything that is said around him, just as you and I can. Therefore, we decided to measure Kanzi's language capacity not by what he could say but by what he could understand.

Comprehending the sentences of another person is as complex an ability as producing those sentences; in fact, many regard it as more complex. In most cases, when we speak we know what we want to say. However, the situation is different when we listen to others. Often we do not really know what they want to say. Our only option is to do our best to understand what they say. Most people do not realize the complexities involved, since when they learn language they are too small and too young to appreciate the difficulty of the exercise.

When we are slightly older, we become familiar with written language. Because we see words written as independent entities, we tend to think of them as discrete units that sound essentially the same every time we hear them. This perception is an illusion. If one looks at a spectrographic analysis or a picture of the vibrations of air molecules as a function of speech, it is clear that there are no neat separations of words. It is impossible to tell by visual inspection alone precisely where one word begins and another ends. Moreover, if we encounter the same word in several different sentences, it never looks the same on the spectrogram.

Knowing what a given pronunciation of "banana" looks like on a spectrogram will not enable you to inspect other spectrograms and identify additional instances of "banana." Yet it is just this sort of feat that we have little trouble accomplishing when we listen to speech or when we read a written text. Knowing what the word "banana" sounds like will enable us to identify it in any novel sample of speech. Similarly, knowing how the word "banana" is written will help us identify it in a novel sample of text, even if we are completely unfamiliar with the rest of the language.

Since spectrograms are not the products of a conventional system of writing but are mechanically produced representations of the physical properties of sound, we have no way of "reading" them. This is one reason why it is so difficult to build a computer that can reliably decode human speech. When one looks at the representation of speech sounds in a spectrogram, it is virtually impossible to tell where each word begins and ends, as there are none of the breaks between words that we are familiar with from writing. Instead, each word appears to merge into the next in a steady stream of represented noise. Yet when one replays the very speech that produced that spectrogram, the word units are easily recognized.

Since Kanzi's ears were okay, we decided to measure his comprehension of language and use our findings as an index of his syntactic capacity. For understanding the utterances of others requires as great a knowledge of syntax as does producing one's own utterance, if not more. We began by noting whenever we observed in ordinary daily events that Kanzi clearly understood something said to him. If people spoke to Kanzi but had to help him understand by pointing or showing him what to do, we took note that such assistance was needed. As we analyzed the data, we concentrated on determining the kind of things he seemed able to grasp without such assistance.

This method limited us to recording instances that could be objectively validated. For example, if we were cooking potatoes and asked Kanzi to help by getting some out of the refrigerator, we could observe his actions to determine whether or not he had understood our request. However, if we told Kanzi we would have some potatoes later at the A-frame, it was not as easy to be certain that he understood this by watching his ensuing actions. Still more abstract sentences—such as "Kanzi, don't you know that potatoes are good for you?"—provided us with virtually no way of measuring Kanzi's comprehension by observing what he did after we spoke. For this reason, we limited our data gathering to sentences relating to actions that could be carried out immediately by Kanzi.

The method also encountered difficulty when Kanzi elected not to do what he was asked to do, even though we believed that he understood our requests perfectly well, or when he elected to do precisely the opposite thing in order to tease us. Nonetheless, we persisted, because when our requests were clear and when Kanzi was cooperative, it was as though a window opened into his mind that gave us a picture of a far more complex creature than we could have discerned by noting only the utterances that he produced.

Our observations suggested that Kanzi understood a wide variety of complex sentences. For example, when he heard "Would you put some grapes in the swimming pool?" he got out of the swimming pool, walked over to where a number of foods were placed on a towel, and picked up the grapes and tossed them in the water. When he knew we were playing a game of hiding surprises, and he heard a clue such as "I hid the surprise by my foot" or "Rose hid the surprise under her shirt," he immediately raced to the correct location and retrieved his surprise. When asked on a walk in the woods, "Would you please give Panbanisha an onion?" Kanzi looked around for a patch of onions and, when he found one, pulled out a bunch and took it back to Panbanisha. When he had a new ball that he wanted to take into the colony room with him when he went to visit Matata, but he was told "Your ball stays here"; he placed it by the door while visiting Matata but of course retrieved it immediately after he left.

One day when Kanzi was visiting Austin, he wanted some cereal that had been prepared specifically for Austin. He was told, "You can have some cereal if you give Austin your monster mask to play with." Kanzi immediately found his monster mask and handed it to Austin, then pointed to Austin's cereal. When told "Let's go to the trailer and make a water balloon," Kanzi went to the trailer, got a balloon out of the backpack, and held it under the water faucet. He needed help fitting it on the faucet and filling it with water, but he had clearly understood the sentence. Even sentences with general terms such as "it" or "this" were easy for Kanzi. For example, sentences like "If you don't want the juice put it back in the backpack" were readily responded to, as were sentences like "Get some water, put it in your mouth."

These examples, and thousands more, nearly all different, collected systematically across time, began to paint a more complete picture of Kanzi's abilities. Kanzi could understand language at least as well as a child two to three years old, perhaps better if the topic was of keen interest to him. These examples suggested that Kanzi had an understanding of grammatical relationships that went considerably beyond the simple combinations he was able to produce.

Moreover, we noted that when Kanzi heard a sentence like "Can you throw a potato to the turtle," he never made mistakes such as throwing both items or throwing the turtle toward the potato. Typically, he either responded correctly, or in some way that suggested he had not clearly heard a specific word but had nonetheless grasped the general gist of what was said. For example, he might throw a tomato to the turtle, rather than a potato, if he were not listening carefully. However, he almost never made grammatical errors, such as throwing the turtle at the potato. Similarly, in sentences like "Get the hot dogs and put them in the hot water," Kanzi never seemed to think the term "them" should apply to anything other than the noun mentioned previously in the same sentence.

Had Kanzi responded only to simple two-word combinations such as "ball chase" or "go A-frame," his ability to understand grammatical relationships would have remained somewhat questionable. However, when he responded appropriately to sentences such as "Let's play ball chase at the A-frame" by going to the A-frame and then initiating a game of chasing with the ball, it left little doubt that he understood a great deal about relationships between words, even though his own combinations were far less complex.

However, the belief that animals are incapable of such high-level mental activities remained so strong that few critics accepted Kanzi's responses to such sentences as evidence of the true capacity of his mind. They suggested that Kanzi was somehow figuring out what to do based on contextual information, or that subtle, if unintentional, cues were aiding him in undetermined ways.

In response to these concerns, a comprehension test was designed that would permit us to rule out such extraneous factors. I sat behind a one-way mirror and asked Kanzi to carry out a sequence of novel requests. I selected only requests that differed from the kinds of things that Kanzi might hear in the course of his normal daily activities, and I repeated each request only once. Thus, Kanzi could not depend on something he had learned previously, in order to respond appropriately. Kanzi was also the only party who could hear my request, since the other individuals in the room wore headphones that played loud music to drown out anything I said from behind the mirror. Each sentence was presented only one time, and 660 different sentences were presented. Kanzi's response to each request was videotaped.

This test, given to Kanzi when he was nine years old, not only validated my previous impressions of his ability to understand complex sentences but also indicated that earlier data, taken when he was six years old, had underrepresented the range and complexity of the sentence types he had come to comprehend. More important, many of the requests were so unusual that it would have been impossible for him to have responded appropriately the first time he had ever heard such a sentence by any means other than understanding what was said to him. Examples of some of these unusual sentences include:

Put the collar in the water.
Tickle Rose with the sparklers.
Put the tomatoes in the melon.
Give the doggie [a toy dog] some yogurt.
Put a sparkler in the coke can.
Put the toothbrush in the lemonade.
Take the snake [a plastic snake] outdoors.
Put the chicken in the potty.
Put the raisins in the shoe.
Go scare Matata with the snake.

Can you pour the ice water in the potty?
Can you take the gorilla [a stuffed toy] to the bedroom?
Can you brush Liz's hair?
Can you take Rose's shoe off?
Go get the balloon that's in the microwave.
Can you put the blanket on the doggie?
Can you put the bunny [a puppet] on your hand?
Make the snake bite Linda.
Tickle Rose with the bunny.
Drink the coffee that's hot.
Drink the iced coffee.
Go get the noodles that are in the bedroom.
Liz is going to tickle Kanzi.
Go vacuum Liz.
Put on the monster mask and scare Linda.
I want Kanzi to grab Rose.
Use the toothbrush and brush Liz's teeth.
Tickle Liz with the umbrella.
Stab the ball with the sparklers.
Pour the Coke in the lemonade.
Pour the lemonade in the Coke.
Knife the doggie.
Hide the toy gorilla.

Kanzi did not get every single sentence correct, but he was able to properly carry out 72 percent of the requests. His ability to understand such sentences compared favorably with that of a two-and-a-half-year-old child named Alia. Alia responded appropriately to 66 percent of the same sentences. Sometimes Kanzi responded to some of the sentences in a most unexpected manner, but one that was nonetheless correct. For example, when I asked him to "put some water on the carrot," he tossed the carrot outdoors. At first I thought this was a mistake until I reflected on the fact that it was raining very heavily at that moment, and tossing the carrot out into the rain was certainly a satisfactory means of getting it wet. Another time, I asked him to "put some water on the vacuum cleaner," and he picked up a glass of water and began to drink it. Again, I thought he was wrong until I realized that he had not swallowed the water but had filled his mouth full of water and was using his mouth to carry the water to the vacuum, where he then leaned over and dribbled the water out of his mouth into a small hole in the top of the vacuum cleaner.

Sometimes Kanzi misunderstood one or more of the words in the sentence, as his ensuing behavior made clear. For example, when I asked him to "take Liz to the bedroom," he seemed to think I had said the word "knives" instead of "Liz," as both words have a "zz" sound on the end. He picked up a large handful of knives, but I tried to correct him by repeating "Liz, Liz." He then understood the word "Liz" but apparently thought I also wanted him to take the knives as well, so he kept them and headed toward Liz with a handful of knives. This was a bit frightening for Liz, as Kanzi was quite large and was walking bipedally straight toward her with a handful of knives. Since she did not know what I had said (as the test required that she did not hear any utterance) rather spontaneously backed away from Kanzi. This made Kanzi think that perhaps he had not understood me correctly with regard to the word "Liz," so he turned and headed back again toward the bedroom with his knives. I then said, "Get Liz by the hand and take her to the bedroom." In response, Kanzi turned and approached Liz again with his hand held out kindly toward her. This time Liz was not so startled and did not move backward, and Kanzi took her by the hand and led her into the bedroom.

Kanzi also had trouble with the word "can." This is an interesting word in that it is used as a means of forming a question in sentences like "*Can* you open the juice?"; as a modifier, as in "can of Coke"; and as part of a proper noun, as in "can opener" and "trash can." All these different usages seemed to befuddle Kanzi, and he had difficulty ascertaining what was meant when we used the word "can." Consequently, sentences like "Can you use the can opener to open a can of Coke?" left Kanzi dumbfounded. However, more unusual sentences, such as "Can you put the chicken in the potty?" were carried out appropriately, since the puzzling word "can" was not used in several different ways in the same sentence.

Similarly, the word "trash" seemed to be a mystery for Kanzi. We frequently asked him to pick up his "trash" and put it in the backpack when we were outdoors. We also asked him to put things in the "trash can" when we were inside. The only common element of these two different situations was that the word "trash" referred to things that we did not want left in the location where they were. But putting "trash" in a backpack and putting a banana peel in the "trash can" were concepts that constantly confused Kanzi, because we were using the same word in ways that did not seem similar to him at all. Apparently, the idea that we would have a name for things that were going to be thrown away later in time was a concept that lay outside his understanding of how the world worked. Bonobos typically drop their trash wherever they find themselves. If they put something in a container, it is because they want to keep it, not because they want to throw it away later. Kanzi never seemed to understand why some things went in the trash and others did not. Often the trash looked very attractive to him and he wanted to take things out of the trash and play with them. Thus, our idea of what was to be discarded also differed significantly from Kanzi's, further complicating his task of discerning what we meant when we uttered words like "trash can."

Such difficulties should not be taken to imply that Kanzi was unable to cope when the same word was used in different ways. With some words he was able to do this quite well. He had no trouble at all with "water" or "watermelon," for example, or with "dog," "hot," and "hot dog." In each of these cases, even though the same word was used in different ways, the referents for the different words were more concrete and hence more readily grasped by Kanzi.

Alia had similar problems with some abstract words. For example, when she was asked to bring an object during the test, she sometimes brought several things instead of just the item she was asked to retrieve. Her mother attempted to get her to bring only one object by saying, "Just one, Alia, just one." However, Alia did not grasp the idea that "just one" referred to number. She assumed that "just one," was the name of an object, so she brought even more things back to her mother, trying to figure out which thing it was that her mother was calling "just one." The more her mother emphasized "just one," the more objects Alia returned with, in hopes of bringing the right thing. She would hand her mother the objects one at a time, saying "dustin," "dustin," as though to figure out which object was called "dustin." Her mother, exasperated, kept repeating "just one," holding up one finger to try to convey this idea to Alia. But even though this scenario was repeated multiple times during the test situation, Alia never discerned the meaning of "dustin." Some months after she had started to learn to count, the meaning of "just one" did, of course, become clear to her.

Most of the mistakes that Kanzi and Alia made on the test resulted from their failure to grasp the complete meaning that was intended. Typically, their mistakes resulted from confusions between words that were similar in sound, such as "tomato" and "potato" or "orange" and "orang." Other confusions occurred between words that sounded quite different but represented things that, to them, seemed very similar, such as "clay" and "paint."

When either of them made mistakes of this type, they often insisted that they were correct. For example, when I asked Kanzi to "put the paint in the potty," he put the clay in the potty instead. I then tried to help him by saying, "But what about the paint?" emphasizing the word "paint." Kanzi responded by placing additional clay in the potty. I then commented, "Thank you, that was the clay, now could you put the paint, the paint, in the potty." Kanzi then pulled the potty over in front of me and tilted it toward me to show me that, as far as he was concerned, he had done exactly as I had requested. Realizing that he thought clay and paint were essentially interchangeable items, I thanked him for his help and moved on to the next sentence.

Rarely did either Kanzi or Alia make mistakes that indicated a lack of understanding of the basic grammatical structure of the sentences. Both of them readily differentiated between requests to retrieve objects from locations ("Go to location X and get object Y") and requests to take objects to locations ("Take object X to location Y"). They also understood the difference between sentences that required them to move through space in addition to acting on objects and sentences that required them to act on the objects in some way without moving about. The grammatical structure of some sentences was very simple, for example, "Give the ball to Rose." Others were much more complex, such as "See if you can make the doggie bite your ball" or "Show me the ball that's on TV." Switching between these different levels of grammatical complexity seemed to pose few difficulties for either Kanzi or Alia.

Of particular interest, from a grammatical standpoint, was whether or not sentences of the form "Show (or give) me X and Y" (for example, "Show me the ball and the cereal") would be easier for Kanzi than those that were grammatically more complex. To respond correctly to sentences such as "Show me X and Y" requires an understanding that the verb "show" or "give" applies to both objects, but apart from this requirement the sentences are very simple. The listener can show or give the objects to the speaker in any order, and he or she does not have to construct any sort of relationship between the word "ball" and the word "cereal."

In contrast, a sentence like "Put your ball in the cereal" requires the listener to construct a specific relationship between ball and cereal. A more complex sentence such as "Get the ball that's in the cereal" requires the listener to decode the relationship between ball and cereal that is made manifest by the sentence and to look for a specific instance in the world about him where ball and cereal hold that relationship to each other. If there are balls and bowls of cereal lying about that do not hold this sort of relationship to one another, the listener must not be confused by them, but must look instead for those objects whose extant relationship is precisely that specified by the sentence.

Sentences of this type (Get the X that's in Y) also require an understanding of the principle that subunits of the sentence, for example, "that's in Y," act to modify the meaning of other subunits of the same sentence. In this case, Kanzi must not look for just any ball, but for the ball that is in the cereal. That is to say, the phrase "that's in the cereal" determines how Kanzi must interpret the word "ball"—that is, not just any ball, but a specific one. Linguists typically call such syntactic devices "embedded phrases." In this example, the true meaning intended by the word "ball" cannot be understood without realizing that its meaning is embedded within the phrase "that's in the cereal."

Linguists maintain that only human beings are able to process symbolic information that is structured in such a complex interdependent manner. Kanzi, however, did quite well on such sentences. In fact, he responded correctly to 77 percent of the sentences presented with this structure, while Alia responded properly to only 52 percent of these sentences. The assumption that only human beings can understand complex structural and categorical relationships clearly deserves reevaluation in light of Kanzi's ability to understand such sentences.

Quite unexpectedly, Kanzi experienced the greatest difficulty with sentences that had the simplest grammatical structure, the "Give (or show) someone X and Y" sentences. In these sentences, Kanzi's only task was to listen and give me the two objects mentioned in the sentence. Surprisingly, most of the time, he could remember only one thing. Kanzi correctly responded by giving both things on only 33 percent of such sentences, a performance far lower than he had achieved on other more "grammatically difficult" sentences. Kanzi's problem with these sentences was not a failure to understand but a memory failure.

Kanzi always gave me at least one of the items that I mentioned. Never did he make the error of giving one correct item and one incorrect item. When he responded with only one item to a sentence like "Show me the milk and the doggie," I had only to mention the forgotten item by saying "and the milk," and Kanzi would immediately pick up the milk and show that to me also. It was not necessary to repeat the verb to remind Kanzi that he was to show the object to me.

The fact that Kanzi found grammatically difficult sentences easier to respond to than simple ones suggests that, contrary to the expectations of linguists, structural relationships between words helped Kanzi to decode the speaker's intent. When faced with a sentence that was structurally simple but required that he keep two items in short-term memory while he looked around and decided which ones he was supposed to give, he had trouble remembering both things. Consequently, a sentence like "Show me the doggie and the milk" was more difficult for him than a sentence like "Feed the doggie some milk."

When Kanzi is asked to feed the doggie some milk, an inherent relationship is constructed between dog and milk, which revolves around the action of feeding. However, when Kanzi is merely asked to show these items, no inherent relationship is constructed which would link the dog to the milk. The items simply form a short list. Kanzi's differential performance on sentences with similar words but different structural content indicates that grammatical relationships actually facilitated sentence comprehension and recall for Kanzi, as opposed to making these things more difficult.

In instances where an ape does not perform as well as a child, the difficulties seem to reside either in the ape's failure to comprehend the semantic content of words—for example, "trash can,"—or in a failure to hold in short-term memory a list of unrelated items. The ape's difficulties do not appear to be primarily due to grammatical constraints on sentences uttered naturally by English speakers. Although some grammatical problems may be documented in the future, it is probable that they will arise from a more basic semantic failure to grasp some concept encoded by the grammatical relationships, that is, time, possession, and so forth.

Kanzi's ability to understand language greatly exceeds his ability to produce it. In large measure, this must be because the language he understands is spoken English. However, he cannot speak, so in order to communicate he must point to symbols. The number of symbols available is limited, and to use any one of them, he must search to find what he wants to say. This means that "talking" is far more difficult for Kanzi. If Kanzi could produce vocal speech, he would produce many more complex utterances than he currently does. Perhaps, in the future, a way around this limitation can be found.

What Kanzi Tells Us

In the past, when people have attempted to communicate with animals, they have often focused on teaching the animal to talk. They have taught a vocabulary and then tried to get the animal to use this vocabulary to tell them things. The reason this method has met with such limited success is now clear. Language is learned, not through speaking, but by coming to understand what others say to us. There is enormous complexity in the speech to which children are exposed, and they are immersed in a world of speech for a year or more before they begin to speak at all.

During the first year of life, children cannot speak, even if they understand words, because their vocal-laryngeal tract is too immature to produce all the sounds that characterize human language. Throughout this year, however, people are constantly speaking to them and expecting them to respond in some way to what is said. By the time a child begins to speak its first words, it is already aware of the communicational potential of speech and it has already been exposed to hundreds of thousands of words and sentences. From these early experiences, the child has learned how to recognize verbal units of various sizes and can understand some of these units in combination with one another.

From this point on, language learning becomes a matter of refining this core of knowledge. By listening to what others say and trying to interpret their intent, the child is presented with all the information needed to figure out language. However, we cannot see the child listening to others, nor can we see it attempting to figure out what they are trying to say. Sometimes, we can tell what it is that children do not understand, because we see them doing something that does not correspond to what they have been asked to do; however, most of the time we do not know what they do or do not comprehend.

While children are being brought up they undergo a long period of exposure to speech, and to its interactional functions, at a time when their brains are rapidly expanding in size and complexity. This exposure provides a sort of experience very different from those that previous investigators interested in language capacities of animals have provided for their animal subjects. Instead of talking to the ape throughout a sensitive developmental period, investigators have typically waited until the ape was old enough to be weaned and then have rewarded it in some way for correctly executing proper responses of some type when shown various objects. Given this enormous difference in the methods of exposure to language, perhaps we should not be surprised that children typically learn language without any special instruction and that, prior to Kanzi, no animal had done so.

What Kanzi tells us is that humans are not the only species that can acquire language if exposed to it at an early age. Humans simply appear to be the only species that can make the proper sounds to actually speak, and thus the only species that has exploited the sound system to a significant degree for communicating novel messages to conspecifics. Perhaps animals other than Kanzi could also understand spoken language if brought up in a similar fashion.

PART II

THEORETICAL AND PHILOSOPHICAL IMPLICATIONS

CHAPTER 2

Philosophical Preconceptions

Would it be absolutely impossible to teach the ape a language? I do not think so. I should choose a large ape in preference to any other, until by some good fortune another kind should be discovered, more like us, for nothing prevents there being such a one in regions unknown to us.

Julien Offray de la Mettrie, *L'Homme Machine,* 1748

In the previous chapter, Savage-Rumbaugh makes a strong case for the claim that Kanzi's communicational skills are not observably different from that of the two-and-a-half-year-old human child named Alia. This claim—like virtually all those attributing a linguistic skill to a nonhuman primate—has not been generally accepted in the scientific community. Indeed, it has been derisively rejected by some of the leading linguists and cognitive scientists of the day (see *New York Times,* June 1995). Critics of Ape Language Research (ALR), including Pinker (1994) and Wallman (1992), insist that no ape has ever developed truly linguistic skills, and that even the skills that Kanzi has manifested are more accurately termed "performative" and "effective," but certainly *not* "linguistic."

But why do they not say the same thing of Alia's skills? What ground is there to assert that Kanzi's behavior, unlike Alia's, lacks any evidence of possession of an "internalized grammar," even though their performances in comprehension tests were roughly equivalent? What exactly is this "evidence" that is invisibly *present* in the two-and-a-half-year-old child's behavior but is equally invisibly *absent* from Kanzi's? Kanzi also produces two- and three-string requests similar to those produced by a two-and-a-half-year-old child. However, it is said that "in the case of children, there is evidence that underlying this reduced utterance is a complete syntactic structure that, for reasons of linguistic and/or cognitive immaturity, cannot yet be expressed in its entirety" (Wallman 1992, 96). But the same cannot be assumed for Kanzi. We are told that the children may regularly omit one or another of the major consitituents in a sentence, but that they will "reliably sequence the other two elements in the order they take in the full, underlying representation" (96). But the same will not be granted of Kanzi.

And why, by the same token, can we not say that Kanzi's grasp that the agent doing an action comes first and the recipient of the action comes after the verb is comparable to a two-and-a-half-year-old child's grasp of simple grammatical rules? If we can describe Kanzi as grasping the same relational statements as a two-and-a-half-year-old child (see Tomasello 1994), we are left with the question of why the so-called *rules of evidence* seem to be so different in the two contexts. Why is the ALR scientist compelled to *prove* that Kanzi's placing the agent first and the subject after the verb is not just a "lexical position habit," whereas in the case of the two-and-a-half-year-old child the linguist is permitted to take it as a given that when the child says "Give my toy to Mommy" she *understands* what she is saying? That is, why is there no parallel need to *prove* that it is justified to speak of two-and-a-half-year-old children as referring, as meaning, as intending, as understanding each other, and so forth?

Those with an interest in the implications of ALR soon learn that such questions are asked in vain. No matter how much evidence Savage-Rumbaugh might amass, the skeptic will always respond that Kanzi is not *really* "encoding" and "decoding" propositions; he just acts as if he is. An animal, the skeptic assures us, may possibly be conditioned or taught to use sounds to obtain certain ends, but by no means can it acquire *language*: the ability to use sentences to communicate thoughts. And it would appear that nothing that Savage-Rumbaugh has done—or *can* do—could refute this argument. For the supposed impossibility this argument asserts is logical, not empirical. The assertion is not based on an exhaustive study of apes' linguistic or neurological capacities; in fact, it doesn't have much to do with apes at all. Rather, it is a consequence of a characteristically modern picture of language as our uniquely human birthright. Thus, regardless of what Kanzi can do, or can be brought to do, it *cannot* be described as language, simply because he does not share in that birthright.

True, the fact that Kanzi acts as if he understands sentences forces the critic of ALR to come up with a different explanation of this behavior. Thus we are told that Kanzi possesses remarkable problem-solving abilities. We even get the argument that Kanzi may understand the meaning of specific words. But he doesn't— he *couldn't*—possess syntax. Instead, his "apparent" grasp of sentences is to be explained in terms of his atomistic grasp of the meaning of the words in an utterance. Apparently, the nature of these words is such that he is left no choice but to execute the desired action. For example, there is said to be "only one pragmatically sensible way" in which to respond to the words "give," "trash," and "Jeannine." "No ability to decipher syntactic structure is required in order to respond appropriately" (Wallman 1992, 103). Accordingly,

> [t]he testing of Kanzi's sentence comprehension . . . demonstrates that he is able to put together the object or objects and the action mentioned in the way that is appropriate given the properties of the objects involved, what he typically does with them, or both. His performance provides no evidence, however, that he was attending to even so simple a syntactic feature as word order. (104)

The ALR critic concludes, "What appears to be the case is that the ape is competent in some or all of the collateral areas but devoid of a language faculty"

(Wallman 1992, 112). This is the crucial point in the skeptical argument. The *appearance of continuity* is due to the fact that there are these areas of "collateral" cognitive or social skills. The more ALR advances, the more we can hope to learn about the various *nonlinguistic* aspects of communicative behavior that may be present in or accompany linguistic interactions. But the transformation into a true linguistic agent involves the activation of an "internalized grammar" that is imprinted on the brain of *Homo sapiens sapiens* and only the brain of *Homo sapiens sapiens*. Ape Language Research may be able to teach us a great deal about the development of nonverbal communicative skills, therefore, but it will never be able to teach us anything about the nature of language, or indeed, the development of the human mind.

One of the most intriguing, and most deceptive aspects of this, the "ape language debate," is that its roots extend far back into the texts and contexts of the Western intellectual tradition. Indeed, the problems that cognitive and linguistic developmentalists are grappling with today are little changed from the concerns of the eighteenth-century philosophe: in particular from his interest in how a child makes the transition from natural expressive behavior to linguistic interaction. Moreover, just as orangutans—the "men of the woods"—posed such a dilemma for philosophes such as LaMettrie and Rousseau, so too Kanzi and Panbanisha have proved an extremely awkward problem for modern linguists and cognitive scientists. These latter-day philosophes are forced to accept that some remarkable breakthroughs have occurred at Savage-Rumbaugh's Language Research Center: that nonhuman primates have been shown to possess far more sophisticated cognitive and communicative capabilities than has hitherto been documented by ape language theorists. Yet there remains a dogmatic refusal to accept the possibility that Kanzi possesses primitive linguistic skills. Does the source of this debate really lie, as the ALR critics would have it, in Savage-Rumbaugh's and others' "rampant over-interpretation of the evidence"? Or does it rather lie in the peculiar pattern of philosophical preconceptions and rhetorical tendencies that characterizes the modern Western tradition in thinking about language and cognition? To answer this question, we need to look closely at the origin, development, and foundations of that tradition.

The Cartesian Revolution

Perhaps the best way of elucidating the peculiar nature of Western thinking about the relation between language and cognition is to begin with the revolutionary works of René Descartes. Virtually all of Descartes's texts were subversive; but historically speaking, perhaps the most seditious of his published works was the first: the *Discourse on Method*. The *Discourse* epitomizes, and was widely seen by Descartes's contemporaries as having inspired, the enormous social, scientific, and religious changes taking place in the Enlightenment. It represents the appeal to reason over authority, be it theological or scholastic. But Descartes was not just challenging the hegemony of revelation; he was also championing the autonomy of the individual.

The emphasis in the *Discourse* is placed squarely on the thoughts of René Descartes: a solitary intellectual who had come to distrust scholasticism; who decided to continue his studies by reading from the "great book of the world" rather than the classics; and whose "real education" taught him to accept as certain only those ideas that he could see clearly and distinctly *in his own mind's eye*. It is in this respect that the *Discourse on Method* is such a revolutionary text: the paradigm of a modern revolutionary text. The very style in which it is written—the intrusion of the first-person voice—marks a radical break from the conventions of scholasticism. But the most revolutionary part of the *Discourse* lay in the argument spelled out in part 5.

After reiterating the orthodox position that there is a continuum of intelligence leading from man through the angels up to God, Descartes insists that, contrary to received opinion, there is a radical break between animals and man. That is, man is not only superior to the animals: he is totally different from them. For man, Descartes insists, is unlike the brutes in that he possesses a mind. What man has in common with animals is simply the fact that the human body, as in animals, is a machine.[1] But man, unlike animals, is also endowed with the ability to reason and reflect, to exercise moral choice, to direct the actions of his body, to be conscious of his mental states, to speak a language, and to live in a society. These cognitive, moral, social, and linguistic abilities cannot be possessed in degrees, nor can they be acquired by any nonhuman species. That is, animals do not enjoy nor can they develop the higher attributes of man.

In other words, Descartes postulates a hiatus between animals and man that *cannot* be filled by a "missing link." His use of "cannot" often sounds as if it is logical, not empirical—that this postulation is not a scientific hypothesis that could be overturned by travelers' stories of the "tailed men" dwelling in the Dark Continent but is a logical thesis—a premise subject to proof only through philosophical argument. Any incidents of supposed "animal intelligence" would thus have to be explained away by showing either that the "animal" in question was really a species of man or that the so-called "intelligent" behavior in question was really the result of instinct. For Descartes's picture of man was built on the foundation of his *discontinuity thesis*: the postulation of a radical discontinuity between animals and man.

In order to elevate man, therefore, Descartes repudiated the Great Chain of Being: the ancient doctrine that all of nature is organized in an unbroken series that progresses from inorganic matter and plants, through simple organisms and animals, to man, and then beyond man to spiritual beings, and ultimately, God. The Great Chain of Being took as its prototype something like the natural number series: beginning with the lowest possible integer we slowly increase toward infinity, one unit at a time. There can no more be "gaps" on the cognitive than on the arithmetic continuum; for this would amount to suggesting that God might occasionally be guilty of an oversight (which is strictly incoherent). Hence, to understand man—his mental powers and limitations—is to understand his place on the continuum (as revealed by the Bible and clarified by the sages). There is little scope here for independent cognitive development, or for individual variations (although cultural biases could still be maintained by assigning a subject race to a lower position on the continuum); and no sense in supposing, as Descartes does, that the mind of an individual creates its own world.

The *Discourse* thus heralded what can truly be described as a Copernican revolution in philosophy. For Descartes's universe, unlike that of the ancients, is bifurcated. At its center stands neither the Earth, nor the Sun, but man. Indeed, as we shall see in the following section, at the center of Descartes's universe stands the mind of the individual—responding to, and literally creating, the world around it. When Aristotle argued that man is by nature a political animal, or Seneca that man is a reasoning animal, the emphasis was very much on *animal*: one analyzes human nature in terms of the natural order. Man is a part of that natural order. But all this is changed in the *Discourse*. The body of man may be a machine, but with his mind man has the power, not just to rise above and control his animal instincts, but to construct the very reality that he inhabits. Unlike the medieval king, who was very much a member of the society over which he ruled, man is set apart from—and above—all of nature.

The shock waves that this argument set off—and that it was intended to set off—were enormous. The Great Chain of Being was not a doctrine Western thinkers were about to abandon without a struggle. Gassendi swiftly reaffirmed the classical line, insisting that "although [animals] do not reason so perfectly or about as many subjects as man, they still reason, and the difference seems to be merely one of degree" (Cottingham 1986, 2: 189). Similarly, the objections compiled by Mersenne (in the Sixth Set) defend the Great Chain of Being on the basis of the very epistemological skepticism that has come to be seen as the hallmark of Cartesianism (279). And in the third book of the *Essay Concerning Human Understanding* we find Locke arguing, "In all the visible corporeal world we see no chasms or gaps. All quite down from us the descent is by easy steps, and a continued series that in each remove differ very little one from the other." The crucial corollary of this argument is that "[t]here are some brutes that seem to have as much reason and knowledge as some that are called men; and the animal and vegetable kingdoms are so nearly joined, that if you will take the lowest of one and the highest of the other, there will scarce be perceived any great difference between them" (Locke 1690, 3, 6, sec. 12).

This orthodox defense of the Great Chain of Being prompted the contrary—materialist—response that man could indeed be treated in the same terms as animals, but only insofar as the behavior of neither should be explained in mentalist terms.[2] Significantly, when the infamous mechanist La Mettrie ridiculed "all the insignificant philosophers—poor jesters, and poor imitators of Locke," it was not for defending the principle of continuity, but for doing so on the wrong terms (La Mettrie 1748, 142–43). According to La Mettrie, the real lesson to be learned from Descartes's "proof that animals are pure machines" is that "these proud and vain beings, more distinguished by their pride than by the name of men however much they may wish to exalt themselves, are at bottom only animals and machines which, though upright, go on all fours" (143).

Descartes's attack on the Great Chain of Being thus provoked three distinct responses: first, there were those who fully embraced his discontinuity thesis and used it to justify such practices as dissecting live animals without anesthesia (in order to discover how the body maintains a state of thermal equilibrium). Second, there were those who defended the orthodox conception of the Great Chain of Being and maintained that Descartes had produced no convincing reason why the same terms that apply to man should not be extended to animals (or, in a more poetic vein, argued that there was no reason to so degrade the animals as to discredit them as possessing human qualities). And third, there were those who accepted Descartes's mechanist account of animal behavior but argued that exactly the same terms should be applied to man.

Thus, the *Discourse* inspired two diametrically opposed attempts to defend the principle of continuity: one group, the vitalists, set out to show how the behavior of animals is intelligent and purposive, while the other group, the mechanists, sought to demonstrate that human behavior is entirely reflexive. Vitalists sought to blur the lines between the higher animals and man by positing a *continuum of sentience*: all behavior, whether animal or human, was thought to be caused by sensations. Mechanists sought to blur the lines between the higher animals and man by eschewing any appeal to vital forces or mental states in the explanation of human action: all behavior, whether animal or human, was thought to be caused by internal or external stimuli.

The conflict between vitalism and mechanism quickly superseded the battle between Ancients and Moderns. Perhaps the greatest irony in this conflict is that both sides claimed Descartes as their guide. One reason why this confusion persisted is that it is never quite clear from his writings whether Descartes intended his argument to be seen as a *weak* (an empirical) or as a *strong* (a logical) skeptical thesis (see Taylor 1992). That is, it is never quite clear whether he is arguing empirically, that we lack sufficient evidence to attribute mental states to animals, or logically, that *animal* behavior is properly described in mechanical terms. Sometimes he merely seems to be saying that no one has ever presented any convincing evidence of animal intelligence; but sometimes he appears to want to make the stronger claim that the nature of animals is distorted if their behavior is described in mentalist terms.

This vacillation on what, to us, seems such a crucial point may simply be a reflection of the lack of importance that Descartes himself assigned to the issue; for what really mattered to Descartes was not how animals should be described, but rather, how man should be treated. Nonetheless, as the writings of the philosophes demonstrated, the distinction between weak and strong skepticism turned out to be an enormously important point. If Descartes was taken as making the weak skeptical point that we lack sufficient evidence to describe animal behavior in mentalist terms, then one could argue that not only do we possess sufficient evidence to describe human beings as possessing a mind, but indeed, that it is this very fact that licenses the mechanomorphic description of lower animal behavior. For the notion that we *lack sufficient evidence* to describe animal behavior in mentalist terms presupposes situations where we *possess sufficient evidence* to describe another organism's (i.e., a human's) behavior in mentalist terms. In that case, one could always challenge Descartes's account of higher animal behavior should new evidence about animal intelligence be forthcoming. Hence we find spirited debates in the eighteenth century about the reasoning capacities of beavers, apes, and elephants.

If, however, Descartes is taken as making the strong skeptical point that animal behavior is properly described in mechanical terms, then the door is opened to the mechanist corollary that the same strictures should be applied to man. For given that mental states are, on the Cartesian view, epistemically private, then someone who insists—in the name of "scientific rigor"—that animal behavior should be described in mechanical terms (since mental terms are said to be vacuous or completely nonexplanatory) can then insist that the same rigor extends to the psychological description of human behavior. Thus, a modern skeptic like Quine concludes that, since one can never be certain what another agent means or intends—given that *meaning* and *intention* are construed as epistemically private mental states—then the scientific explanation of linguistic behavior, or of purposive behavior, should not make any appeal to "meanings" or "intentions" but instead should be conducted in terms of stimulus conditions or cerebral events (see Shanker 1997b).

Eliminative materialism, the thesis that all mental terms can be replaced with descriptions of (manifest) behavior or (hidden) physical processes, was not to become a serious philosophical movement until the middle of the nineteenth century (with the rise of mechanist reductionism and scientific materialism; see Shanker 1997a). La Mettrie, as we saw above, toyed with this argument in *L'Homme Machine*, but more perhaps for its rhetorical effect than any strong materialist convictions. The more common form that the strong skeptical interpretation took in the eighteenth century was to treat any compelling evidence of putative "animal intelligence" as forcing us to reclassify the status of the "animal" in question. Thus La Mettrie concludes in *Traité de l'Âme* that the "orangoutans of Africa" are really "*hommes sauvages*" (Hastings 1936, 112). And Rousseau argues in his *Second Discourse* that apes are really men who have not yet developed from the primitive state—that is, men who have not yet learned how to talk.[3]

The philosophes' concern was not so much with our understanding of apes, however, as with our understanding of man. That is, "[r]ather than existing as a simple, isolated scientific problem, the contemplation of apes as wild men align[ed] itself with the more general philosophical problem of man's nature" (Hastings 1936, 110). The philosophes accepted Descartes's view that there is a sharp discontinuity between animals and man, but denied that it was in terms of the possession of mind. For animals, they argued, clearly have senses, and with senses come ideas. They concluded that what separated animals from man was the possession not of mind but of free will. For with free will comes not just the power to choose how one will act, but also the power to choose signs to refer to those ideas. Thus, the philosophes exploited Descartes's picture of volition in order to present what they saw as the explanation for why animals lack language, and thus, the real locus of discontinuity. It was only because man possessed free will that he was able to acquire the communicative means to congregate, which in turn resulted in the rapid (and symbiotic) development of both thought and language, leading ultimately to the dramatic disparity between the mental powers of animals and that of modern man (see Rousseau 1755, 91).

One can see, therefore, how Descartes's attack on the Great Chain of Being greatly stimulated interest in a variety of problems. To begin with, the philosophes became interested in the origins and nature of thought and language. From this followed a growing interest in the nature of animal communication, the nature of speech, and the relation between thought and speech (e.g., whether one is prior to the other, whether the development of one influences the development of the other, whether they are interdependent, whether the structure of one determines the structure of the other, whether some languages are superior to others as a means of *analyzing* and *communicating* ideas). This interest in turn led to a growing concern over the imperfections of language as a vehicle for the communication of thought (these "imperfections" were roughly divided into two broad categories: human carelessness or laziness, and shortcomings of the medium itself). And finally, the philosophes explored the relation between society and language (e.g., whether the formation of society was necessary for the emergence of language).[4]

This list of problems reveals the significant impact which the *Discourse on Method* had on eighteenth-century views of the nature of language and its relation to thought. Perhaps the surest sign of a genuine paradigm revolution is that a new set of problems are created and a new set of presuppositions are accepted. That is not to say that Descartes should be seen—as many proponents on both sides of the vitalist-mechanist debate argued—as the author of everything that goes by the name of Cartesianism. For Descartes was no Moses-like figure who emerged from complete isolation with a fully worked-out revolutionary doctrine. On the contrary, he was articulating—and to some extent synthesizing—a number of familiar epistemological themes.

After all, Descartes's inductive model of science was first formulated by Bacon, and one can find Descartes's view that words stand for ideas in Bacon's *Essay on the Dignity and the Advancement of Learning* (and, for that matter, in Hobbes's *Leviathan*). Moreover, arguments about the epistemic privacy of the mind and the privileged access one has to the mind's operations via introspection were a commonplace in scholastic writings, and can be traced back to the Greeks (see Everson 1991). Where Descartes was so significant was rather in tying this archetypal picture of mental privacy to the Baconian model of science. The result was a dramatic new conception of cognition as an *active mental process* whereby the individual mind *makes sense* of the world around it (which, on this conception, is a blooming, buzzing chaos). From this picture of cognition followed, almost as a corollary, Descartes's conception of animals as machines. It was the reasons that Descartes presented in order to substantiate his discontinuity thesis, which will be discussed hereafter, that created the set of problems and assumptions about the nature of language and its relation to the mind that were so influential in the next century: and, as we will show in this chapter, have continued to dominate attitudes toward language and cognition, in both humans and nonhuman primates, right up to the present.

Praedicet Ergo Est: It Predicts, Therefore It Is

Epistemological skepticism lies at the very heart of the Cartesian revolution. To be sure, Descartes did not invent the concept of epistemic privacy—that is, the idea that an agent is perceptually acquainted with her own mental states but can only infer what another agent is thinking or feeling. But he capitalized on the problem of other minds in order to institute a revolutionary theory of cognition. And it is this theory of cognition that forms the cornerstone of his discontinuity thesis.

In his second Meditation Descartes remarks:

> If I look out of the window and see men crossing the square, as I just happen to have done, I normally say that I see the men themselves, just as I say that I see the wax. Yet do I see any more than hats and coats which could conceal automatons? I judge that they are men. And so something which I thought I was seeing with my eyes is in fact grasped solely by the faculty of judgement which is in my mind. (Descartes 1641, 2: 21)

This last sentence is crucial to understanding Descartes's theory of cognition. He is arguing that we cannot see the internal causes of someone else's behavior, and there is nothing in the behavior itself that displays whether it is mentally caused. Yet we normally talk and act as though the people with whom we are dealing are conscious human beings and not automatons. What this means, Descartes concludes, is that, unbeknownst to us, our mind must infer—or rather, the faculty of judgment in our mind must infer—on the basis of the similarity it observes between an organism's behavior and our own behavior, that S's actions are mentally caused.

This is an extraordinary argument. Descartes exploits the problem of other minds as a means of convincing us that cognition is an unconscious inductive process performed by a "faculty of judgment." The logic of the argument is: Given that all that we see is "mere behavior," and given that we take it for granted that genuine human interaction occurs, it follows that the mind must infer that human actions are mentally caused. This is what our taking it for granted that other human beings have minds consists in: inferring that S is doing such-and-such because S "wants," "intends," "believes" such-and-such.

The crux of Descartes's theory of social perception is that the mind constructs concepts of "mental states" (like *desire*, *intention*, and *belief*) on the basis of self-observations, and then uses these concepts to make sense of or to predict the behavior of other human beings. This argument is distinct from but internally related to Descartes's dualist picture of the mental causes of bodily movements. The latter argument turns on the premise that all bodily movements are caused by "agitations in the brain" that are triggered by two different kinds of events: external objects impinging on the senses, or internal mental states. Accordingly, there are said to be two different kinds of movements: reflex or involuntary, and volitional or voluntary. Those that are involuntary are said to occur "without any intervention of the will," while "the movements which we call 'voluntary'" are those that "the soul determines" (Descartes 1649, 1: 315).

This argument inspired three centuries of debate over what these "volitions" are and how they bring about behavior (see Shanker 1992). Only recently have philosophers and psychologists begun to examine how Cartesian dualism interacts with Descartes's theory of cognition. According to Descartes, voluntary and involuntary movements *look exactly the same*: for example, an arm rising looks just like an arm being raised. It is only because volitions are "transparent to reason"—that is, it is only because each individual is able to see his own volitions "in his mind's eye"—that the mind is able to conceive of this fundamental distinction between *voluntary* and *involuntary* movements. For example, it is because I am able to distinguish between raising my arm and feeling my arm rise that I am able to construct the concept of a *voluntary action*. And it is because our fellow humans behave much as we do, and what is more, often report that one of their actions was voluntary or involuntary, that we are warranted in our analogical extension of what we see in ourselves to their behavior. But it remains within our power to override the unconscious inferences formulated by our faculty of judgment if we should consciously decide to treat human behavior differently.

This argument underpins Descartes's attack on the Great Chain of Being. The very fact that every individual has privileged access to his own thoughts and feelings entails that man occupies a privileged position on the *scala naturae*: not just because animals, no less than nature, are there to serve his needs, but more fundamentally, because it is up to man to decide how to see animals or his fellow man. That is, *perception* is an inferential process that is based on implicit assumptions that may derive from previous experiences, or from social conditioning; but we are not compelled to follow these assumptions. The inference that "S is doing such-and-such because S 'wants' x" is—qua inference—a voluntary mental act. We can alter these assumptions—we can see an organism's movements differently—should we so choose. Thus, Descartes's attack on the Great Chain of Being comes down to the claim that the concepts that man (i.e., his mind) constructs in order to make sense of his own behavior and that of other human beings need not and should not be applied to lower organisms.

Descartes is not saying that we should *treat* animals like machines: he is arguing that, if freed from false (i.e., anthropomorphic)[5] assumptions, we will literally *see* animals as machines. Just as there are cases (e.g., reflexes) where it would be totally inappropriate to see human behavior as mentally caused, so too we should be careful to avoid importing mental properties into the perception of similar behavior in animals (e.g., by interpreting their movements as actions, which as such are willed). The question this argument naturally raises is, why, according to Descartes, was he the first to have recognized this putative fact? Why wasn't this common knowledge? Descartes's answer is that cognition, qua inferential process, is subject to the authority wielded by a priori or *institutionalized* theories. We may overinterpret what we see because we are taught to see animal behavior in mentalist terms. So Descartes is urging us to throw off the anthropomorphic assumptions that color our perceptions of animal behavior and recognize that all that we actually *see* are machines.

The reason he gives to back up this radical thesis is simply that animals cannot talk. That is, he insists that because animals cannot tell us what they are thinking or experiencing, there are insufficient grounds for the mind to apply its mental-causal concepts to their behavior. According to Descartes, all that the mind sees when observing human or animal movements is "mere behavior." As far as the observer is concerned, the behavior of other human beings stands on precisely the same epistemological footing as that of animals: all could be machines. But the symmetry ends here. For the fact is that "there are no men so dull-witted or stupid . . . that they are incapable of arranging various words together and forming an utterance from them in order to make their thoughts understood." Human beings can always tell us what is going on inside them: even if it is only by gestures or signs. But "there is no other animal, however perfect and well-endowed it may be, that can do the like" (Descartes 1637, 1: 140).

There are two different ways to read this argument. On the one hand, Descartes can be taken to be saying that while we are licensed to frame mental-causal concepts to predict the behavior of human beings, there is no similar warrant to extend this model to animals. But then, this leaves open the possibility of discovering, or indeed cultivating, sufficient evidence of animal intelligence. On this reading, Descartes is taken to be arguing that we should see animal behavior in mechanomorphic terms because to do so is scientifically *prudent*. (Since we can never be certain that Fido understands the meaning of the command "Come," it is *safer* to assume that he is merely responding to the sound.) On the other hand, Descartes can be taken as saying that no amount of evidence would suffice to speak of "animal intelligence": that to do so would be a straightforward contradiction in terms. If we know a priori that discontinuity exists—if animals are *defined* as machines—then our task is to find an appropriate theoretical model in which to explain animal movements. On this reading, the description of animal behavior is limited to mechanical terms because to do so is *correct*. (Thus "understanding" is an idly turning wheel in the explanation of Fido's behavior; the *proper* explanation must be in terms of innate or conditioned responses to stimuli.)

The defenders of the Great Chain of Being adopted the former reading. Thus, not surprisingly, they were quick to respond that animals do indeed speak a language—do indeed tell each other what they are thinking or experiencing—but it is a language that we cannot understand. The argument whereby Descartes sought to meet this objection may come as something of a surprise to a modern reader. For Descartes's criticisms could easily have been written by any opponent of strong artificial intelligence (AI), or any modern critic of ALR.

Descartes insists that, even if we were capable of building automata that looked and acted like human beings, there would still be "two very certain means of recognizing that they were not real men." One means at our disposal would be to ascertain whether the organism in question was capable of responding to unforeseen circumstances. Descartes's point here is simply that, however sophisticated it might be, an automaton will only be able to execute the tasks for which it has been designed. Hence there will always be situations where the machine breaks down. This, according to Descartes,

> would reveal that they were acting not through understanding but only from the disposition of their organs. For whereas reason is a universal instrument which can be used in all kinds of situations, these organs need some particular disposition for each particular action; hence it is for all practical purposes impossible for a machine to have enough different organs to make it act in all the contingencies of life in the way in which our reason makes us act. (Descartes 1637: 1, 141)

Descartes is arguing that the ability to adjust to changing circumstances, or to learn from past experiences, or to anticipate future events, requires the ability to think. In other words, he is insisting on a categorial distinction between problem-solving and self-regulation. Moreover, the use of the term "organs" reminds us that it is not so much artifacts that Descartes is thinking of here as animals.[6] Since reason is absent in animals by definition, we are compelled to treat instances of so-called intelligent animal behavior in terms of innate dispositions. Thus, we have an early hint here of the twentieth-century ethological principle that animal behavior is governed by "fixed action patterns" that are "released" by stimuli.

The other reason Descartes gives as to why we could always be certain that we were dealing with a machine is that an automaton "could *never* use words, or put together other signs, as we do in order to declare our thoughts to others" (Descartes 1637: 1, 141). He is ready to concede the possibility of building a machine that "utters words, and even utters words which correspond to bodily actions causing a change in its organs (e.g. if you touch it in one spot it asks what you want of it, if you touch it in another it cries out that you are hurting it, and so on)." But, he insists, "it is not conceivable that such a machine should produce different arrangements of words so as to give an appropriately meaningful answer to whatever is said in its presence, as the most of man can do" (141). In other words, it is not conceivable that a machine could possess or aquire grammar.

Descartes shifts back and forth between the empirical and the logical here. When he insists that we cannot conceive of a machine producing different arrangements of words so as to give an appropriately meaningful answer to whatever is said in its presence, does he mean that it is *psychologically impossible* for us to conceive of such a machine, or that it makes no sense to speak of a "machine" as being linguistically creative? Were the argument empirical, one could argue that Descartes's pessimism was simply unwarranted: both in regard to ape language studies and in regard to the development of expert systems. Indeed, such a response is a characteristic feature of both ALR and AI writings. But if Descartes's use of "never" or "not conceivable" is logical—if, for example, the argument turns on his definition of "machine"—then this premise invites the sort of argument that one finds in Turing that "at the end of the century the use of words and general educated opinion will have altered so much that one will be able to speak of machines thinking without expecting to be contradicted" (Turing 1950, 133,142) insofar as the definition of 'machine' will have changed (see Shanker 1998).

Descartes lays great weight on the distinction, common in the seventeenth and eighteenth centuries, between *speech* and what was commonly described as *natural language*. The latter term was used to refer to natural expressive behavior (e.g., crying "ouch") or what was called the "language of gesture" (e.g., deictic pointing). Descartes is drawing a categorial distinction between this sort of primitive expressive behavior and speech on the grounds that primitive expressive behavior is "mechanical" (i.e., reflexive or automatic), whereas speech is accompanied by mental states. In order to constitute speech, a subject's utterances must be used to communicate her ideas or thoughts. It is a necessary condition of speech that it be underpinned by thought; the mere articulation of sounds without this mental accompaniment no more constitutes speech than a pianola "reading off" the notes on a roll constitutes *playing music*.

Descartes presents us with two reasons why animals cannot be said to possess the capacity to speak. The first is that, given the nature of thought (whatever this might be), sentences can only serve as a vehicle for its communication if they are articulated. That is, the ability to communicate thought verbally, and to understand someone else's utterances, requires the ability to produce or respond to "different arrangements of words." If we relate this point to Descartes's theory of cognition, we can see that he is saying that, without evidence that an organism possesses grammar, we have no reason to treat the organism's vocalizations as speech, as opposed to natural expressive behavior.

Still, the foregoing argument only presents us with a reason for saying that animals cannot speak our language, not that they do not possess their own language which we cannot understand. The further reason that Descartes gives for why animals cannot speak is that, if they had this capacity, they would be able to devise some way of telling us what they are thinking. The fact that animals cannot do so is clearly not because they are physically incapable of it; "for we see that magpies and parrots can utter words as we do, and yet they cannot speak as we do: that is, they cannot show that they are thinking what they are saying. On the other hand, men born deaf and dumb, and thus deprived of speech-organs as much as the beasts or even more so, normally invent their own signs to make themselves understood by those who, being regularly in their company, have the time to learn their language. This shows not merely that the beasts have less reason than men, but that they have no reason at all" (Descartes 1637, 1: 140). Thus we should not think, "like some of the ancients, that the beasts speak, although we do not understand their language. For if that were true, then since they have many organs that correspond to ours, they could make themselves understood by us as well as by their fellows" (141).

Descartes warns that, in the case of some animals, it may indeed be possible, because of their ability to imitate sounds and to adjust to the changing contingencies of their environment, to train them to produce what look like the appropriate "words" for a given situation. But this behavior is merely the effect of what today we would call *conditioning*. That is, you can train an animal to produce certain sounds that may strike the untrained observer as the appropriate words for that situation, but closer examination reveals that the animal does not understand the meaning we attach to those sounds: it does not use those sounds to refer to ideas.

The argument ultimately rests, therefore, on a form of circularity: animals cannot learn how to speak because they have no thoughts, and we know they have no thoughts because they have not learnt how to speak.[7] The defender of the Great Chain of Being thus had two options: to try to meet Descartes's objections and show that animals can combine words appropriately (i.e., grammatically) and can tell us what they are thinking (in their own "words", e.g., by various barks or calls); or to argue that Descartes had laid undue stress on speech as a criterion for assigning intelligence. After all, if speech were merely *evidence* of intelligence, then it would still be possible for animals to have mental states without being able to communicate them, or to communicate them to each other nonverbally, or indeed, "telepathically." But if to have a mind somehow necessitates the ability (and the desire) to express one's thoughts, then Descartes can be taken to be saying that not only does describing S as "truly speaking" presuppose that S is able to think, but conversely, that to describe S as "able to think" entails that S can speak—in a way that can be understood by human beings.

It would be tempting—and indeed, it has tempted many—to dismiss this argument as a victim of anthropocentric bias. But Descartes's argument is far more subtle than to do so would suggest. To see its subtlety, one need only think back to the case of judging that S raised his arm voluntarily, an inference said to be warranted by the fact that S behaves much as I do and uses the words "voluntary" and "involuntary" in much the same way that I do. In order to infer that S experiences similar volitions to my own, I must also infer that S has formed a concept similar to my own of a *voluntary action*. In other words, if the role of the faculty of judgment is to make sense of the world, then the inference that S has a mind amounts to the inference that S possesses a faculty of judgment that is doing exactly the same thing when it looks at me that mine is doing when I look him.

The manner in which Descartes views animals is no different from the manner in which he views human beings. His conclusion is ultimately that we—that our minds—are not given sufficient evidence to infer that animals are conscious of what they are doing or what is happening to them (see Descartes 1970, 36). Nor do they do the same thing that we do when we look at the world: form concepts to make sense of the world, and use words or signs to refer to those concepts. The locus of this argument is not man: it is the mind. For the mind takes its own operations as the metric whereby to categorize the world.

In short, the crux of Descartes's discontinuity thesis is that the very terms that lead us to speak of—and refute—skepticism of other minds lead us to see that the same mental concepts cannot be applied to animals. Thus, we can begin to appreciate why his attack on the Great Chain of Being had such a profound impact on those who worried, not just about the relationship of man to the higher animals, but about the very nature of thought and language. For Descartes's denial that the study of animal behavior could shed any light on the origins of thought and language was the consequence of a bold new view of how the mind works and what sort of window language provides onto the operations of the mind. As we will soon show, this picture of cognition and its relation to language constitutes the starting point for modern Cartesianism.

The Cartesian Mind as "Folk" Theorist

Epistemological circularity lies at the very heart of Cartesianism. Descartes drew his picture of cognition from the Baconian model of science, and then set out to justify the Baconian model of science by showing how it was the natural product of cognition as so conceived. Cognition is thus defined in terms of *observation* and *induction*: that is, the mind frames concepts about the patterns it observes.

Physics and psychology are then construed as natural extensions of the sort of protoscientific activities in which the mind is constantly engaged.

According to Cartesianism, what an agent sees, thinks, wants, or feels is not just a matter of instinct or predisposition, but is in large part determined by the situations in which the agent begins to exercise her mental faculties. The concern with ontogenesis, which has been so prominent a feature of cognitive psychology over the past thirty years, is an integral aspect of Cartesianism. Cartesianism treats it as an ontogenesis of *theory-construction*. The Cartesian developmentalist begins with the paradigm of the scientific mind and works backward through a descending level of "mental constructs" to arrive at the neonate who, in Piagetian terms, immediately begins to conduct experiments on the world around it (see Shanker 1998).

What this means is that the neonate's actions—for they are indeed *actions*—are seen as far more deliberate than we might at first realize. The neonate is said to be seeking, testing, hypothesizing, remembering. Its actions are purposeful because cognition itself is an active mental process: a *mental act*. We tend to overlook the significance which this term originally carried: the fact that it wasn't just a metaphor but was used to signify that the human being directs her mental processes, just as she directs her physical movements.

These mental processes may be epistemically private, but they can be experimentally explored; and to do so becomes the chief task of psychology as conceived by the Cartesian. The Cartesian picture of psychology is grounded, therefore, in the Cartesian picture of the mind. Psychology is conceived of as having the task of sharpening our understanding of the inductive processes whereby human beings make sense of the world. Psychology is thus seen as simply a more comprehensive and systematic version of what every human being does when she looks at reality.

For the Cartesian, ordinary discourse about the mind constitutes a "folk psychology," while ordinary discourse about the world constitutes a "naive physics." Just as a child must be trained in its society's theories about nature, so too it must be trained in its society's inchoate theories about the mind. Thus, the child learning how to use mental terms is seen as learning the rudiments of a "theory of mind." For example, we talk about never being certain of what someone else is thinking. We teach a child that only it can know what it intends. And to be on guard with strangers, since it can never know for sure when someone is lying, or in pain. We correct the child who wonders what plants believe by explaining that only humans have beliefs. In all these cases, and countless more, Cartesianism treats the simple commonplaces of psychological discourse as *empirical hypotheses*: as all part of the causal-explanatory framework that each of us must acquire if we are to make sense of ourselves and of the social behavior of those around us.

The origins of Cartesianism, therefore, both as a theory of cognition and as a theory of psychological explanation, lie in a picture of ordinary psychological discourse as consisting in reports of private mental operations of induction and prediction. The mind, according to this view, is constantly scanning for regularities in order to anticipate actions or events: constantly "abstracting and generalizing" from experience. Psychology and physics are seen as interdependent extensions of this innate disposition to theorize. But then, just as both sciences are constantly evolving, why could there not be a phylogenetic continuum of mental induction? Why could one not argue that, just as the rigorous theories of a scientist are more advanced than the lay theories of an adult, or those of the adult are more sophisticated than those of a child, so too the theories of the human primate are more complex than those of the nonhuman primate, and so on down the continuum, until one arrives at the crude "theories" of simple organisms? In other words, why should Descartes's picture of cognition compel Cartesians to accept his vision of a bifurcated universe?

The answer to this question lies in the fundamental distinction that Descartes stressed between involuntary and voluntary movements. For eighteenth-century Cartesians, the term "involuntary" came to encompass everything mechanical: not just reflexes or conditioned responses, but also, any mental event that happens to us unbidden and uncontrolled (e.g., the association of ideas). The term "voluntary" referred to any mental or physical act that we will. Indeed, what is *voluntary* in a voluntary act (e.g., raising one's arm) is the *act of will* (what William James called the "fiat") that causes that bodily action. Thus, the distinction between involuntary and voluntary movements is really underpinned by a distinction between passive mental states and voluntary mental acts. All conscious activities were thought to fall under the latter category: that is, when we think, infer, know, decide, reflect, remember, attend, believe, perceive, and so on, we *act mentally*. (Recall Descartes's argument, already discussed, that it is up to us to *choose* how we shall see animals.)

For eighteenth-century Cartesians, bifurcationism did not create a phylogenetic problem. The philosophes were agreed that, although they had senses, and thus ideas, animals could not think, which for them meant: could not summon up ideas at will, and hence, recombine ideas in order to form new thoughts. But the involuntary/voluntary distinction did create an anthropological problem: namely, when did man begin to think, and how did this come about? What seemed indisputable to the philosophes was that only once he had acquired free will did man begin to think (only then were "all our faculties developed, memory and imagination brought into play, pride stimulated, reason made active" [Rousseau 1755, 118]). But when and how did man first acquire free will, and thus, begin to *exercise* his mental faculties? That is, when did man's behavior cease to be passive (reflexive, instinctive, appetitive, conditioned) and start to become active?

The philosophes felt that, while science could only speculate about how the transition from involuntary to voluntary behavior might have occurred in the distant mists of man's early history (see Rousseau's *Second Discourse*), it could learn how the child makes this transition by close observation (see Rousseau's *Émile*) and perhaps thereby deepen our understanding of man's transition from a primitive, passive state where his actions were governed primarily by instincts and appetites into a being with free will. Thus was born a new, ontogenetic version of bifurcationism: namely, when does a child begin to think, and how does this come about? And, of course, Descartes had highlighted an important key to answering this latter question: namely, when the child begins to speak.

Given that speech, according to Cartesianism, must be accompanied by—must, by definition, be used to communicate—thoughts, the emergence of speech becomes the crucial indicator for whether, and if so when, the transition from *react-ing* to *acting* has occurred. The child's transition from cries and gestures to ver-bal interaction was thought to mirror primitive man's transition from *natural lan-guage* to *speech*. In both cases, the transition was thought to rest on the emergence of free will. For the decision to use a word to refer to an idea—which was seen as the foundation of speech—was itself regarded as an act of free will. Indeed, some philosophes felt that the child first creates sounds that its parents imitate, and then invents words that its parents incorporate into their speech (see Juliard 1970, 42–43). To be sure, the child learning how to speak is subject to all sorts of coer-cion from its society about how to govern its speech. But from Locke onward, Cartesians regarded the link between words and ideas as voluntary and private (see Taylor 1992; Harris and Taylor 1989).

With Condillac we get the further argument that speech enables man to exer-cise voluntary control over the ideas coursing through his mind. Speech, unlike natural language, forces one (because of the linear form of its sentences) to ana-lyze one's thoughts: to break down complex thoughts into their component parts. Thus, Condillac argues in the *Essai sur l'Origine des Connaissances Humaines* (I: 2, §4) that "a man who has only accidental and natural signs, has none at all at his command. . . . Hence we may conclude that brutes have no memory; and that they have only an imagination which they cannot command as they please" (quoted in Harris and Taylor 1989, 120). If, for example, an animal returns to a spot where it had found food the previous day, it is not because it remembers this incident, but only because a chain of mental events (i.e., the sensation of hunger connected with the idea of the place) has led it, unknowingly, back to that location. "But as soon as a man comes to connect ideas with signs of his own choosing, we find his memory is formed" (120). Were the same thing to happen to a man in possession of speech, his returning to the spot would probably be the result of his remember-ing the incident. For the creation of artificial signs enables man to break complex thoughts down into their component ideas, which can then be named, recognized, recalled, reflected on, recombined, and of course, communicated. Moreover, it is only if the agent possesses speech (e.g., tells us why she returned to that spot) that we are licensed to infer that she *remembered* the previous day's events.

Without speech, animals would not be capable of analyzing their ideas; that is, would not be capable of thinking. Without speech, there is insufficient evidence to infer that animals possess free will: that is, to infer that their actions are purpo-sive, that they are capable of mental acts. Hence apparent counterinstances of animals behaving in what appears to be a purposive manner have to be explained away (e.g., in terms of instincts or the association of ideas).

It is highly significant that, the more they learned about anthropoids—and, especially, orangutans—the more uncertain the philosophes were as to how to classify them. Apes not only looked a great deal like men, but what is more, dis-played a number of highly human traits (e.g., a similar anatomy, tool use, some sort of social structure). The problem was that these "men of the woods" did not speak. Some wondered if perhaps they chose to remain silent for fear that, if they spoke and thus revealed their intelligence, they would be enslaved. Rousseau speculated that they were a primitive race of men that, "with no opportunity to develop any of its potential faculties, had not acquired any measure of perfection, and was still found in the primitive state of nature" (Rousseau 1755, 155). What was clear to these early Cartesian anthropologists, however, was that, without speech, these creatures could not be classified as sentient beings. For only with the acquisition of speech did man acquire voluntary control over the operations of his mind, and thence, his actions.

Thus for eighteenth-century Cartesians, what separated man from the beasts was indeed speech, but at a deeper level, it was the emergence of free will on which the ability to engage in speech depends that separated man from beast, and ultimately, the possession of an immaterial soul, which was seen as the source of free will. After all, many animals possessed organs of speech; thus, if they failed to speak, it had to be because they lacked the will to do so. What remained an utter mystery, however, was how primitive man took the prodigious step from natural language to speech: how he was able to acquire the free will that enabled him to develop artificial language, and thence, his thought processes and society.

Cartesian Bifurcation versus Mechanist Continuity

Of course, if apes could speak our special place in the universe would be imperil-led, but the cardinal de Polignac, for one, felt no real danger to his faith when he approached the chimpanzee in the glass cage at the Jardin du roi and proclaimed, "Parle, et je te baptise."
                    Robert Wokler, *The Ape Debates in Enlightenment Anthropology*

The nineteenth and early part of the twentieth century was marked by the rapid growth of mechanism as a serious alternative to Cartesianism. This development was sparked off partly by the great mechanist successes in the life sciences and partly by Cartesianism's continuing failure to explain the mystery of man's transition from an involuntary to a voluntary state. Mechanism responded to this mystery by seeking to remove the involuntary/voluntary distinction altogether (see Shanker 1997a).

To this day, psychology remains deeply divided over the question of what constitutes a proper scientific explanation of human behavior: that is, whether to adopt a bifurcationist picture of both phylogenetic and ontogenetic development, or some version of the continuum picture (e.g., computationalism or connectionism). Psychologists remain divided over the question of whether the mentalist terms of the bifurcationist picture are essential to the manner in which human beings categorize the world, or whether the mechanisms of "categorization" are no different from the mechanisms of adaptation and habituation. But the one thing on which both sides are agreed is that the idea of a third option—a cognitive continuum, in which psychological terms can be freely ascribed to all organisms—is illicit. According to Cartesians this is anthropomorphic; according to mechanists, it is mentalist. But despite their differing views of why it is illegitimate to apply psychological terms to lower animals, both sides are agreed that mechanism constitutes the appropriate theoretical framework for explaining animal behavior.

Thus, the continuing clash between Cartesian bifurcationism and mechanist continuity comes down to the question of whether the continuum picture can be extended to explain human as well as animal behavior, or whether there must be some point of phylogenetic and ontogenetic discontinuity demanding a new set of terms for the proper explanation of human behavior: some point at which stimulus-response connections are displaced by abstraction and generalization; or instrumental conditioning is supplanted by the construction of theories; or "sensorimotor schemes" are transformed into "cognitive representations"; or at which a Language Acquisition Device (LAD) is suddenly activated (i.e., when the brain, or certain faculties, reach some threshold of experience). Bifurcationist thinking has long been the great regulative force of Cartesianism: not simply because it dogmatically excludes any light that the study of animals might shed on some domain in the study of human cognition, but more important, because it compels the Cartesian psychologist to develop theories of mind or of language that can substantiate the discontinuities that are postulated.

In the radical conception of bifurcationism, the study of animal behavior is excluded from all aspects of the study of (human) cognition, and the postulation of cognitive processes is prohibited from all aspects of the study of animal behavior. For since animals do not possess the ability to speak, we are said to have no grounds to infer that they are capable of gaining control over their environment by abstracting regularities and constructing theories to predict future events (or further, of experiencing any form of joint awareness or mutual understanding, since they must also lack the ability to predict what each other will do in different situations). The task facing a Cartesian science of animal behavior is clear: to extirpate any vestiges of anthropomorphism by demonstrating that all supposed instances of intelligence are the result of purely reflexive responses to stimuli. If one is interested in the study of animals in their natural surroundings, one is restricted to examining how their behavior is determined by a number of drives that affect their responses to external stimuli.

This mechanist outlook constituted the starting point for classical ethology. All the work done on *vacuum behaviors* ("action patterns" triggered in the absence of appropriate stimuli) was designed to subvert what was seen as the anthropomorphic belief that animals might experience certain human emotions or thought processes. Getting a turkey hen to attack one of its offspring by playing the sound of a predator in the nest, and conversely, getting it to nurture a predator by playing the sound of one of its chicks, was taken as demonstrating that it makes no sense to speak of a hen as *bonding* with her chicks, but rather, that these are simply instances of "innate releasing mechanisms" set off or triggered by stimuli.

It is important to recognize the extent to which ethology has left its mark on contemporary attitudes toward animal cognition and ALR. As its name implies, the study of animal cognition challenges the most basic tenet of radical bifurcationism. Yet as Herb Terrace, perhaps the best-known ape language skeptic, admits, most scientists of animal cognition accept that mental predicates have to be reduced to nonmental terms if one is to succeed in "[e]xorcising the ghosts of consciousness and introspection" from the study of animal cognition (Terrace 1984, 8).

Terrace embraces the Cartesian assumption that research in animal cognition—*qua research in cognition*—is confronted with the basic problem "of studying processes which cannot be observed directly" (Terrace 1984, 7). Indeed, he accepts the fundamental Cartesian premise that the absence of speech among animals forces us to accept "a possible discontinuity between animal and human cognition" (8). The result is a modified Cartesian theory that might be called *moderate bifurcationism*, which holds that animals can indeed think and construct concepts, but they cannot name those concepts: cannot use language to communicate their thoughts.

The moderate bifurcationist believes that both animal cognition and human cognition are primarily unconscious affairs. But in the study of human cognition, verbal behavior constitutes one of the key factors in "inferring the critical features of unobservable processes" (Terrace 1984, 8). Hence, "[t]he unavailability of language as a medium of cognition for animals dictates that models of animal cognition will differ in many important respects from their human counterparts. When studying animal cognition, it seems prudent to keep in mind Piaget's many demonstrations of the differences between a child's and an adult's mode of thought" (9). In effect, Terrace is subordinating anthropomorphism to psychologism. He is telling us: Do not read human mental processes into an animal's mental processes, and do not assume that animals share the same categorization processes or the same concept taxonomies as humans.

Terrace is well known for his repudiation of ALR (see Terrace 1979). But he is no behaviorist, and his rejection of ALR is clearly not based on radical bifurcationist principles. On the contrary, he is fully committed to the premise that an animal's behavior is often guided by mental representations (i.e., that not all animal behavior can be explained by reflex theory). Nor is his attitude to ALR dogmatic; all he says is that "[i]t has yet to be shown . . . that even the most intelligent of animals could learn enough about language to name their thoughts and to use such names as mnemonics" (Terrace 1986, x). Above all, Terrace wants to present animals as active rather than passive organisms: that is, as *choosing x*, or *intending to* ϕ. Thus, contrary to the eighteenth-century argument that since animals lack speech we lack sufficient grounds to infer that they are capable of memory, Terrace insists that it is possible to gather sufficient evidence that animals, who cannot speak, are indeed capable of remembering things.

To substantiate this claim, he cites the example of how pigeons and monkeys can perform successfully on tests where they are shown a long series of photographs and then shown a "problem" photograph that either matches or does not match one of the earlier photos. To earn a food reward the animal must press a "yes" button when there is a match and a "no" button when there isn't. To explain pigeons' and monkeys' success in this experiment, Terrace argues: "The subject must somehow recall the photographs he has seen. A correct choice can occur only if the subject is able to compare its representations of the previously shown photographs with the probe on hand. Such a mental comparison does occur: the greater the number of photographs on the list, the longer it takes for the subject to decide if it had seen the probe" (Terrace 1986, x).

The problem with this argument is that it impales Terrace on the horns of a dilemma. By his own standards, it is not enough to explain the animal's success by saying "It remembered that it had seen x" or "It knows that it hadn't seen x":

according to Terrace, we need to explain the mechanics of this "unconscious mental comparison process." But the problem with such an explanation is that either it fails to remove the mentalist terms, only pushing them to a lower level, or the argument collapses into mechanism, in which case there are insufficient grounds to postulate cognitive processes to explain the animals' behavior.

To see this point, consider the question Terrace sets out to answer: How did the pigeons and monkeys *recognize* that the photograph matched item x on the earlier list? From the radical bifurcationist perspective, an anthropomorphic response to this question merely resorts to using disguised mental terms: for example, using "match" as a psychological verb, or speaking, as Terrace does, of the "mental comparison" that occurs. Hence the anthropomorphic response fails to explain how the animal *knows* that such-and-such a mental representation is the *same* as the probe on hand. To be sure, to say that a human being made a *correct choice* is to say that he *remembered* seeing x; but then, such judgments are fundamentally tied to the *reasons* which the agent gives for why he chose x. Thus, the radical bifurcationist will insist that, in the case of animal behavior, one can only speak of a "representational match" in the same way that one speaks of there being a match between a key and the lock that it opens: that is, if the pieces fit together, this fit causes the animal to φ. That is, cognition doesn't enter at all in the case of animals, and a fortiori, normativity doesn't enter at all; for without the ability to tell us why they chose such-and-such a photo, there are insufficient grounds to speak of the pigeons or monkeys as *making a choice*, let alone *making a correct choice*. Thus, we must conclude that an animal is "guided by its mental representations" in exactly the same way that a missile is guided by its internal settings and feedback cues.

The dilemma in which scientists of animal cognition find themselves is really part of a larger skeptical problem facing anyone who starts out from the Cartesian conception of cognition. For why should we not compare the turkey hen experiment mentioned earlier with the role that oxytocin or phenylethylamine play in human behavior?[8] Perhaps it no more makes sense to speak of a mother as *bonding* with her baby than a hen as bonding with her chicks? Of course, the mother, unlike the hen, can tell us about the emotions she is feeling.[9] But then, the behaviorist has no qualms about reducing verbal behavior to stimulus-response terms. So perhaps the real moral that must be drawn here is that skeptical attacks on animal cognition and communication can be applied just as forcefully to the study of human cognition and communication? Perhaps the arguments that underpin the skeptic's charge of anthropomorphism ultimately force us into the arms of eliminative materialism and Skinnerian theories of verbal conditioning?

Moreover, what are we to say now about moderate bifurcationism's own standing in light of its attack on ALR? After all, the basic premise in the moderate bifurcationist's reluctance to sanction ALR is that positing such "mental states" as understanding, meaning, or reference adds nothing to our understanding of apes' communicative behavior. But exactly the same point should apply to the study of animal cognition. In other words, ALR and animal cognition research stand or fall together.

The point here is not that to describe the behavior of an animal in cognitive terms entails that it must be credited with linguistic abilities; rather, it is that the epistemological basis of the skeptical attack on ALR can just as well be applied to the study of animal cognition. For the same reasons that convince a moderate bifurcationist to adopt a skeptical attitude toward Kanzi's linguistic abilities must, with equal force, compel him to adopt a skeptical attitude toward Kanzi's cognitive abilities. In both cases we are trying, in Terrace's words, to infer the "critical features of unobservable processes." But the only reason we are given for why the pigeons and monkeys should be described as *remembering* what they had seen is that they consistently pick out the right photographs and reject the wrong ones. But then, how different is this reason from the criteria Savage-Rumbaugh uses to justify the claim that Kanzi understands the statement "Put the ball in the box"? Don't the sort of criteria Terrace takes to justify his description of pigeons' and monkeys' cognitive abilities equally justify Savage-Rumbaugh's description of Kanzi's linguistic abilities?

The question all this raises is: Why have scientists of animal cognition adopted a dual standard toward their own research and ALR? The answer lies in the fact that moderate bifurcationism is grounded in a Cartesian conception of cognition together with a Cartesian conception of language. As far as moderate bifurcationism is concerned, the issue raised by ALR solely concerns the "law of parsimony," which, in practice, translates into the following precept: No matter what communicative skills apes might acquire, these can always be described in non-linguistic terms. For example, word-order regularities can be explained away as *lexical position habits*. The common refrain here is that ALR theorists are guilty of "elevating to linguistic status behavior more cogently explained in simpler terms" (Wallman 1992, 31). And, significantly, the critic takes this "rampant overinterpretation" to be the consequence of a "limited, at times crude, understanding of language" (36). That is, ALR is committed, according to moderate bifurcationism, to a behaviorist "reduction of language to problem-solving" (37).

Moderate bifurcationists oppose *their* understanding of the "crude theory of language that one finds in ALR" with a Cartesian picture of language: words are mapped onto concepts, enabling one to communicate one's thoughts, "albeit imperfectly," to another language-speaker (Wallman 1992, 49). This *telementational* view of language goes hand in hand with the nativist argument that language is not something that can be *learned*: it is something that *grows*. Language must already be "in" young children, enabling them to "distill the syntactic pattern out of the speech of their parents" (Pinker 1994, 22).

Nativists base their argument on the following themes:

- the universality of language
- the universal attributes of language
- the fact that language emerges in all children at roughly the same age
- the apparently uniform sequence of language development
- the relative insignifance of practice, reinforcement, or IQ on language acquisition
- the fact that the child must deal with grammatically incorrect sentences, slips of the tongue, and incomplete sentences
- the child's ability to understand or utter infinitely many novel sentences

- the child's ability to learn myriad rules of grammar
- the child's ability to create grammatical complexity where none exists

None of these themes, according to the nativist, could be explained on the basis of the relatively meager linguistic data to which the child is exposed. The child must therefore be endowed with knowledge of all the possible forms that grammar can take. That is, the child must come into the world possessing a set of "super rules" that make all these otherwise extraordinary feats possible. Only thus can we explain "how children's grammar explodes into adultlike complexity in so short a time. They are not acquiring dozens or hundreds of rules; they are just setting a few mental switches" (Pinter 1994, 112). Hence language is not something which an animal could *develop* (through training or observation). Language is rather an integral and unique part of the human birthright: an "endowment of the species" (Wallman 1992, 77). It is simply not possible, therefore, for a bonobo to *acquire* the ability to convey his or her thoughts linguistically.

Nativists may accept the developmental interactionist model that one finds in ALR as far as the early stages of protolanguage are concerned. They may even concede that the ability to use sounds to mark one's intentions emerges in this prelinguistic stage. But "[t]he first words may not *have* any meaning in the conventional sense. Instead, their utterance may be merely a ritualized part of recurrent activity contexts, only nominally more linguistic than the nonverbal behaviors that also define these contexts, or it may be an attention-directing behavior, or both" (Wallman 1992, 51). In the case of humans—and only in the case of humans—a crucial transformation takes place when the subject acquires language: vocalizations get transformed into *linguistic symbols* when the child begins to use sounds, not just to do things (e.g., to initiate routines or to get another subject's attention) but to *signify* its mental representations (see Wallman 1992, 50).

Discontinuity between nonhuman and human primates is located, according to moderate bifurcationism, at precisely this point of transformation. Apes can be brought to the verge of this threshold, but for genetic reasons, they cannot cross over it; for they lack the organ (or faculty, or gene) that enables human beings to map concepts onto words, or to combine words into sentences, or to embed sentences in other sentences. The moderate bifurcationist may accept that "the apes' concepts are not qualitatively different in focus or extent from their counterparts in young children." But he insists that "a distinction should be drawn between concepts and their linguistic expression in reference," where "reference" is said to be "the cognitive event in which some entity in mind is specified through linguistic means" (Wallman 1992, 64). Ape utterances (whether these be vocalizations, gestures, or sign uses) "are better characterized as performative than referential . . . [i.e.,] a repertoire of habits that [a]re *effective* rather than *meaningful*" (77).

Becoming a Person

Twentieth-century Cartesians have not been immune to the pressures emanating from the ascendancy of mechanist theories, beginning with behaviorism, followed by cybernetics and automata theory, and culminating in AI. They have responded that perhaps we can speak of lower organisms in some of the same terms as higher organisms: that is, as having sensations and some first-order mental states. But modern Cartesianism has sought to turn this concession to its own advantage. Thus it speaks of the problems involved in getting inside the mind of a monkey, or a bat, or perhaps, of a slug. For why should the problem of other minds not be extended to the problem of other species? Indeed, perhaps the problem of other minds is exemplified by the problem of knowing how bats or monkeys see the world. But these moderate bifurcationists will hasten to add that, even if it is true that there is a *sentient continuum*, that does not undermine the fundamental principle of discontinuity between animals and man. Thus, the modern Cartesian continues to insist on there being a point of bifurcation: not in Descartes's crude mechanical/mental terms, nor the philosophes' possession of free will, but rather, in terms of *being a person.*

"Being a human being," we are told, "is necessary for true personhood, but it is not sufficient. To be a human being is to have a biological status: It entails certain physical characteristics and capacities. Human infants are human beings, but they are not yet fully persons. They have the potential to become persons, but attaining full personhood requires a gradual process of development founded on interaction with others" (Shatz 1994, 6). This picture of a developmental process whereby the child crosses over the point of bifurcation and enters the society of humanity proper recalls the philosophes' picture of the process whereby primitive man must have made the transition from his savage, nonlinguistic state into a primitive social state in which speech emerged. The source of this continuity lies in the Cartesian view of language and its relation to cognition. For the essence of language, according to Cartesianism, is that it is a representational system that enables the transmission of thoughts from the mind of one agent to that of another. As we will show in the next section, the psychological implications of this view of language reinforce the bifurcationist thesis.

To begin with, one need only think of Ferdinand de Saussure's picture of the "speech circuit."

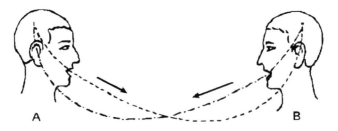

In order to identify what role *langue* plays within the totality of language, we must consider the individual act of speech and trace what takes place in the speech circuit. This act requires at least two individuals: without this minimum the circuit would not be complete. Suppose, then, we have two people, A and B, talking to each other. . . . All the individuals linguistically linked in this manner will establish among themselves a kind of mean; all of them will reproduce—doubtless not exactly, but approximately—the same signs linked to the same concepts. (Saussure 1916, 11–13)

Communication, according to Saussure, takes place when A successfully transmits her concepts to B. Saussure takes it as a given that communication does at least sometimes occur. His own concern is with the properties that langue must possess in order to make this communication possible (see Taylor 1992, 70–72). But we can also tease out a psychological thesis from this argument. For it must be the case that, for two speakers to communicate with one another, each must have a mind; and for any speaker to believe that he or she is communicating with another, he or she must believe that the other agent has a mind. That is, both speakers in the "speech circuit" must believe—given that they assume that they are communicating—that the other understands what they are saying (has decoded their thoughts) and that when the other talks he or she is describing (encoding) his or her thoughts. But what is it to believe that another agent has a mind?

This question is already implicit in Descartes's picture of cognition. Recall that it is Descartes's mind that infers that the figures crossing the square are men and not automatons: that is, the mind extrapolates from its own experiences and applies the resulting concepts to similar-looking behavior. But on Descartes's argument, to infer that other beings have minds is not simply to infer that their actions are voluntary: it is also to infer that they go through the same process that I go through when they observe my behavior. This connection would mean that the question of whether another organism has a mind doesn't simply rest on the question of whether it experiences mental states: it also rests on the question of whether that organism has framed a *theory of mind* on the basis of its acquaintance with its own mental states.

In effect, moderate bifurcationism argues that Descartes's radical bifurcationist argument is guilty of conflating first-order mental states and higher-order "metacognitive" concepts. The moderate bifurcationist argues that, to infer that an organism possesses metacognitive concepts does indeed, as Descartes suggested, presuppose the ability to speak. But speech is not necessary to infer that an organism experiences first-level mental states. Accordingly, the moderate bifurcationist can argue that, even if one infers that animals experience mental states, this inference does not compel one to accept that animals are capable of possessing language: of grasping that arbitrary symbols can be used to transmit thoughts. To establish the latter and much larger thesis, the ALR scientist has to demonstrate that apes possess a theory of mind.

It is no surprise, therefore, that the debate over ALR has shifted in recent years to this issue (see Premack and Woodruff 1978). For the moderate bifurcationist can maintain that, even if it is the case that Kanzi's comprehension skills are comparable to a two-and-a-half-year-old child's, and his production skills are comparable to a fifteen-month-old's, these facts do not suffice to show that he is capable of understanding language, or of combining lexigrams to communicate *linguistically*, any more than an eighteen-month-old, who is beginning to acquire words quite rapidly, is capable of putting those words together into sentences in order to speak rationally and intelligibly. Bifurcationists feel that if they can prove that

Kanzi does not have a theory of mind, such proof would reinforce the argument that Kanzi does not possess and cannot acquire language.

The key to this argument lies in the categorial distinction that Cartesianism draws between *natural expressive behavior* and *linguistic behavior*. We showed how the critic of ALR is prepared to accept that Kanzi, like a fifteen-month-old child, may have acquired the use of some words. But this, the critic feels, does not constitute language use; for these "words may not *have* any meaning in the conventional sense. Instead, their utterance may be merely a ritualized part of recurrent activity contexts, only nominally more linguistic than the nonverbal behaviors that also define these contexts, or it may be an attention-directing behavior, or both" (Wallman 1992, 51). These first words are seen as providing the building blocks out of which the language-learning process can proceed. *Language learning* is regarded as a process of experimentation in which the child actively begins to use primitive verbal skills in order to learn more about language. And it is precisely this process which is said to be missing in Kanzi.

Once again, there is a residue here of eighteenth-century ideas. Recall Condillac's argument that the acquisition of speech enabled man to analyze and exercise voluntary control over the ideas coursing through his mind. One finds a similar picture of a "bootstrapping process" in the theory of mind literature. Children are seen as *working* at language learning, as *consciously* developing strategies for learning more about language: "They seek information and confirmation from helpful adults, they practice, and they listen to and revise their own productions" (Shatz 1994, 9). But "[l]earning a language involves more than just learning vocabulary and the rules of grammar. Children must learn rules of discourse: when and how to speak so that they seem to be recognizing the same implicit beliefs that organize the social and mental lives of others in their society. In learning to use a language, a child learns what justifications and explanations of behavior are comprehensible and acceptable, and how important it is to communicate unobservable mental states" (7–8).

If one goes back to the Saussurean diagram one can see that, taken as a picture of linguistic communication, far more is involved than two talking heads, each mapping sounds onto internal representations and responding in a Turing machine–like manner to the sounds issuing out of the other's head. For *language*, according to Cartesianism, presupposes being able "to act and communicate as a rational member of a society—one who understands and uses social means to interact with others in mutually comprehensible ways" (Shatz 1994, 6). This is very much an eighteenth-century view: the child must use its emerging language skills to *become a person*, where "[b]eing a person means one can be trusted to behave rationally, as 'rational' behavior is defined by the community. Through one's use of language, a person conveys his or her acceptance of that covenant" (8). The child not only has to figure out the extensions of terms and grasp the rules for combining words: it also has to figure out how its community defines "rational behavior," and then show that it understands and is willing to conform with those conventions.

For the Cartesian, we are ultimately free to choose the theoretical framework that governs our social perceptions. Indeed, not surprisingly, Cartesianism itself is said to be just such a framework. Thus, the moderate bifurcationist explains that "[t]o be a person, one has to be able to give culturally acceptable explanations for why people behave the way they do and to make accurate predictions about how others will respond in various situations. At least in Western societies, such explanations are based on the belief that unobservable internal states can be the causes of an individual's behavior. Persons in such societies must be able to make reasonable inferences about the internal states of others" (Shatz 1994, 10). In other words, the question of when a child in our culture begins to communicate linguistically with others hinges on when the child acquires a (Cartesian) theory of mind.

The acquisition of a theory of mind, and a fortiori language, is seen as a relatively late phenomenon in the child's cognitive development, occurring some time between the ages of three and four. Unlike the case that Terrace describes, where it is possible to devise tests to discern whether a nonlinguistic animal experiences first-order mental states, the possession of a theory of mind is demonstrated by the ability to understand questions that draw on such a theory. The classic example of such a test is the "false belief" task:

> Imagine that the following story is acted out for a child: A boy comes home, places some chocolate in a cupboard, and then leaves the room. While he is gone, his mother comes in and happens to move the chocolate to another cupboard. Later, the boy returns and wants to eat the chocolate. Where will the boy look? Notice that a correct answer to this question depends on the child knowing something about the beliefs of the boy in the story. In other words, it depends on the child having a "Theory of Mind" . . . that is, an understanding that people have mental states including thoughts, beliefs, and desires. (Frye and Moore 1991)

On the classical Cartesian account, to possess a *mind* is to exercise a number of active mental processes, to initiate various sorts of actions, to experience a variety of passive mental states, to be aware of all of these phenomena, and to develop representations of reality that enable a subject to predict external events. Modern Cartesianism superimposes on this picture the further argument that to possess a theory of mind is to construct *meta-representations* of mental representations or states that enable a subject to predict the thoughts and actions of other agents, and to describe one's thoughts to other agents and to understand their descriptions of their thoughts. The human mind is not only a thing that thinks, sees, feels, desires, intends, believes, refers, means, and understands, but as the very argument of the second Meditation demonstrates, it is a thing that knows that (and when) it is doing all these things. But then, what is it to *know* that one experiences these "mental processes" or "states"?

Cartesianism sees this use of the cognitive operator as tacitly signifying that it is not enough only to witness these ongoings *in foro interno*: one must also *possess the concepts* of thought, perception, sensation, desire, intention, belief, reference, meaning, and comprehension. For one must be able to identify "This experience I am having right now" as an instance of x, y, or z. That is, one doesn't perceive one's *intention to φ* as such; rather, one has an experience that the mind classifies as an instance of *intending to φ*. But by the same token, one can only be said to possess these concepts if one is able to apply them to the behavior of other agents as well as to oneself: to classify *their* behavior as instances of x, y, or z.

Thus, to possess these concepts is to have built up a theoretical representation of the types of behavior—in any organism—that are indicative of *thought, desire, intention, belief, perception, sensation, reference, meaning,* and *understanding.*

This argument leads inexorably to the thesis that a child in our culture must develop a theory of mind if it is to *become a person.* For in the early stages of language learning a child uses action verbs indiscriminately: it uses psychological terms to describe the behavior of objects, and it uses physical terms to describe psychological phenomena. (For example, a young child treats dreams as things that others can see if the lights are on or will just as readily talk of a cloud trying to cross the sky as a man trying to cross the street.) This indiscrimination, according to the advocate of the theory of mind thesis, is grounds for saying that the young child is incapable of being aware of the subjectivity and privacy of its own experience. Thus, the young child is said to be incapable of distinguishing between "thoughts and things," or between dreams and reality. This statement supposedly amounts to saying that the young child lacks an understanding of the "fundamental, ontological distinction . . . between internal mental phenomena on the one hand and external physical and behavioral phenomena on the other. This is the bedrock on which a Theory of Mind is built" (Wellman 1990, 13).

The picture that modern Cartesianism paints, therefore, is one in which to be a person is not only to possess all of the faculties that Descartes outlines in the second Meditation, but, at a bare minimum, to possess the concepts of desire, intention, and belief, to attribute these mental states to other agents, and to govern one's interactions with these other agents accordingly—in other words, to possess the rudiments of what is literally a Cartesian *theory of mind.*

For instance, Cartesianism holds that in order to have built up a theoretical representation of *belief,* a child must not only be capable of *believing x,* but must also be able to identify a mental state that it is experiencing as an instance of *belief.* But a child can only be said to possess the concept of belief if it is able to apply this construct to the behavior of other agents as well as to itself: to classify their behavior as instances of *belief.* Thus, to possess this concept is to have built up a theoretical representation, on the basis of its own experiences, of the types of behavior that are indicative of *belief.* But a child can only predict another agent's actions on the basis of its beliefs if the child grasps how mental states cause behavior. And a child can only have reached this level of understanding if it has constructed a theory of the "fundamental, ontological distinction . . . between internal mental phenomena on the one hand and external physical and behavioral phenomena on the other" (Wellman 1992, 51). Only when a child has reached this level of cognitive development can it be said to have crossed over the point of bifurcation and become a person.

The modern Cartesian conception of the point of bifurcation, therefore, is that *to be a person is to have constructed a theory of mind*: a "naive" or "tacit" or "inchoate" theory of *what a mind is* and *what a mind does.* To be sure, we are said to be operating in the realm of "tacit knowledge" here. The ordinary layperson, much less the four-year old child, is hardly likely to be able to formulate such a theory. But to say that the child has acquired an "understanding that people have mental states including thoughts, beliefs, and desires" is treated as equivalent to saying that the child has built up a theory of the following facts:

1. Mind is private
2. Mind is distinct from body
3. Mind represents reality
4. Minds are possessed by others
5. Thoughts are different from things (Wellman 1990; see Astington 1993)

The point of bifurcation, whether it be anthropologically, phylogenetically, or ontogenetically conceived (i.e., between primitive and modern human beings, or between animals and humans, or between the child who cannot and the child who can pass the false belief test) lies at the human being's ability to construct a theory of those aspects of *mind* that Descartes spells out in the second Meditation. Descartes himself should be seen, not as the discoverer of a hidden continent, but as mapping out a theory that all of us must master if we are "to act and communicate as a rational member of [our] society—one who understands and uses social means to interact with others in mutually comprehensible ways" (Shatz 1994, 6).

Thus, the ability to understand questions concerning true and false belief, as demonstrated by the ability to respond appropriately to tests like the "false belief" task, is essential for the inference that the child has constructed a theory of mind, and a fortiori, that the child has taken the crucial step from prelinguistic (instrumental) behavior into the society of language users. For Cartesianism postulates an internal relation between the telementational model of language and the theory of mind thesis. To endeavor to communicate—*to encode one's thoughts in words in order to convey these thoughts to B*—A must not only believe that B has a mind: A must also believe that B possesses a theory of mind, so as to treat A's utterances as *linguistic* (which, as such, need to be decoded). In other words, A must look at B in exactly the same way that the critic of ALR looks at Kanzi. B must *prove* to A that B grasps what a mind is and what a mind does before A will go to the bother of speaking to B or treating B's utterances as linguistic (i.e., before trying to infer what B is referring to or what B means). In other words, for A and B to undertake to communicate with one another, each of them must not only be protoscientists, but also must be satisfied that the other is a like-minded protoscientist. A meeting of any two speakers is thus a miniature version of a meeting of the American Psychological Association. Of course, ordinary speakers, being the lax folk scientists that they are, may be totally oblivious of all this. But from this Cartesian perspective, what is perhaps most surprising is not that ALR critics should be so reluctant to treat Kanzi's behavior as linguistic, but rather, that they should be willing to suspend their robust skepticism in the case of anyone at all.

The "Charm" of the Theory of Mind Thesis

In her *Ape Language*, Savage-Rumbaugh asserts that the common chimpanzees, Sherman and Austin, would communicate knowledge to one another that they knew the other didn't possess. For example, on one occasion Savage-Rumbaugh baited a container of food with Peter Pan peanut butter in front of Austin while Sherman waited in another room. But instead of allowing Austin to use the lexigram board to tell Sherman what was in the container she scattered a bunch of different food labels on the floor. What she wanted to know was whether Austin would understand that he needed to tell Sherman what was in the container, since he alone had witnessed this event; whether he would realize that he needed to find some other way of communicating this knowledge to Sherman, since the lexigram board was turned off; whether he would recognize the Peter Pan label, which he had often seen on the jar, lying on the floor; whether he would realize that he could use the label to communicate to Sherman what was in the container; and whether Sherman would grasp Austin's communicative intent, if indeed Austin showed him the label. The answer is that Austin quickly looked for and found the Peter Pan label, which he immediately showed to Sherman (see Savage-Rumbaugh 1986).

The first chapter of this book is filled with similar stories about Kanzi's even more impressive communicative and cognitive abilities. As this narrative makes clear, Kanzi frequently imparts information that he thinks someone else doesn't possess; he conceals his intentions on occasion and knows when others are doing the same; he delights in playing pretend games, and is aware that they are pretend games; he is fully capable of taking advantage of inexperienced LRC staff, for example, getting them to take him somewhere in the forest where he knows he is ordinarily not allowed to go. It is even fair to say that Kanzi has a mind of his own. Savage-Rumbaugh tells us how Kanzi frequently doesn't believe her when he can't understand the reason for what she's said; that he has to find out for himself whether she's right or wrong. The story that she tells of his hiding the screwdriver under the blanket and then putting it into the electrical outlet despite her repeated warnings is the story of any little boy who knows precisely what his caregiver intends and chooses to disregard it.

Yet one would hardly want to say, on the basis of this account of Kanzi's cognitive and communicative abilities, that Kanzi grasps that:

1. Minds are private
2. Minds are distinct from body
3. Minds represent reality
4. Others possess minds
5. Thoughts are different from things

The "theory of mind" criterion thus creates an interesting dilemma; for while one would most certainly agree with the moderate bifurcationist that Kanzi has not mastered this kind of Cartesian theory, there are nonetheless countless occasions where one wants to say that it is clear that Kanzi knows what someone else is thinking, or wants, or what they intend, or even, what they believe. Is one forced to conclude, therefore—in light of Morgan's Canon[10]—that if the former proposition does not obtain, then the latter description of Kanzi's behavior is ipso facto "illicit" or "anthropomorphic"?

The "law of parsimony" is represented by the Cartesian critic of ALR as nothing more than scientific prudence. For according to Cartesianism, all we *ever* see—

in both human and animal behavior—are "colorless movements," and there is neither need nor warrant for describing animals as possessing linguistic abilities or as possessing a theory of mind. This argument is a slightly watered-down version of the classical ethological attack on animal cognition. Critics of ALR may not speak of Kanzi's behavior in terms of complex nests of innate releasing mechanisms,[11] yet the latter type of objection has left its mark. For there is a lingering feeling among some cognitivists that Savage-Rumbaugh's methodology is "suspect." After all, she never attempts to expose Kanzi or Panbanisha to situations that are designed to decompose the stimuli affecting them so as to identify 'fixed action patterns' in their behavior. Moreover, her approach to studying apes is totally opposed to generic description. Not only does she focus on solitary subjects, and give them names, and allow them to proceed as they please so that the "experiments" take on the form of unstructured interactions; and not only does she rely heavily on anecdotal evidence and use action verbs and mental predicates to describe the animals' behavior; more to the point, she treats Kanzi and Panbanisha as agents: indeed, in some respects, as persons.

Far more is involved here than a simple challenge to the canons of ethology. It is really the epistemological picture underpinning the "law of parsimony" that Savage-Rumbaugh's work can be seen as attacking. Strong skeptics of animal cognition insist that all they are demanding is a *theory-neutral vocabulary* with which to arrive at a more objective description of animal behavior. But, as Eileen Crist points out, "a technical language of behavior does not lead to an objective or neutral portrayal of the animal but rather, creates a mechanomorphic portrait of the animal" (see Crist forthcoming). If I describe a baseball game solely in terms of the players' reflexes and musculoskeletal processes, excluding any mention of their goals or intentions, I will not arrive at a *more objective* account of what the players are doing, but rather, a totally different view of the activity: one that is barred from treating it *as a game*. Such a physiological description might well have considerable interest in the context of an anatomy class, but it does not provide a more rigorous analysis of a baseball game: of what the players are *really* doing.

The very notion of a "generic description" (which eschews mentalist terms whenever an action can be interpreted as the outcome of purely mechanical factors) is theory-laden—the consequence of mechanist thinking. As AI has clearly shown, any behavior can always be so interpreted, provided that one accepts the reductionist thesis that all actions are the end result of cognitive processes that are built up out of noncognitive units. But the *meaning* of an action can only be understood in the context in which it occurs, and in terms of the agent's intentions (see Coulter 1989). Thus, to deny the relevance of the circumstances in which an agent øs, or the agent's intention in øing, is to exclude *ab initio* the possibility of grasping the significance of that agent's or animal's actions—to grasp that behavior *as an action* rather than seeing it as the "release of action-specific energy."

The source of this picture of what constitutes "scientific rigor" in the behavioral sciences lies in the fundamental Cartesian assumption that the *same* movements can be categorized in either mental or mechanical terms—that we can describe the same behavior in either the ordinary vernacular terms that we use to characterize each other's actions or in a technical language that excludes mentalist terms. The basic premise here is that *behavior* can be treated as a category-neutral phenomenon—a "colorless set of movements"—that, as such, can be described in either causal or psychological terms. This premise entails that the science of behavior must choose which language will best serve its needs—in human as much as animal studies. But if anthropomorphism is the illicit attribution of human mental experience to animals,[12] then mechanomorphism is the no less illicit misrepresentation of animal (or human) behavior as mechanical.

But what if it is not a matter of *choosing* between anthropomorphism or mechanomorphism, or of *settling* for a possibly less rich understanding of Kanzi's behavior as the price that must be paid for removing the temptation to indulge in "rampant overinterpretation"? What if the issue is simply: *What is Kanzi doing?* What if the question "Should Kanzi's social interactions be described in terms of instrumental conditioning or problem-solving strategies?" is not asking whether this question is linguistically possible or desirable but instead is asking: "Is this the sort of behavior which is *properly* described in mechanical or noncognitive terms?" In that case, the specter of epistemological skepticism about Kanzi's "mental processes" doesn't enter; for the question is simply whether Kanzi behaves in a manner that satisfies the criteria for describing him as understanding what other people think, or feel, or want, or even believe. Savage-Rumbaugh and her colleagues presented a thorough account of Kanzi's comprehension skills in *Language Comprehension in Ape and Child* (Savage-Rumbaugh et al. 1993).[13] The fact that this work failed to convince hard-core critics of ALR to modify their views must lead one to question whether their objections are grounded in scientific skepticism, or are rather the product of cognitivist presuppositions.

It is somewhat ironic that, in an important sense, cognitivism is very like anthropomorphism: only it is not human psychological attributes that the cognitivist reads into the behavior of an organism, but those of the cognitive scientist! What Kanzi therefore forces one to recognize is just how dogmatic a theory cognitivism is. For there is no substantial difference between Kanzi's behavior and that of a young child to whom we freely ascribe the ability to distinguish between its own perspective and that of another agent. The point here is not that Kanzi should be treated in the same cognitivist terms as the young child, but instead, that we need to consider whether even a four-year-old child behaves in such a way as to warrant describing it as possessing a theory of mind. And if not, whether this prohibits us from describing, not just the four-year-old, but the younger child, and indeed Kanzi, as understanding what others think, feel, want, or believe.

Admittedly, it is hard not to be sympathetic to the original impetus behind the "law of parsimony" when one reads through some of the more exuberant examples of naturalist writings from the turn of the century. But to attribute the sort of theory of mind just outlined to a four-year-old child solely on the basis of its ability to anticipate which cupboard the boy will open in the Wimmer-Perner test surely rivals anything the early naturalists may have written. Nonetheless, what is most striking is how, despite the obvious discomfort the term "theory of mind" causes even those who are sympathetic to the argument (see, e.g., Frye and Moore 1991), Cartesians are nonetheless drawn to describing a child's ability to understand what another agent thinks, wants, intends, or believes, as the result of its possessing a quasi-scientific theory.

This "charm" exerted by the theory of mind thesis stems from the Cartesian picture of cognition: the idea that the world is seen through a conceptual grid that an organism constructs on the basis of its interactions with reality. The next step is the claim that an isolated concept cannot perform this function of cognitive economy on its own; instead, "the meaning and significance of a concept" must be "determined by its role in an interrelated web of other constructs and terms" (Wellman 1990, 6). That is, "concepts within a theory—theoretical terms—get their meaning through their interconnections with other terms in the theory, by virtue of their place in a context of cohesive propositions" (6, 7). The principle here is that "a theory provides a causal-explanatory framework to account for, make understandable, and make predictable phenomena in its domain" (7). Thus, the thinking underlying the theory of mind is that psychological concepts are organized in just such a causal-explanatory framework whereby a subject makes sense of—interprets and predicts—human behavior: "The notions invoked there— thoughts, dreams, beliefs, and desires—form an interconnected coherent body of concepts; they rest on, or indeed define, basic ontological conceptions; and the theory provides a causal-explanatory account of a domain of phenomena: human action and thought" (9).

Unlike customary scientific theories, however, the naive psychological theories an organism constructs are portrayed as *epistemically private*: another agent's theory (or indeed, an agent's own theory) can only be *inferred* from that agent's behavior. Hence, we are apparently confronted in our everyday interactions with the problem of discovering whether another agent's theory of mind is the same as our own. The task of any interlocutor, much less that of the cognitive psychologist, becomes akin to that of the cultural anthropologist as construed on the paradigm of Quine's radical translator (see Shanker 1997b). In all these cases, "the aim is to understand a worldview that might prove different from our own" (Wellman 1990, 2). The concepts that mediate a subject's interactions with the world, or the theories in which those concepts subsist, or the logic whereby those theories are organized and applied, may be totally foreign to our own way of thinking.

The Cartesian insists that possession of the concept of belief presupposes that the child possesses such concepts as causality, self, agency, desire, and intention. But what motivates this insistence? It is the Cartesian's treatment of (what Wittgenstein [1953] calls) "the grammatical" as empirical. For it is true that it makes no sense to describe a subject as "thinking that 'S believes such-and-such'" unless it also makes sense to describe that subject as "thinking that p causes q" or as "recognizing herself in a mirror." But this meta-linguistic observation is a "grammatical" remark: that is, it stipulates how the expression "S possesses the concept of belief" *is to be used*. Yet this grammatical remark is treated by the modern Cartesian as if it were really an empirical proposition—a psychological hypothesis about the genesis of theory-construction (i.e., first the child must develop a representation of causality, then a representation of self, then of agency, etc., at each step modifying its earlier representations).

Accordingly, the Cartesian concludes that there must be a definite temporal process in which a child constructs its theory of mind. The picture here is of a linear progression, with more primitive concepts providing the foundation for the next higher concept in the child's cognitive development. The charm of the "theory-theory" therefore lies in the fact that this "mental process" is construed as the same that occurs in the growth of any scientific theory. The child is really just a little (Cartesian) psychologist: the child's mind both revises and augments the interconnected body of psychological constructs whereby it understands or explains or predicts human behavior. In so doing, the child grasps the "fundamental, ontological distinction . . . between internal mental phenomena on the one hand and external physical and behavioral phenomena on the other" (Wellman 1990). The whole interest in the false belief paradigm for bifurcationists lies in the idea that it enables them to zero in on this critical point. There have, of course, been other candidates proposed to fill this role (e.g., desire, intention). But whatever pivotal concept (or cluster of concepts) the theory of mind ultimately settles on, the basic hope will remain that this concept exposes what is, in essence, the point of bifurcation.

Thus, rather than trying to define the point of bifurcation in terms of the *possession of a faculty*, the modern Cartesian approaches discontinuity in terms of the *possession of a concept*. The very idea of designing a verbal test to establish whether or not a subject possesses a given concept is Cartesian. If the subject fails the Wimmer-Perner "false belief" test, then *ex hypothesi* the subject doesn't possess the concept of belief, but must base his or her predictions of other agents' behavior on some simpler antecedent construct (e.g., desire). The possession of mental concepts is treated as a zero-sum affair: either the subject does or she does not possess the concept ø, and a suitable test will reveal that possession or not in the same way that a reagent will tell us whether or not a given substance is present in some compound. Given the nature of *belief*, such a test must involve the use of psychological terms. If the Wimmer-Perner test reveals that the subject does not possess the concept ø, we can proceed to simpler tests to establish whether S possesses the more primitive concept ψ (and so on down the logical hierarchy of psychological concepts).

The stress that theory of mind proponents—like all Cartesians—place on speech raises an important question. Is it really the case that a child's grasp of what other agents are thinking, or what they want, or intend to do, or believe, can only be determined in light of its mastery of psychological terms (or at least, the type of question being asked in the Wimmer-Perner test)? In the last few years developmental psychologists have shown that young children's comprehension skills may far exceed their production skills and, perhaps, pave the way for the latter. There are myriad criteria for establishing this fact—the child's gaze, attention, gestures, and vocalizations. Moreover, Savage-Rumbaugh has shown how the same point applies to Kanzi. Kanzi learned how to interact with the other members of the Language Research Center group in exactly the same way that he learned what they were saying: *before* he approached the lexigram board on that fateful day when Matata had been removed. The route into his becoming a member of the linguistic community led as much through understanding what others were thinking or feeling as what they were saying (see Savage-Rumbaugh et al. 1993).

Judy Dunn rightly wonders, "If preschool children are so limited in their ability to understand others, how do they manage to function effectively in the complex world of the family?" (Dunn 1991, 98) Is it not the case that young children who are incapable of understanding the question posed to them in the Wimmer-Perner test must nonetheless have some understanding of what other family members think and feel and believe? Savage-Rumbaugh asks precisely the same thing, not only about Kanzi and Panbanisha, but indeed, about bonobos living in the wild. For so much of their behavior—whether it be feeding, traveling, sexual, or social—needs to be *coordinated*. The last chapter of this book discusses some of the signals that bonobos in the wild use to communicate with one another: leaves strategically trampled on one side at a juncture in a path, twigs pointing in the direction one should proceed (including up), a log placed at the point where one should ford a stream, a branch buried two inches in the ground surrounded by holes where the other members of the group had all dug for an insect found about two inches below the ground. Such behavior forces us to ask the same question about nonhuman primate behavior that Dunn asks about preschool behavior: How is it that these nonhuman primates are able to function so effectively as a social unit in their complex group activities? In *Ape Language* Savage-Rumbaugh described how Austin and Sherman were able to adapt effortlessly to the test described above in which the labels on familiar jars were removed and they had to use the label to convey which food they wanted (see Savage-Rumbaugh 1986). Perhaps the question one should be asking here is: Was this some skill that Savage-Rumbaugh laboriously cultivated in her laboratory, or was it rather the case that she brought Austin and Sherman to transfer skills that chimpanzees in the wild possess to the artificial situation of using a Peter Pan label to convey information that they knew the other was lacking?

However, bifurcationists reply that the criteria that Dunn or Savage-Rumbaugh might cite to substantiate the case for the young child's or the bonobo's social understanding in fact only amount to instances of (what the Cartesian calls) *natural expressive behavior*, and they note that missing from these critieria are the crucial signs of linguistic behavior that are required as evidence for the possession of a theory of mind. They conclude that while natural expressive behavior may serve as evidence for the possession of more primitive psychological concepts, possession of a theory of mind presupposes the possession of "true" (i.e., syntactic) language.

This issue is addressed later in the section "The Ascent of Pan." For the moment, it is important to note the modern Cartesian's presupposition that psychological terms can be treated as standing for *theoretical notions* that a child constructs in order to predict human behavior. Yet recent research on the child's acquisition of psychological terms suggests that a child's earliest uses of psychological terms are spontaneous, and occur well before the ability to pass anything like the false belief test. Typically, a child seems to capture some aspect of a term's use but can in no way be said to have mastered the concept. Often, a child will use a term simply because of its effect (e.g., the child discovers that saying "I'm sorry" or "I didn't mean to" serves to placate its caregiver). It is generally impossible to state categorically when a child has begun to grasp the meaning of a psychological term that it has been using for some time. This isn't a matter that can be resolved by closer observation, or carefully scripted laboratory tests, for this "constitutional uncertainty" in the use of psychological terms is a reflection of the unique nature of psychological discourse: of the marked categorical difference between the "naive" use of psychological terms and the use of theoretical constructs in cognitive science.

The source of this reading of psychological terms lies in what is perhaps the heart of Cartesianism: the interpretation of the metadiscursive commonplaces of psychological discourse as a species of lay psychological theorizing. Recall Descartes's remarks about looking out his window at the figures crossing the square below. Descartes treats the statement that one cannot see what another agent is thinking or what his intentions are as an empirical generalization. On this basis he concludes that his mind must unconsciously project certain mental states in order to predict the movements of the passing figures. The key to this argument is the idea that one observes *colorless movements* that one *infers* are caused by such-and-such *mental states*. But the theory of mind is not concerned with the question of whether or how desires, intentions, or beliefs might *set in motion* or *bring about* the actions they are said to cause. It merely insists that the nature of psychology is such that it is compelled to make use of the concepts of *desire*, *intention*, or *belief*; for if one is to explain how an agent makes sense of the world, how could one possibly bypass the basic constructs whereby he or she does so?

Thus, one mustn't forget that proponents of the theory of mind do not overtly commit *themselves* to an orthodox Cartesian theory of the mind. Instead, in a classic case of displacement, they claim that it is *the child* who applies a Cartesian theory of mind in learning how to make sense of human behavior. The child is the one pictured as the committed Cartesian (albeit tacitly), while the theory of mind proponents portrays their own perspective as simply that of a neutral observer: a chronicler of "folk" psychological theories. Yet, clearly, this distinction is not nearly the straightforward matter that the theory of mind proponents assume. For the argument that Cartesianism is merely the child's way of making sense of the world is itself grounded in the fundamental Cartesian assumption that the world is something that the child needs to make sense of.

In some ways, the theory of mind can be seen as marking a deconstructionist phase in the evolution of Cartesianism. Perhaps the greatest service it has performed is that it draws attention to the nature of Cartesianism as a grammar of psychological discourse: what Taylor has in mind when he speaks of the "larger sense of 'Rhetoric'" (see Taylor 1992). The theory of mind is not a consequence of the Cartesian's attitude toward concept theory; it is rather the other way round, insofar as the theory of mind has been implicit in Cartesianism from the start. The Cartesian conception of the fundamental affinity between psychology and physics is grounded in a picture of what an organism must do in order to make sense of its world. Organisms must constantly construct theories that enable them to predict and anticipate events. Mental states—like theoretical constructs—are postulated in order to predict human behavior. When one says that a child learns—or suddenly grasps—that doing such-and-such is evidence of *believing such-and-such*, what one is really saying, according to Cartesianism, is that the child learns or suddenly grasps the utility of the construct *believing such-and-such* for predicting human behavior. Thus, Cartesianism is really a metric whereby ordinary language users, as much as psychologists, are assumed to categorize an organism's behavior. The very fact that Kanzi fits so awkwardly into this framework may turn out to be one of the most important benefits of Savage-Rumbaugh's research, for it forces us to look objectively at the framework—to see it *as a framework*, guiding the sorts of questions that psychology asks and the sorts of theories that are deemed explanatory.

The Cartesian Hierarchy of Psychological Concepts

Modern Cartesianism sees the question of how an organism's actions should be described or classified as a function of what concepts the organism can be judged to possess. Concepts, according to Cartesianism, are epistemically private mental constructs whose existence and nature are inferred from the organism's "overt behavior." In essence, a statement that applies a psychological expression to describe an organism's behavior is thought to assume that the organism possesses (has constructed) such-and-such a concept, which in turn presupposes that the subject possesses the appropriate set of "prior" concepts. For example, the statement "Kanzi thinks that Sue is going to punish Tamuli" would be said to assume that Kanzi possesses the concept of punishment, which in turn presupposes that he possesses the concepts of agency, intention, responsibility, and so on. To determine whether this statement is legitimately asserted, one would first have to establish whether or not Kanzi possesses the requisite subconcepts. Only once such tests had all been passed could one go on to consider whether it is legitimate to assert that "Kanzi thinks that Sue is going to punish Tamuli."

In other words, Cartesianism treats the proposition "The assertion that 'S possesses the concept ϕ presupposes that S possesses the concepts $\emptyset, \gamma, \zeta, \varepsilon$" as an empirical hypothesis. Thus, the statement "Kanzi thinks that Sue is going to punish Tamuli" is broken down into the hypothesis that he possesses the cluster of prior psychological concepts out of which *punishment* is said to be composed (e.g., agency, intention, responsibility, etc). Given that it can be determinately established that Kanzi possesses each of these subconcepts, one can then go on to test whether or not it is legitimate to describe Kanzi as "possessing the concept ϕ (as "thinking that Sue is going to punish Tamuli"), where this, too, is a matter that can be answered in a yes-or-no fashion by experimental and replicable methods.

The thinking here is epitomized by the classical Piagetian view that developmental psychology has to engage in concept analysis—has to delineate the order in which concepts must be acquired—before attempting to map behavior onto these logical patterns. According to this outlook, there is a fixed order in which concepts must be acquired. The behavioral anomalies that inevitably result from this kind of a priori approach (i.e., with one child skipping over some of the preordained stages of cognitive development while another child actually seems to reverse some of the stages) can all be explained away by exploiting some such notion as *décalage* or *content effects*. But determining whether a subject possesses a given concept at any given stage is thought, in principle, to be a fairly clear-cut matter: if analysis dictates that doing x, y, z constitutes sufficient evidence for stating that "S possesses the concept ø," then the psychologist has to establish whether or not S can do x, y, z. Just doing x is not enough: there is no such thing as having *partial* possession of ø, or possessing *part of ø*.

Cartesianism thus postulates, on the basis of the priority assigned to logical analysis, a discrete hierarchy of psychological concepts. The Cartesian developmentalist sees his or her job as that of deciding whether an organism's behavior constitutes sufficient evidence for saying that it possesses the higher concept ø or the lower-order concept ψ, where there is a clear break between ø and ψ. For example, one of the key points frequently made in discussions of the false belief paradigm is that the concepts of *pretense* (ψ) and *lying* (ø) fall on either side of the theory of mind barrier. To be capable of pretense a subject need only believe that doing x will lead to getting y, but to be capable of lying a subject has to believe that if he or she does or says x another agent will believe something false and act accordingly. To achieve the latter cognitive level a subject must be able to represent another agent's mental states. There is no conceptual intermediary between *pretense* and *lying*. If a subject is unable to pass the Wimmer-Perner test it is impossible for that subject to lie (where this is thought to be a psychological generalization about the relation between two mental states: lying and pretending).

This putative logical gap between pretending and lying entails that an organism must make a *cognitive leap* to get from pretending to lying. Indeed, Cartesianism postulates a whole series of discontinuities—between nonlinguistic and linguistic behavior, or between being an agent (having beliefs, desires, and intentions) and possessing the various concepts of agency (i.e., a theory of mind), or, in general, between any two concepts thought to lie on different levels in a "concept hierarchy" (where this term might refer to the relation between subordinate, basic level, and superordinate concepts, or to the relation between primary and secondary concepts). Moreover, the discontinuities between nonlinguistic and linguistic behavior, and between being an agent and possessing a theory of mind, are thought to be intimately connected with one another. If one goes back to the point raised at the end of the previous section about the emergence of the child's ability to use psychological terms, one can see how, according to Cartesianism, a child cannot begin to use a word like "lie" *meaningfully*—to refer to the concept— before it can use the word "pretend" meaningfully, for the child must construct the relevant psychological concepts before it can map these onto words. So, for example, long before the child grasps the concept of lying she may discover that saying to her mother that her brother lied will result in her brother's being punished. For the Cartesian, this usage only confirms that the child's use of "lie" is merely *instrumental*, not *linguistic*.

Similarly, the bifurcationist can see no verbal evidence that Kanzi possesses grammar or the requisite higher concepts that would license the inference that his use of the lexigram board belongs to the category of *meaningful language* rather than to that of *natural expressive behavior*. The reasoning here is thought to be exactly the same as applies to a young child. In order for its utterances to be truly meaningful, both child and bonobo must grasp that what they say will not just have an effect on what their caregivers *do*, but will have an effect on what the caregivers *think* or *believe*. That is, whether child or bonobo, they must possess the basic mental concepts. Thus, in order to be judged capable of *linguistic* behavior they must be judged to possess a theory of mind. Even understanding the question asked in the Wimmer-Perner test is only thought to give partial evidence of possession of the concept of false belief. Without the concomitant ability to use psychological expressions appropriately—in third-person as well as first-person contexts—Cartesians will insist that they lack sufficient evidence to infer that either the child or the bonobo possesses the interconnected cluster of psychological concepts that are necessary to enable it to distinguish between its own perspective of the world and that of another agent.

It is within such a context that one may begin to appreciate the very different perspective taken by Savage-Rumbaugh. For she argues that what is most significant about her work is not simply that Kanzi has reached a higher level of comprehension than other apes, or that he has mastered simple relational constructions, or that this came about by his being reared in an unstructured linguistic environment. Rather, it is that we can learn from Kanzi how primitive linguistic behavior emerges from prelinguistic behavior, largely as a means of augmenting and amplifying interindividual routines.

In other words, Savage-Rumbaugh is not merely confronting us with a different picture of the *cognitive precursors of language*—one that applies to nonhuman primates as much as human infants—but with a different picture of *language*: one in which words are seen not as names (of mental representations or concepts) but as tools that are used for all different sorts of communicational purposes (see Canfield 1993, 1995). And just as there are many different kinds of words, so, too, sentences should not all be treated as descriptions (e.g., of thoughts that language speakers must encode and decode). For there are countless different kinds of sentences, used to do all sorts of things (e.g., to promise, order, request, command, invite, threaten, chide, etc.). But it is not just Kanzi's comprehension and production skills, or his mastery of simple grammatical rules, or his spontaneous acquisition of new words, or his linguistic creativity that make it so compelling to describe him as having acquired *primitive linguistic skills*; on top of all these, it is that because Kanzi shares in so much of the "form of life" involved in language speaking that he poses such a challenge for Cartesian theories.[14]

The more one watches Kanzi, the more clear it becomes how difficult is to pigeonhole his cognitive or linguistic abilities. In some respects he seems to have the comprehension skills of a two-and-a-half-year-old child, but in other areas he displays the cognitive and motor skills of a seven- or an eight-year-old. Moreover, the areas where he is "weak" (e.g., his failure to respond in the same way as we would to conjunctives) are not at all where one might expect, given his facility with similar constructions (e.g., disjunctives); and the areas where he is "strong" (e.g., tool-making, or his remarkable performance playing video games) can be quite startling to see. But the fact that Kanzi cannot be assigned to any specific cognitive or linguistic "level" hardly means that there is insufficient evidence to "get inside his mind"; and the fact that Kanzi seems to be near the apex of his cognitive and linguistic development, whereas the two-and-a-half-year-old is just starting out, hardly seems to constitute satisfactory grounds for assigning Kanzi to one side of a "language barrier" and the two-and-a-half-year-old to the other, when both possess virtually the same comprehension skills—when both satisfy the same criteria for describing them as understanding the meaning of a sentence (of a request, or a question, or a command, or a simple observation).

This statement is not meant to embrace a behaviorist reduction of the concept of language; on the contrary, it is to argue that the characterization of Kanzi's linguistic behavior as "merely effective" is itself behaviorist. Savage-Rumbaugh is fully aware of just how complex an ape's behavior must be to satisfy the criteria for describing him or her as "understanding the meaning of p." In *Language Comprehension in Ape and Child* she remarks:

> It is easy to train an ape to say *apple* in order to get an apple but difficult to teach it to use *apple* to describe a food that it is not allowed to eat, a food that it sees someone else eating, a food that it does not like, a food that is found in a particular location, etc. Such usages, common in children, are seen in apes only when symbols are "decontextualized" from the events associated with symbol learning. It then becomes possible for the ape to recognize that the symbol *apple* can be employed to indicate something about a particular fruit that has little to do with the "reward value" of receiving an apple. (Savage-Rumbaugh et al. 1993, 15)

Kanzi's upbringing represents the optimal "decontextualized" environment since, after all, Savage-Rumbaugh was not even aware that Kanzi was attending to the training sessions with Matata, let alone trying to teach him the symbols. And Kanzi does indeed possess these sorts of skills with an extensive lexigram vocabulary, covering a wide range of word types (e.g., names of foods, proper names, names of locations, object names, action verbs, activity verbs, prepositions, logical conjunctions). He responds appropriately to simple questions, requests, commands, and descriptions. He is capable of following a simple conversation—even when he is not directly involved in it himself. And he is capable of putting together novel combinations to make unexpected sentences.[15]

Despite all this, bifurcationist critics remain unconvinced, for bifurcationist critics refuse to be convinced. Thus, they insist that responding to a request to "fetch the ball" by finding the ball among the toys in the lab and bringing it over is only evidence of—admittedly advanced—*problem-solving* behavior. Or else the critic concedes that Kanzi may indeed have acquired some words (i.e., mapped the lexigrams onto the appropriate concept), but objects that he cannot put these together into sentences. Or else the critic concedes that Kanzi may indeed grasp some simple relational constructions, but objects that he lacks the more complex syntactical (e.g., subject-verb-object) knowledge that is *implicit* in a two-and-a-half-year-old's utterances. Or the critic concedes that Kanzi's comprehension abilities may indeed be judged comparable to a two-and-a-half-year-old's, but objects that he lacks the sort of curiosity about language that the child displays. Or perhaps the critic concludes that there is no real substantial difference between Kanzi's language skills and a two-and-a-half-year-old child's, but since neither possesses a theory of mind, neither can be properly described as "understanding *language*." And so on.

The important point is that the Cartesian is *always* going to be able to come up with some criterion to define a point of bifurcation if he or she so chooses— always going to come up with some test for the possession of some concept that is deemed to be the critical concept vis-à-vis discontinuity. And none of this thinking is in any way incoherent. Certainly ALR scientists must feel this way, for otherwise they wouldn't go to so much trouble trying to meet whatever the latest objection is. What would be most unfortunate, however, is if the mounting successes of ALR only served to relocate the point of bifurcation rather than to change our attitudes toward the nature of language and its relation to thought, and indeed, to psychology. But for the latter shift to be possible, one must first get clear on how Cartesianism conceives itself, and why it is that ALR has put Cartesianism on the defensive, and not the other way round.

Cartesianism insists that psychology must carefully script tests to determine whether or not an organism possesses the concept ø. But no matter how stringent these tests are made, one can "never be certain whether and how the effects we obtain and the behaviors we observe are related to the ever-intangible underlying cognitive processes and mental representations" (Waxman 1990, 109). Behaviorism accepted this Cartesian picture of the mental but insisted that, because mental states are not just hidden but are epistemically private, one's only hope of establishing psychology on a sound scientific footing is to pursue it as a species of social engineering. From a bifurcationist perspective, where behaviorism was useful (even if to be useful in this way was not its intention) was in bringing psychologists to see the importance of comparing the behavior of the lower life forms with machines, forcing psychologists to recognize that the stronger the analogy, the more unfitting it is to use psychological terms to describe the movements of an organism. The reason why this perception was so important, according to Cartesianism, is that understanding the limits involved in applying psychological terms is essential for the accurate classification of an organism's cognitive abilities. Cartesianism assumes that we know that such limits exist (atemporally and acontextually), and that one of developmental psychology's tasks, when dealing with borderline cognitive behaviors, is to discover where the limits (the discontinuities) are.

Bifurcationism insists that the description of animal behavior in cognitive or linguistic terms is neither licensed by any neurophysiological similarities that may exist between lower and higher organisms nor canceled should it be discovered that the neurophysiological processes between lower and higher organisms are dissimilar. Do pigeons recognize landmarks? Do dogs understand commands? Do apes understand words and sentences? These are not the sorts of questions that can be answered by studying cerebral phenomena (or computer programs). Yet neither, the Cartesian insists, are they the sorts of questions that can be answered by looking carefully at what other sorts of things pigeons and dogs and apes can do or can be brought to do. For example, when a dog digs up a bone that it buried the previous week, does it *remember* that it had buried it there, or should its action be compared to that of a squirrel, which is guided by its sense of smell to dig up nuts that it buried the previous winter? To answer this question it is not enough to look more carefully at other aspects of dogs' behavior to see, for example, whether dogs ever *forget* where they buried a bone and hunt around for it; whether they get *confused* if a bone is moved; whether they are ever *certain* that this is where their bone was; whether they *remember* other things: people or places or sounds or other dogs; whether they begin to have more and more trouble *remembering* things as they grow older. For in each of these cases, we have simply shifted the original problem to a different location.

In other words, from the Cartesian perspective, an ordinary language approach to these questions is just as unsatisfactory as an AI or an eliminative materialist approach; the former simply replaces one anthropomorphic problem with another, while the latter denies the genuine cognitive problem that arises about the manner in which organisms make sense of the world. Nevertheless, Cartesianism insists that there are indeed—waiting for us but as yet undiscovered—answers to such questions as whether pigeons can recognize landmarks or monkeys can remember photographs or apes can understand language. Once we can get clear on the concepts that an organism must possess in order to be described as "recognizing such-and-such" or "remembering such-and-such" or "understanding such-and-such," we can then set about designing suitable tests for determining whether the species can be judged capable of possessing the construct in question.

Thus, as far as the Cartesian is concerned, the fact of the matter is that either Kanzi does or Kanzi does not possess a language faculty. Since, according to the nativist view of language, this faculty is not something that Kanzi could have *acquired*, and since there is no evidence of bonobos in the wild possessing a language faculty, it follows that we *must* explain Kanzi's so-called comprehension and production skills in nonlinguistic terms. To be sure, we can learn a great deal about the plasticity of nonhuman primate cognitive processes from studying Kanzi: but that is all.

The implications of the challenge that Savage-Rumbaugh's work poses to this outlook are far-reaching. If one is to make sense of her demonstration that a nonhuman species can, if exposed to a linguistic environment from birth, acquire primitive linguistic skills, and more generally, if one is to make sense of the idea that not only is it not the case that speech is the sine qua non for inferring that a subject understands language, but indeed, that comprehension forms the foundation for acquiring language, then one must radically alter one's views about the nature of language and its relation to thought. No such problems arose with earlier ape language studies. Washoe or Sarah or Lana could all do some remarkable things, but there was always a feeling that one was still dealing with *training*. With Kanzi it is completely different: not just because training has largely been removed from the picture, but more important, because the critic of ALR cannot make a compelling case for treating Kanzi's comprehension and production skills solely in terms of conditioning or imitation. Thus one sees bifurcationists shifting their tactics and appealing to "action-schemata." And this area is but one where Cartesianism is being forced to give ground. For the truth is that Cartesianism is under assault from several different quarters (see Button et al. 1995). One is reminded here of the last days of the Shah of Iran. In the face of the growing insurgency he kept giving way to the demands of the Hezbollah. But in retrospect it is clear that his days were numbered long before he was actually overthrown. For it was never his control over the military-industrial complex that was in jeopardy; it was his political authority throughout the country that he had lost. So too, one begins to suspect, Cartesianism is beginning to lose its grip on the manner in which psychologists look at the manner in which the human mind develops.

The Ascent of Pan

In *Ape Language*, Savage-Rumbaugh recounts:

> As Sherman and Austin moved from the simplest discrimination tasks to complex spontaneous communications, it became increasingly apparent that they were continually learning to do far more than they were being taught. The issue of whether or not they had achieved "true" human language was never the goal. The goal was to improve their communicative competence and in doing so to more clearly define the skills involved, both at the behavioral and at the cognitive levels. (Savage-Rumbaugh 1986, 404)

Earlier in the book, she describes how "[a]fter the many training paradigms centered around giving, requesting, naming, retrieving, problem solving, and the complex tasks which drew upon these separate skills, Sherman and Austin began to produce truly indicative exchanges in which they announced what they were going to do" (326). In other words, Sherman and Austin not only acquired advanced reception, comprehension, and production skills: they actually became able to express and act on their intentions. Indeed, Savage-Rumbaugh reports:

> When a training task was begun, instead of waiting for the teacher to ask that certain items be given or labeled, the chimpanzees began naming items spontaneously and then showing the named item to the teacher. As the chimpanzees decided which objects were to be named and shown, they also incorporated many aspects of the teacher's role into their own behavior. They initiated trials, singled out objects, and actively engaged in behaviors designed to draw the teacher's attention to what they were saying. Moreover, these indicative behaviors, once they appeared, were not limited to training contexts. (326)

The implication of this account is that intentional terms—instead of causal terms—are justified in describing Sherman and Austin's communicative interactions; that is, their behavior became too complex to be described in the limited terms of instrumental conditioning or as affect-driven vocalizations—without, that is, distorting the very nature of what is meant by *instrumental behavior*. But in the process of accomplishing these important results, Savage-Rumbaugh raised a further and, even from her own perspective, unexpected problem: Could Sherman and Austin's behavior also be described in *normative* terms as "rule-governed"? Had they acquired a range of communicational skills that warrants describing them as using and combining symbols *correctly* or *incorrectly*? Indeed, the larger question that *Ape Language* raises is: Can Sherman and Austin be described as having acquired "primitive linguistic skills"?

Savage-Rumbaugh recognized that this is as much a question about the nature of language—about what is meant by "linguistic skills"—as a question about Sherman and Austin's communicational abilities. Moreover, it is a question that forces one to address some of the most basic tenets in contemporary attitudes toward language studies. Savage-Rumbaugh approached this issue circumspectly. She argued that "we can learn a great deal about the phenomenon of language itself as we attempt to produce it in apes" (Savage-Rumbaugh 1986, 34). And in her "Retrospect on the Ape-language Controversy" she returned to this point that "[a]pe-language research has taught us a great deal about dimensions of language that likely would never have been teased out in the study of normal children" (383). This statement can be read in either a negative or a positive light—as arguing that we can learn as much from what Sherman and Austin are incapable of doing (e.g., learning simple grammatical rules, acquiring reflexive language skills) as from what they are capable of doing. The very fact that their mastery of new lexigrams was so laborious tells us that we are not dealing with humanlike language learning. Yet when we look at the totality of their communicative behaviors we can discern subtle aspects of language use that are crucial to our understanding of the nature of language.

Savage-Rumbaugh describes how "[u]ntil we studied the taped sequences, we were unaware that Austin and Sherman had worked out their own means of signaling who was to use the keyboard, or who was to give the food. We also did not realize the highly specific and deliberate roles that gestures had come to play in the general coordination of behavioral events" (Savage-Rumbaugh 1986, 224). This account is reminiscent of the account of vervet communication that Cheney and Seyfarth present in *How Monkeys See the World*. The problem of understanding the complexities of vervet communication is not just a matter of learning to distinguish subtle differences between vocalizations that are difficult for the human ear to pick up. This problem is further compounded by the number of different modalities involved in vervet communication—posture, gesture, context, frequency, tone, and the identity of the subject all seem to contribute to the significance of a vocalization. But most of all, the problem lies in understanding how vervets see the world and each other (see Cheney and Seyfarth 1990).

One finds exactly the same problem when one studies film of the bonobos feeding at Wamba. If one is not actually looking for coordinated group interaction, one is apt to see the bonobos' behavior as the result of excitement at the sudden prospect of feeding. But watching the film in slow motion reveals a startlingly different picture: what had previously seemed to be random acts of branch-dragging or excited gesticulations suddenly appears as part of a highly structured activity, overseen by the dominant male of the group, who decides when feeding can commence and who ensures orderly conduct. In one fascinating sequence, one of the younger males steals into the feeding site before he has been given permission. His transgression is quickly noted, and the dominant male summons him with an imperious gesture. The younger male immediately submits to the latter's authority and is subjected to a symbolic display of that authority. While all this is going on it is possible to discern several distinctive types of vocalizations, whose significance one can at this stage only guess at.

Savage-Rumbaugh is saying more, however, than just that even primatologists may have underestimated the complexity of nonhuman primate communication (see Harris 1983). Lying behind her observation of the nonverbal aspects of communicative interaction is a radically different perspective of "the phenomenon of language" from the Cartesian telementational model. The picture that emerges in *Ape Language* is not of two chimpanzees laboriously acquiring an abstract symbol system whereby they became able to communicate (or, as the Cartesian would say, "encode") their previously incommunicable thoughts and intentions. Instead, the story that Savage-Rumbaugh tells is one in which Sherman and Austin's interactions were slowly enhanced and extended by their growing mastery of lexigrams. This process enabled them to develop new types of communicational exchanges of suprising complexity, and, perhaps, licensed the description of their activities in normative terms.

A notable example is the tool-use paradigm. Sherman was placed in a room in which there were a number of boxes baited with different kinds of food. Each box could only be opened by using a different kind of tool, and Austin was placed in another room with all the tools. Though a window Austin could see all the different foods in the boxes, and he would signal to Sherman which it was that he wanted. Sherman responded by using the lexigram board to tell Austin which tool he needed to open that box. Austin would select the appropriate tool (e.g., a key or a wrench) and pass this through a small hole to Sherman. Sherman would then open the right box and pass the food through to Austin (eating a small portion of it along the way).

The point of the experiment was to establish whether Sherman and Austin "could: (1) attend to one another, (2) coordinate their communications, (3) exchange roles of tool-requester and tool-provider, (4) comprehend the function and intentionality of their communications, and (5) share their access to tools and the food obtained through tool use" (Savage-Rumbaugh 1986, 193). What was perhaps most significant about this task was not the ease with which Sherman and Austin were able to perform it, but that "Joint regard, amplification of symbols with gestures, and spontaneous correction of errors were behaviors that emerged out of the interindividual interactions between Sherman and Austin" (203). It is particularly significant that they were quick to correct their own and each other's lexigram mistakes.

> For example, on one trial Sherman erroneously requested a key when he needed a wrench and he watched as Austin searched the tool kit. When Austin started to pick up a key, Sherman looked over his shoulder toward his keyboard. When he saw that he had selected the symbol for "key" (which was still displayed on the projectors) he rushed back to his keyboard, lighted "wrench" instead, and tapped on the projected wrench symbol to draw Austin's attention to the fact that he had just changed his request. Austin looked up, dropped the key, picked up the wrench, and handed it to Sherman. (201–2)

Thus, Sherman and Austin had reached the point where they were able to do such things as use 'p' correctly, respond appropriately to its use by others, initiate spontaneous exchanges using 'p', extend the use of 'p' to novel (but suitable) circumstances, and even correct their own or each other's mistaken uses of 'p'. The critic of ALR will—rightly—insist that this achievement is not nearly enough to describe them as fully fledged linguistic agents: not simply because they "lacked grammar" but also because of the limited range of their communicative acts. But still, these are very much the sorts of skills that satisfy the criteria for describing a subject as "understanding the meaning of 'p'." Thus, however one might answer the following question, the important point is simply that it becomes legitimate—and problematic—to ask: Can one say that Sherman and Austin acquired *primitive linguistic skills*?

To answer this question affirmatively clearly requires a different understanding of the nature of language from what one finds using the Cartesian approach. The picture of language presented in *Ape Language* is one in which "[v]erbal behavior emerges from and with nonverbal behavior, and as it does, it provides for a new means of coordinating interindividual object-oriented behaviors. We cannot completely understand the verbal system without going back to its roots, which are in the nonverbal system. . . . Interindividual interactions come to be coordinated through the use of words" (Savage-Rumbaugh 1986, 31). There are several important points to be made about this argument:

1. "Language learning is not an individual accomplishment, but an interindividual *process*" (32). The child should not be seen as an isolated organism, trying to infer the referents of the sounds that the linguistic agents around it make, or trying to distill the syntactic patterns in their utterances. Rather, the child develops linguistic skills through interindividual interactions with its caregivers. This includes "grammar," which the child begins to comprehend even before its caregivers do such things as respond differentially to the child's grammatical and ungrammatical utterances.

2. It is highly problematic to draw a hard and fast line—a categorial distinction—between *nonverbal* communicative behavior and *primitive linguistic* behavior, or between *primitive linguistic behavior* and *language speaking proper*. For some purposes one might draw such a distinction here; for other purposes there. This variability is an essential aspect of our metadiscursive language practices.

3. The impetus for regarding syntax as an "abstract system" distinct from semantics is removed; and so too, a fortiori, is the need for some sort of universal grammar to explain how a child is able to acquire an "abstract syntactical system" from the limited "linguistic input" to which it is exposed.

4. The description of Sherman and Austin as acquiring "primitive linguistic skills," as these are defined in *Ape Language*, does not expose one to worrisome skeptical objections.

Each of these points needs to be examined in turn.

The picture of language learning presented here is one in which the routinized interactions in which an infant and its caregiver engage are the seed from which language grows. Dyadic interactions between (both nonhuman primate and human) infants and their caregivers are initially effected by the use of sounds and gaze to establish and maintain joint attention, and are then supplemented by natural gestures and then sounds to initiate or coordinate interindividual routines. The infant starts to look where its caregiver wants and starts to attend to objects and situations. Soon afterward the infant begins to use gaze and gestures to direct its caregiver's attention, and then to use gestures and conventionalized sounds to initiate exchanges. The child is trying to get its ball, to stand up, to be fed, to get attention, to go to point B; and it is exploring means or soliciting help for attaining these ends. The gradual development of language skills is integral to the child's growing ability to satisfy its needs or expectations and to express its desires or intentions.

In the early stages of language learning, a child is learning how to use sounds to augment gestural signals and to coordinate increasingly complex social interactions. Savage-Rumbaugh provides a detailed account of some of the key elements in this process in *Language Comprehension in Ape and Child*. She first describes how effective caregivers often mark their own actions prior to engaging in them by posture, gesture, expression, or vocalization, and mark an ape's or child's actions as soon as it becomes apparent what they are going to be. They actively structure events in such a way as to determine an ape or a child's actions, again marking the actions just before they occur. Throughout this process the caregiver is monitoring the subject to ensure that the purpose of the marker has been understood; if not, the caregiver will fall back on further markers, and if necessary, actually perform the action in an exaggerated or emphatic fashion in order to ensure that the significance of the marker is grasped. This behavior primarily occurs in the context of specific routines, with the ape or the child's behavior manifesting when the significance of the marker has been learned. This achievement is often followed by the ape or the child using the marker itself to initiate the routine. As Savage-Rumbaugh puts it, "In so doing, children or apes begin the move from the role of a responder during routines to that of a primitive initiator and then to that of a symbolic communicator capable of announcing their intentions to another party" (Savage-Rumbaugh et al. 1993, 30). Dyadic interactions between an infant and its caretaker are thus initially governed by the use of sounds and gaze to establish and maintain joint attention and to engage in interindividual routines, and are then supplemented by natural gestures and then by words.

Savage-Rumbaugh provides a vivid illustration of this process in *Language Comprehension in Ape and Child*. The "bubbles routine" is initiated by a caretaker blowing bubbles in front of an ape or a child, while various verbal or gestural markers accompany and are used to initiate the routine. As they learn the nature of the game, the apes or children begin to respond to these verbal and gestural markers. For example, at the utterance "bubbles" they might be observed to glance at the wand, to grasp and orient it in front of their mouth, to pucker their lips and blow on it. But the word "bubbles," or the bottle, should not be seen as stimuli setting off a behavioral response. For not only does the ape or child, seeing a bottle of bubbles, begin to initiate the routine itself—by picking up the bottle and looking at the caregiver, or by pointing to the bottle—the ape or child will also use the lexigram or the word when no bottle is present to indicate its desire to engage in the bubbles routine.

The bubbles routine can be seen as a primitive language game, in which the apes or the child come to master the *meaning* of "bubbles." An important point underpinning such a description of this routine is that the apes never pointed at the bottle when no one else was present, or when only one of the lab dogs was in the room with them. Nor were they continually amazed when, after pointing at the bottle, Savage-Rumbaugh began to blow bubbles. Instead, they learned that they could use a specific gesture when they were with Savage-Rumbaugh to express what they wanted her to do, and that she understood what it was that they wanted when they did so; and that if she denied their request it was because she didn't want to comply, and not because she didn't understand what they were asking for.

Cartesian critics of ALR will object that not nearly enough has been said here to warrant speaking about "learning the meaning of 'bubbles.'" They will no doubt point out that a "routine" is precisely something based on habit and regularity: that is, on conditioned behavior. But the argument presented in *Language Comprehension in Ape and Child* suggests that Kanzi and Panbanisha did indeed learn several things in this routine. They did not simply learn that uttering "bubbles," or pointing at the bottle, would usually be followed by Savage-Rumbaugh's opening the bottle and blowing soap bubbles. What the apes learned was that they could ask Savage-Rumbaugh to blow bubbles by pointing at the bottle—they learned that they could communicate their desire in this manner. They also learned that that didn't mean the desire would always be satisfied; sometimes other activities took precedence, and sometimes Savage-Rumbaugh simply wasn't in the mood to start blowing bubbles. What Kanzi and Panbanisha were learning here, like all infants, was that expressing their desires did not always result in their satisfaction.

The critic of ALR cannot accept any of the terms used in this description of what the apes learned; for there is no room in the discontinuity view of language for Savage-Rumbaugh's account of *primitive linguistic skills*: either "bubbles" is an element in a problem-solving strategy, or else the ape grasps it as the *name* of a mental representation. And since nothing has been said here to describe the apes as using "bubbles" in well-formed-sentences, or in novel combinations, one must conclude that the apes' use of the word is confined to problem-solving strategies. But Savage-Rumbaugh is not suggesting that once the apes were able to grasp the significance of "bubbles" in this routine they had become fully competent language users; she is arguing that there is no hard and fast line between what is called "primitive linguistic behavior" and what is called "linguistic behavior." Not only is it perfectly legitimate to describe Kanzi and Panbanisha as "asking for x" or as "telling S that they want to ø": more important, an insight into the nature of language and the processes involved in language learning emerges as a result of the awareness that it is perfectly legitimate to describe Kanzi's and Panbanisha's actions in this manner.

The implications of this last point vis-à-vis the Cartesian picture of mental privacy need to be spelled out. A certain arm movement by an ape or a child might serve to initiate a tickling routine, which is accompanied by the caregiver's saying "Do you want to be tickled?" Eventually symbols or words are introduced to supplant the gesture (e.g., the ape points to the lexigram for "tickle," the child utters "tickle"). The word "tickle" is introduced in the context of, and becomes an integrated part of, the tickling routine. The actions that constitute speech are continuous with nonverbal behavior. One might say: The *meaning* of the gesture, the lexigram, or the utterance, is constituted by the role it plays in this routine. Accordingly, the gesture becomes a *criterion* for saying that the ape or the child wants to be tickled, rather than *evidence* of some "hidden mental state" (the "desire to be tickled"). It is on the basis of its behavior and the context in which this gesture occurs that one says that the ape or the child wants to be tickled (its gestures, its response to being tickled, the fact that it repeats the gesture as soon as the tickling stops, etc.) The statement "S is telling you that she wants to be tickled" does not license or rest on the inference that the ape or the child experienced some mental state that (1) it first identified, and (2) then chose the word that it thought would best convey that mental state to its caregiver; instead, the statement is grounded in this particular language game.

Using this approach, the child is seen as learning how to use words for a multiplicity of nonreferential, noncausal purposes. The child is seen as learning how to do different kinds of things with words: as learning the rules for participating in different kinds of language games. According to Cartesianism, the child is suddenly able, in the second half of its first year of life, to refer to its mental representations. In place of this description, the child is here seen as gradually learning how to participate in different kinds of social practices (e.g., giving and requesting objects, playing peek-a-boo, asking and answering simple questions, etc.). As its mastery of these practices advances, the child is progressively described as "intending or trying to ø," as "looking or hoping for x," as "thinking or believing p," and so on. The child's gestures, its utterances, and its actions, serve as the critera for what it is thinking or what it understands.

In its broadest terms the point here, as far as language learning is concerned, is that a child is learning the techniques required to engage in different kinds of practices—is learning the circumstances in which it is appropriate to use certain terms. This is not some recondite "metatheoretic" ability: it is a crucial aspect of what is meant by *learning how to speak*. Moreover, as the theory of mind makes clear, a further crucial aspect of language-speaking lies in the ability to determine whether or when another individual is unaware of something—for why tell someone something that they already know? But then, one can see from Savage-Rumbaugh's work with Sherman and Austin, Kanzi and Panbanisha, and from the films of the bonobos at Wamba, that this ability is already evident at the level of so-called nonverbal communicative behavior. For the tapes of Sherman and Austin, Kanzi and Panbanisha, and the bonobos at Wamba show that not only are apes aware that others may not see or know the same things as themselves, but that they employ various gestures, and even symbols, to communicate such knowledge to the other.

When learning how to speak is seen as learning how to do things with words—when language is seen as emerging as a means of augmenting the gestures and sounds that are used to coordinate interactions between adults and children—it follows that there is little point in trying to draw a hard and fast line where one can say "this is where nonverbal behavior ends and verbal behavior begins." In other words, the concept of language cannot be drawn with sharply demarcated boundaries. The point here isn't simply that there are different kinds of languages (a list that includes, among other things, sign languages, artificial languages, formal languages, machine languages, technical languages, pidgins, creoles, and lingua francas), or different varieties and different dialects of the same language, or different modalities of language (e.g., speech, writing, sign language), or varying levels of linguistic ability. More important, there is no sharp break between "non-verbal" and "verbal behavior" such that one can speak of the former as those aspects of communicative behavior that may be present in or accompany linguistic interactions (so-called paralanguage). Rather, "linguistic communication [is] a continuum of interaction which may be manifested both verbally and nonverbally." Indeed, "speech is underpinned by nonverbal communication which is vastly more complex than those simple cases exemplify" (Harris 1990, 44).

This continuity argument does not amount to the thesis that there are *degrees of language-speaking*—a continuum of ever more linguistic behaviors. Instead, the argument draws attention to the simple fact that there are myriad borderline cases—with human infants as much as nonhuman primates—where rival theorists are unable to agree on the proper description of the behavior. This disagreement is patently obvious in the debates over ALR. One side insists that what the apes are doing is primitive linguistic behavior, while the other typically responds—as primatologists frequently complain—by changing the location of the goal posts. But this sort of stalemate does not signify that we lack sufficient evidence to categorize the behavior in question; rather, it provides us with a profound insight into the nature of the metadiscursive discussions about language which themselves constitute an essential part of language. For we distinguish between "learning x" and "being conditioned to do x": a distinction that is variably realized, explained, justified, and enforced. But the (variable) fact of this distinction gives one no justification for assuming that there *must* be a corresponding distinction in the phenomena one is studying, or, a fortiori, that because the linguistic distinction is variable and indeterminate, therefore the phenomenal distinction *must* also be so, with gradient differences between shades of *being conditioned to do x* and *learning x*. Nor is one justified in assuming that, if the phenomenal distinction can't be found in the mind, it must therefore be in the behavior, so that there are gradient variable differences between *behavior that amounts to being conditioned to do x*, and *behavior that amounts to learning x*.

Just as in the case of attributing the possession of a concept to a subject, our judgment of a subject's linguistic abilities is based on how he or she behaves in certain contexts. One is not dealing here with some mysterious realm whose nature we can only infer from the organism's behavior. Rather, one observes (or can at least observe if one looks carefully enough) what an ape or a young child understands. That is, one does not *infer* that Kanzi understands Savage-Rumbaugh's request to "Go wash the potatoes, cut them up, and put them in a pot on the stove" when one observes him turning on the kitchen faucet, washing the potatoes, fetching a knife, cutting the potatoes into pieces, placing them in a pot, filling the pot with water, and then placing it on the stove.[16] This just is what is called "understanding the request." If the critic of ALR insists on further criteria before he is prepared to sanction this description of Kanzi's behavior (e.g., that Kanzi is able to do this activity with different kinds of vegetables, that he can pick out a potato from a table laden with different kinds of vegetables, that he understands the relation between *potato* and *vegetable*, etc.), this requirement merely signifies that the application of "understands the request" may sometimes demand greater behavioral complexity than might be afforded by a simple or a single comprehension task, and not that comprehension is some epistemically private mental process or state hidden behind the veil of an organism's behavior. Thus, the demand for further data may well be legitimate, depending on the context, and assuming the critic can identity what sort of evidence will satisfy his or her concerns.

There simply is no place in this discussion for the kind of epistemological skepticism about "mental processes" that characterizes the Cartesian's approach to ALR. This point is as true of the earlier study with Sherman and Austin as it is of the work that has been done with Kanzi and Panbanisha. Moreover, one should not allow one's natural fascination with Kanzi and Panbanisha's practical abilities to blind one to the theoretical significance of *Ape Language*. Whether or not Sherman and Austin behave in a manner that satisfies the criteria for describing them as possessing rudimentary linguistic skills, what is so interesting about *Ape Language* is its meticulous study of just what sorts of actions would have to be displayed in order to make such an attribution. It is no doubt because the field has still not quite managed to throw off its behaviorist anxieties that the Language Research Center has had to expend so much energy on anticipating objections. Yet such a preoccupation is certainly warranted; for what might look like a straightforward criterion of linguistic competence when viewed in the narrow context of a production or comprehension experiment takes on a much different complexion when one begins to consider what other sorts of actions an agent credited with such a linguistic ability should be able to perform: where infant verbal behavior serves as the paradigm for the sorts of skills that the ALR scientist is seeking to replicate. The consequence of this detailed comparative methodology is an illuminating picture of the complex interaction between overlapping skills and abilities involved in the infant's acquisition of language, the highly specific and deliberate roles that gestures and sounds come to play in the general coordination of behavioral events, and the manner in which these processes bear on ape language studies.

A very different reading of the benefits of comparative primatology thus results when the telementational picture of language—the picture of language as a structured system of arbitrary vocal sounds whereby thoughts are transferred from one person's mind to another—is abandoned, and when formal languages or Natural Language-computer programs no longer serve as the paradigm for what a child must innately possess in order to acquire language. The significance of the enterprise becomes as much conceptual as it is empirical, in a way that has an interesting bearing on what Wittgenstein had in mind when he preached the philosophical benefits of studying primitive language games: "When we look at such simple forms of language the mental mist which seems to enshroud our ordinary use of language disappears" (Wittgenstein 1960, 17). By gradually developing ever more complex language games, Wittgenstein hoped to clarify how our use of causal terms shades into our use of normative terms—that is, to illustrate the grammatical continua that characterize the application of psychological and linguistic terms. Wittgenstein explains in the *Blue Book* how, when one examines primitive language games, "We see activities, reactions, which are clear-cut and transparent. On the other hand we recognize in these simple processes forms of language not separated by a break from our more complicated ones. We see that we can build up the complicated forms from the primitive ones by gradually adding new forms" (17).

If ever there was a case for treating a form of language as a primitive language game, it is to be found in the work conducted at the Language Research Center. And yet, as the debates over Kanzi's comprehension and production skills demonstrate, the mental mist that enshrouds our use of "language" seems to grow ever more dense when one enters the domain of ALR. This confusion may partly be because of the subtlety of the behaviors being examined, but even more than this, it seems to be the result of the conceptual frameworks from which rival theoretical schools view that behavior.

This point returns us to the argument for continuity touched on earlier: but it is not continuity as linearly conceived. Attempts to "situate" the nonhuman primate on a cognitive continuum are all too reminiscent of debates about an organism's location on the *scala naturae*. Why should psychologists or philosophers suppose that an ape can be neatly slotted into some fixed category: say, that of a two-and-a-half-year-old human infant? Why should psychologists and philosophers insist on fixing a boundary between apes' and human infants' cognitive and linguistic capacities: on identifying the difference between apes and humans, rather than the differences (see Diamond 1991)? Mental/nonmental; mechanist/vitalist; voluntary/involuntary; linguistic/nonlinguistic: the dichotomies have seemed rigid and, ultimately, fruitless. Perhaps, then, it is time to abandon the source of the bifurcationist thinking that has overshadowed psychology from its inception.

"The Constitutional Uncertainty of the Mental"

Cartesianism can be seen as a species of metadiscourse whose purpose is to regulate the interpretation of ordinary talk about the mind. Descartes in effect argued that when one says something like "Only I can know what I intend to do" one is making an empirical claim and that, as an empirical claim, such a remark needs to be evaluated accordingly. This metadiscursive injunction might lead one Cartesian scientist to insist that knowledge of one's intentions is "privileged"; or another to challenge the dualist's claim for the infallibility of such knowledge (as Russell did in *The Analysis of Mind*, and more recently, Nisbett and Wilson have done in "Telling More Than We Can Know" [see Shanker 1993]); or yet another to argue that psychology can never hope to be a genuine science until it understands the mechanics of the process whereby this "mental state" (i.e., an intention) is represented in the brain and thence sets an agent's actions into motion (see Shanker 1991). That is, various schools might quarrel over the status, or the implications, of this "fact"—that is, that which is apparently asserted by the remark "Only I can know what I intend to do." But what all Cartesian theories have in common is that they accept that a remark like "Only I can know what I intend to do" is, and so should be evaluated as, an empirical claim.

The essence of Cartesianism, therefore, lies in the fundamental assumption that the simple commonplaces of psychological discourse are empirical hypotheses, and are part of a causal-explanatory framework that each of us must acquire if we are to predict the behavior of the objects or other organisms we encounter. When Cartesianism does introduce a technical concept, or turns some ordinary concept into a technical concept, it is invariably as a consequence of this view that the subject needs to *abstract and generalize* from his or her experiences in order to *make sense* of his or her environment. And since these constructs are seen as epistemically private, there is always room for substantial disagreement over the "proper" characterization of an organism's behavior.

From a philosophical point of view, what is so fascinating about these debates is how they are conducted. If psychology really were akin to physics, then one could indeed hope to be certain some day about how the behaviors of an organism are related to its underlying mental representations. However, the debates themselves—as is clearly demonstrated in that over ALR—are far from the sort of conflicts that one finds in the empirical sciences. In the latter, there is generally a clear understanding of what sorts of results are needed to satisfy a given hypothesis. But psychologists from rival schools are not even able to agree upon this.

Thus, the critic of animal cognition might object that a pigeon who only pecks at round shapes no more knows that they are *circles* than a dog who responds to its name possesses a concept of self- identity. The point of vacuum behavior experiments is to persuade us that, since an animal can be shown to behave inappropriately in some circumstances, it is illegitimate to conclude that it possesses the concept φ simply because it may appear to behave appropriately in some situations. The critic might go on to insist that, in order to credit pigeons with the possession of the concept of circle, they must be able to respond appropriately to the uses of the word "circle," to master the rules for the use of "circle," and to explain the meaning of "circle." The critic hastens to add that that does not mean that the possibility that a pigeon might be taught the concept of circle is being ruled out a priori; only that one needs a clear grasp of just how complex its verbal behavior must be to warrant such an attribution before one can speculate whether a pigeon possesses the concept of circle (see Shanker 1998).

What the critic is really saying in this argument is that doing x, y, z should be treated as the criterion for saying that an organism possesses the concept φ. The critic's insistence that "To possess the concept φ, S must be able to do x, y, z" is not offered as an *inductive generalization*. Rather, it is a *grammatical proposition*, stipulating the circumstances in which it is legitimate to use the expression "S possesses the concept φ." The stipulation "To possess the concept φ one must be able to do x, y, z" (or "Only I can know what I intend to do") is not an empirical claim that could possibly be falsified by any imaginable experience: it makes no sense to try to test its validity. It is not like saying "Bishops are always male" but rather is like saying "The bishop moves diagonally in chess." The latter stipulates how, if one wants to play chess, the piece must be moved. Likewise, if one wants to describe S as possessing the concept φ, then S *must* (grammatical "must") be able to do x, y, z.

If a chess theorist were to come along who insisted that we cannot be certain that this is how a bishop moves—that we need to watch a few thousand games before we can be sure that the bishop moves diagonally—we could only say that he or she is confused about the nature of chess and the significance of the rules whereby we formulate how to play the game. The same point arises when Cartesianism treats grammatical propositions as if they were empirical propositions. For example, Nisbett and Wilson argue that first-person avowals of intention are really hypotheses based on on "implicit, *a priori* theories, or judgments about the extent to which a particular stimulus is a plausible cause of a given response" (Nisbett and Wilson 1977, 231). They conclude that only rigorous testing will resolve the extent to which (or the situations in which) an agent's "hypotheses" are to be trusted (and preliminary results, according to Nisbett and Wilson, indicate that "people's reports about their higher mental processes [are] neither more nor less accurate, in general, than the predictions about such processes made by observers" [249]). But this picture distorts the nature of *being wrong about one's own intentions.* For the latter construction is not used to signify that an agent has made a *mistake* in the same way that one can be wrong about the weather. It is used to indicate that the agent has arrived at a new insight into his or her character, motives, desires, and so on. That is not to deny that Nisbett and Wilson may have established something interesting and important about the manner in which agents might rationalize certain types of actions, but that does not entail that the statement "I intend(ed) to ϕ" is really an empirical hypothesis.

Suppose, however, that our chess theorist were to argue that the bishop should ordinarily be moved diagonally, but when one is in check, vertically as well as diagonally. If we were to debate the merits of adopting this rule, it would be in terms of the effect it would have on the game. That is, our debate about this issue would be pragmatic, not empirical; the issue at stake would not be whether this new rule is somehow "truer to the real nature of chess," but rather, over the consequences for the game of adopting this rule (cf. the debate over the "designated hitter" in professional baseball). Similarly, as is argued in the next chapter, debates between rival schools within the Cartesian framework over how an organism's behavior should be "legitimately" described invariably stem from disagreements over the criteria for applying a psychological term. It is primarily for this reason that these debates go largely unresolved; for the arguments that one school finds convincing are dismissed by those who insist on a different metric with which to measure behavior. Their debates are not therefore about "matters of fact," but rather about which systems of measurement to use in evaluating those "facts."

Thus, if one goes back to the debate over the nature of pigeons' "mental representations," one sees that the critics' argument—that pecking consistently at different sizes of round shapes does not constitute possession of the concept of circle—is grammatical, not empirical. Their point is not that there is insufficient *evidence* to know what a pigeon is thinking; it is rather that *this behavior* does not satisfy the criteria for describing an organism as possessing the concept of circle. But then, what does constitute *such criteria*? One school insists that responding in a consistent manner to circles (e.g., pecking at circles) is a criterion; another that adhering to circular patterns in its behavior (e.g., flying in circles) is a criterion (see Gallistel 1990). No doubt some parents still believe that an infant can be described as understanding what a circle is if it can identify the correct flashcard. Another group insists that, in order to be legitimately described as understanding what a circle is, a child has to be able to use and respond to the use of "circle" correctly, explain what "circle" means (e.g., by pointing to circles), respond appropriately to the command "Gather round in a circle," draw circles when asked to do so, distinguish between circles and squares, and so on. But perhaps the criteria for saying of a child that it possesses the concept of circle should be that it can produce the appropriate Euclidean definition, or can perform simple operations like constructing a circle using a compass, or calculating its area? Perhaps it has to be able to define a circle as a figure that is perfectly round; or as a construction in which every point on the circumference is equidistant from the center; or as a plane curve that is the locus of a point moving at a fixed distance (r) from a given point (the center)? Perhaps we should insist that he needs to know that $(x - a)^2 + (y - b)^2 = (r)^2$ (where r is the radius and (a, b) is the center); or that a circle is a conic with zero eccentricity (i.e., a special case of an ellipse). And so on.

The very question, "What are the criteria for describing a subject as 'possessing the concept ϕ'?" is one that different groups of speakers can and do answer differently, depending on their point of view. In place of the Cartesian notion of "concept taxonomies"—rigid hierarchies of "mental constructs" that can be modelled set-theoretically—one might think instead in terms of overlapping language games which range from primitive to rarefied uses of psychological expressions. As one moves away from paradigmatic uses of a term, the criteria for its use are either relaxed or tightened, and grow ever more dissimilar. The grammar of the term varies according to the circumstances in which it is being used (e.g., who is talking, who they're talking to, what they're talking about, etc.). (Compare, for example, the use of "pretense" when said of a young child to its use in diplomatic circles.)

This integrationist viewpoint suggests a very different way of viewing the relation between "higher" and "lower" psychological concepts: that is, cases where "the possession of ϕ" is said to presuppose "the possession of ψ." One is dealing here with those asymmetric conceptual relations where it makes no sense to describe S as possessing ϕ (as being able to do x, y, z) unless one can also describe S as possessing ψ (as being able to do p, q, r), while the reverse grammatical proposition does not hold. But if one is dealing with a range of uses of "possession of ϕ" and "possession of ψ," one cannot expect to be able to model the relation between ϕ and ψ, as the discontinuity theorist proposes, as sharply demarcated sets. For the uses of "S possesses the concept ψ" will shade into or overlap with uses of "S possesses the concept ϕ," so that there will be many instances where it is not at all clear which is the more appropriate term, and even cases where it is possible to use both. There may, for example, be some cases where a developmentalist will want to state categorically that x constitutes pretending (e.g., playing with a doll) while y constitutes lying (e.g., a child reporting that it was its sibling who broke the vase), yet other cases where it is not at all clear which is the more appropriate term: even when spoken of the same subject (e.g., a child feigning illness to avoid going to school, or some of the cases of primate deception reported in Whiten and Byrne [1988]). Thus, psychology can hardly hope to learn from formal logic alone how a child's mind must develop or how an ape's mind works.

To speak, in this context, of the "structure of language" as "a maze of lines running this way and that" (Waismann 1965, 98) draws attention to the fact that we use the same psychological expressions in a range of language games, all of which have quite different, albeit related grammars. In primitive circumstances, the criteria for applying a psychological term will be quite modest; in advanced contexts, fairly complex. The fact that many psychological terms have primitive uses does not, however, mean that these language games can be extended—as AI proposed—to the point where any form of causal regularity (e.g., a tropism) can be regarded as satisfying the criteria for applying a psychological term (see Shanker 1998). Moreover, the fact that the linguistic distinctions between psychological terms, or between different uses of the same psychological term, are variable and indeterminate is precisely the reason we can engage in endless debates over how best to characterize animal and human behavior.

This observation is part of what Wittgenstein had in mind when he spoke, in *Last Writings on the Philosophy of Psychology*, of the "constitutional uncertainty of the mental": the fact that one is dealing with the normative imposition of different systems of describing behavior by different people, for different purposes, in different contexts, taking account of different "related issues" and analogous language games, and making use of different supporting justifications as to why *this* system is the one that *must* be imposed. Some of these systems draw the line for what satisfies the criteria for describing a subject in such-and-such terms *here*, some draw the line *there*, and some draw no hard and fast line at all. But it is not in autonomous features of the *phenomena to be measured* that a criterion can be found with which to determine which of these systems of measurement is really "the best": the one we *should* impose. Different groups of language speakers can choose to answer this question howsoever they please: provided, of course, that they recognize that deciding on *this system of measurement* entails (all things being equal) certain consequences.

This point helps to clarify what is meant by speaking of the "thickness" or the "opacity" of psychological discourse—the fact that language speakers are free to set the criteria for psychological terms, with the sole proviso that, if one wants to be considered a rational speaker of the language, then one must accept that however one sets the criteria has such-and-such a consequence. Cartesianism insists, however, on the *transparency of language* in talking about mental phenomena. That is, Cartesianism maintains that it is the *facts of the matter* that ultimately decide the criteria for applying psychological terms; language is just a way of representing these "facts." Thus, Cartesianism maintains that there is an answer to all the criterial debates in which rival psychological and philosophical schools engage, and that it lies buried in intangible mental representations and processes whose nature can only be inferred from overt behavior.

One way to see what is wrong with this argument is to look at the converse grammatical proposition "If S can do such-and-such, then S possesses the concept φ." To say "S sees what is common to the exemplars of φ" is not *evidence for* but rather, is a *criterion* for saying "S possesses the concept φ": one could no more know how to respond to someone who insisted that S possesses the concept ø but fails to see what its exemplars have in common than one could know how to respond to someone who insisted that only careful scrutiny will establish whether the bishop moves vertically. But this is just what Cartesianism does, for it treats the grammatical proposition "A minimal criterion for having a concept is that discriminably different objects be treated as similar" as an empirical proposition—as stating: "If S can pick out the exemplars of φ it is *because* S possesses the concept φ." Doing such-and-such is said to be a criterion for possessing the concept φ because φ enables the subject to do such-and-such. In other words, Cartesianism represents the *grammar of mental discourse* as being determined by, or derived from, *language-independent mental phenomena*. Debates between rival schools over the criteria that should be adopted for applying psychological terms then take the form of arguing: this is how we should talk, because this best reflects the underlying mental reality.

Thus, the various grammatical propositions of psychological discourse are invariably represented by Cartesianism as empirical hypotheses. To return to the example of "higher" and "lower" concepts, one speaks metadiscursively of one concept entailing or being a prerequisite for another: one treats it as a rule of grammar that S can only be said to possess the concept φ if S can be said to possess the concept ψ. Put another way, S can only be said to be capable of doing x, y, z (e.g., speak a language) if S can do p, q, r (e.g., understand that he or she knows something that another agent does not). But the Cartesian interprets this rule of grammar as stating the hypothesis that S can only construct the "higher-order" concept φ if S has already constructed the "lower-order" concept ψ. And now one must develop some test, such as the Wimmer-Perner test, to establish whether or not this reified ψ exists in S's mind, and if one gets a positive result, another test to establish whether or not φ exists in S's mind.

If one is to escape this Cartesian framework, then the last thing one wants to do is get involved in a debate with the critics of ALR on their own terms (which are constantly shifting) by arguing that Kanzi's behavior satisfies their demands, or by insisting that Savage-Rumbaugh's work provides us with a different set of criteria for deciding what constitutes (primitive) linguistic behavior. Certainly this is not Savage-Rumbaugh's intention. We quoted in the preceding section her remark from *Ape Language* that "we can learn a great deal about the phenomenon of language itself as we attempt to produce it in apes" (Savage-Rumbaugh 1986, 34). But what exactly is it that we learn? What are the "dimensions of language" to be gleaned from ALR that "likely would never have been teased out in the study of normal children" (383)?

The key to Savage-Rumbaugh's answer lies in her observation of "the highly specific and deliberate roles that gestures . . . play in the general coordination of behavioral events" (Savage-Rumbaugh 1986, 224). She illustrates this point with a striking analogy: "Each sort of interindividual routine is something like a delicate dance with many different scores, the selection of which is being constantly negotiated while the dance is in progress, rather than in advance. Experienced partners know what turns the dance may take, and, more important, they have developed subroutines for negotiating what to do when one or both partners falter in the routine" (Savage-Rumbaugh et al. 1993, 27). Savage-Rumbaugh's thinking here—and indeed, the analogy—are a familiar theme in writings on nonverbal communication. Argyle, for example, describes how "a speaker starts gesticulating and looks away as he starts to speak, and reverses this when he stops. There is an intricate coordination of pausing and looking within turns, followed by head-nods, smiles, and gazes. Interactional synchrony has been called a 'gestural dance,' and likened to a waltz" (Argyle 1988, 118). But Savage-Rumbaugh has something significantly different in mind from what one typically finds in the nonverbal communication (NVC) literature; for unlike the latter, she is challenging the sweeping categorial distinction that Cartesianism draws between "nonverbal" and "verbal" communication.

We are dealing here with what Wittgenstein called "the penetration of gestures into verbal language" (Waismann 1965, 95)—in regard not just to the role that gestures play in language-learning, but also, to the role that they continue to play in verbal communication. For gestures are a constant accompaniment of speech; they serve not only to clarify or embellish what a speaker has in mind (the so-called gestural illustrators) but also to coordinate conversation. But "what is the meaning of a head-nod in a conversation where this is not consciously noted but has the effect of allowing another person to carry on talking?" (Argyle 1988, 7) Argyle suggests that we should speak of its "behavioral meaning." But then, exactly the same question can be asked of the vocalization "Uh-huh" or the words "Go on." Words, no less than gestures, can serve to coordinate conversation and can become automatic. Can gestures (as opposed to the signs of a sign language, which are just words) have a *linguistic* function?

The crucial question here doesn't concern the paralinguistic accompaniments of linguistic interaction; the question Savage-Rumbaugh's work raises concerns the consequences of using the word "language" "as a term applying to everything that serves the end of expression and communication . . . to cover not only verbal language but also gesture language, picture language, the 'language' of maps, the formal 'languages' of mathematics and logic, besides signal systems, and much else" (Waismann 1965, 93). The standard conception of nonverbal communication as that which "takes place whenever one person influences another by means of facial expression, tone of voice, or any of the other [nonverbal] channels" [Argyle 1988, 2] is not under dispute here. Rather, the issue lies in the communicative role that gestures (and perhaps gaze and vocalizations) play in linguistic interaction.

Note that, where Argyle speaks of the nonverbal means by which one speaker *influences* another, Wittgenstein speaks of "everything that serves the end of expression and communication." Both of the terms in Wittgenstein's argument are somewhat problematic. For example, we speak of the *nonverbal expression of emotion* or the *nonverbal communication of attitudes* (by facial expression, tone of voice, posture, etc.). Wittgenstein is clearly not concerned with the manner in which one can make someone uncomfortable by standing too close or staring too intently at them, or encourage a speaker by smiles and head nods. What he has in mind is the gestural expression and communication of thoughts, or of one's desires, intentions, wishes, beliefs, and so on. His primary goal is to clarify the *linguistic* role that gestures can play. To illustrate this point, he cites the role of the deictic gesture in the sentences "Put it here!" and "Put it there!" Or think of the gesture one makes with one's thumb and forefinger when one says: "I'll have this much whiskey." Or think of the significance of a beckoning or shooing-away gesture. And then, of course, there are conventionalized gestures (the so-called gestural emblems); for example, sports fans holding up their index fingers and shouting "We're number one," or the positioning of index fingers on either side of one's forehead to signifiy the devil's horns in order to call someone a cuckold.[17]

The implications of this argument concern more than just the manner in which language is learned; it also affords an essential insight into the relation between language and thought. We need to distinguish between the following:

1. Those nonverbal elements of interindividual interaction that might influence the direction of an interaction which are innate rather than learned, and over which the agents involved have no conscious control and which they are most likely not even aware of doing (e.g., pupil dilation, posture, perspiring);
2. Nonverbal channels of communication that are learned, can be both idiosyncratic and conventionalized, and that may or may not become automatic (e.g., gesture, gaze, and vocalization).

The second, unlike the first, can be just as much a part of *language* as words: can serve just as well to express or communicate what one is thinking, or what one wants, or intends, or believes.

Such a suggestion is, of course, highly problematic if one starts out with the Cartesian view of words as the names of mental representations and sentences as the descriptions of thoughts. But the picture one is trying to get away from here is precisely the Cartesian view of mental privacy that underpins the telementational view of language. As we showed earlier, both words and sentences can serve a multipicity of roles. Thus, a child learns how to use different kinds of words in different kinds of ways ("the great variety of ways in which words are used is equalled by the variety of ways in which their uses are learned" [Waismann 1965, 95]). What Wittgenstein means when he describes the advent of "language [a]s an extension of the more primitive behavior" (Wittgenstein 1980, vol. I, section 151) is that, in learning how to do things with words, and how to respond to what other people do with words, a child learns how to use words, instead of or along with gestures, in order to engage in increasingly complex social interactions, and to express or communicate a greater range of thoughts, intentions, and desires. The avowal "I understand," no less than the vocalization "Uh-huh," is typically an *expression*—a *manifestation*—of understanding, not a *report* on a "mental state." This point is what Wittgenstein had in mind when he described avowals as acquired extensions of natural behavior—the idea that certain forms of first-person utterance are more akin to gestures than to descriptions of a fact (see Malcolm 1982). The utterance "I understand," like the gesture of tapping the side of the forehead with the index finger, or the vocalization "Uh-huh," is treated by language users as a criterion for describing the subject as "understanding p."

In general, what people say and do constitute the justifying grounds for psychological ascriptions. Epistemological skepticism about other minds stems from misconstruing the grammatical propositions whereby one formulates these criterial relations as empirical propositions. For example, the proposition "You cannot observe someone's understanding" is akin to "The bishop moves diagonally." But Cartesianism construes this as a hypothesis. It then draws the conclusion that what one sees are "colorless movements," from which one must infer a "hidden cause" if one is to make sense of that behavior. But one does not see "mere behavior": one sees, for example, that S understands what one is saying. That is, one says of another person that he or she understands what one is saying on the basis of what he or she says or does.

Does that mean that the criteria for saying "S understands p" *fall short* of establishing for certain that S understands? The sense in which this behavior falls short of certainty is solely that it does not *entail* that someone understands something. But this shortfall has nothing to do with epistemological skepticism. For the logical possibility of defeasibility is not itself a defeating condition. The onus is on the skeptic to provide criterial evidence for doubt when the ordinary criteria for understanding are satisfied. One can only undermine a criterial judgment by providing countervailing criteria: not by doubting the strength of that criterial relation.

Now, where the great importance of Savage-Rumbaugh's work with Kanzi and Panbanisha lies is simply in establishing, irrefutably, that animals are indeed capable of satisfying a vast range of the criteria that we ordinarily apply when speaking of the cognitive and linguistic abilities of young children. The work with Kanzi and Panbanisha has thus introduced a crucial new dimension into ALR—not just because Kanzi and Panbanisha have progressed further than other apes in their comprehension and production skills but, more important, because they have done so without any formal language training, in much the same way that human children acquire language. Moreover, the fact that Panzee, a common chimpanzee who was co-reared with Panbanisha, also learned the lexigrams and responds to speech, tells us something crucial about the significance of the environment for cognitive and linguistic development.[18]

At first blush it might seem tempting to conclude that what is important here isn't simply that they were exposed to *informal* language instruction from birth, but that Kanzi and Panbanisha were exposed to a whole new range of communicational problems and goals that do not arise in their natural habitat, and that they spontaneously acquired the comprehension and production skills necessary for dealing with this setting. We discover that Kanzi and Panbanisha possessed the cognitive resources for dealing with the linguistic and cultural environment in which they were raised. But then, it seems odd that such a capacity could lie dormant, as it were, in nonhuman primates in the wild. Thus, we are confronted with two alternatives: either being raised in a linguistic environment enabled Kanzi and Panbanisha to develop hitherto unrealized cognitive and linguistic abilities in their species, or else we have seriously underestimated the social and communicational complexity of nonhuman primate behavior (see chapter 4).

Have we come full circle, then, to the original objection to Descartes's attack on the Great Chain of Being voiced by Gassendi that "although [animals] do not produce human speech (since of course they are not human beings), they still produce their own form of speech, which they employ just as we do ours" (Cottingham 1986, 2: 189)? The problem with this objection lies in the final clause. It is not some aribitrary condition; Gassendi adds the rider that animals employ their language just we do ours because this assumption is integral to our concept of language. And this involves far more than just "learning how to do things with words." But the point that Gassendi seems to have been driving at is not that language should be seen, as formalists have claimed, as a *representational system*. Rather, the problem that he confronts us with is what exactly we mean when we refer to the "normativity of language."

To see what is involved here, one might return to the metaphor of the dance. The child learning how to speak must learn not only how to negotiate its way in the dance, but also how to talk about its participation in the dance. One of the most important things one can learn from Taylor's *Mutual Misunderstanding* (Taylor 1992) is that what a child is learning when it learns how to speak are the techniques required to engage in normative practices. To do so is to learn the circumstances in which it is appropriate to use certain terms, including terms that refer to those normative practices. This is not some recondite ability: it is an essential aspect of what we mean by *learning (human) language*. To become a competent speaker a child must acquire a *reflexive* ability: learning how to talk about this and that involves as an essential component—*essential to our concept of language*—learning how to talk about talking about this and that. How one talks about these practices is not something that can be separated from the contexts in which that talking is done (or the particular purposes for which it is done, or how it is treated in a particular context, etc.). And it is not just metalinguistics that is at issue here: human practices—those that are typically recognized as distinctively human—are also essentially self-conceptualizing and self-regulating (Taylor 1997, ch. 1). To acquire the ability to engage in a *human* practice, a child must acquire the ability to talk about that practice, whether self- or other-performed: this is an essential aspect of our concept of *human practice*.

Do Kanzi and Panbanisha possess these "reflexive abilities"? The question is far more difficult to answer than may at first appear. Certainly, they were exposed to a linguistic environment in which such reflexive exchanges were an essential aspect not only of how Savage-Rumbaugh and her coworkers spoke to one another, but also of how they spoke to Kanzi and Panbanisha (e.g., about the significance of various lexigrams). What one has to look at here is not simply whether Kanzi and Panbanisha already use, or could be taught to use, certain metalinguistic expressions that are crucial to our conception of language. What one really needs to look at is the way they behave in reflexive communicative interactions: how they respond to Savage-Rumbaugh's reflexive remarks, the things that they do to explain what they or someone else means, or to clear up misunderstandings, or to explain to a fellow bonobo what a certain lexigram means, and so on. What one needs most now is not more *data* about what Kanzi and Panbanisha can do with lexigrams, but greater clarity as to how to describe their already quite impressive cognitive and linguistic abilities.

It would seem, then, that the only thing preventing us from appreciating— and indeed, building on—Savage-Rumbaugh's impressive achievements with Kanzi and Panbanisha are *philosophical* preconceptions and objections. If there is to be a genuine paradigm revolution and not just another paradigm shift in the evolution of Cartesianism, what we need to recognize is that when we talk about overthrowing Cartesianism, what we are really calling for is the liberation of psychology from a philosophical outlook that has gripped the Western mind from at least the time of Aristotle (see Sorabji 1993). The reason why so many psychologists have agonized over the fact that psychology is still not seen as a bona fide science is that they start out with a definition of *science* based on the paradigm of physics. Likewise, the reason psychology has suffered so many violent paradigm shifts over the past hundred years is precisely that psychologists have accepted the fundamental Cartesian assumption that their task is to solve *epistemological* problems—the mind-body problem; the problem of other minds; the nature of intentionality, or consciousness, or language; or the problems that have so exercised developmentalists over the past twenty years; for example, the "entry into language" or the acqusition of a "theory of mind." These are philosophical, not psychological problems that, as such, can only be resolved philosophically, not empirically (see Shanker 1992, 1993).

What is so interesting about the research on Kanzi and Panbanisha are the things which the Cartesian dismisses. What matters most isn't what they cannot do, but what they can; and more precisely, the factors that enable these (latent?) capacities to flourish. The very fact that, by being raised in a humanlike environment, Kanzi and Panbanisha should have spontaneously acquired primitive linguistic skills, speaks volumes about both the phylogenesis and the ontogenesis of language: about the social conditions that first led to the emergence of language, and the amount of language that a child understands before it begins to speak.

Perhaps our greatest problem now is that Cartesianism still infects every aspect of our attitudes toward cognition and language. Our whole way of thinking about the mind and about language—the way we present and defend ideas, the questions we ask, the way we try to resolve them—has been thoroughly shaped by the Cartesian framework. But perhaps Kanzi and Panbanisha's small step into the world of human interaction and communication is the spark that is needed to ignite the paradigm revolution that will lead us beyond Cartesianism. Watching Kanzi and Panbanisha, one can see how myths like that of the LAD, or the language instinct, distort what occurs when human beings learn how to speak. Even worse, such myths reinforce the conceptual myopia that prevents us from seeing and appreciating the richness and complexity of animal life. Kanzi's and Panbanisha's entry into the world of human interaction and communication was made so effortlessly, and so inconspicuously, that if not for a series of fortuitous events, it might not even have been noticed. It is our great fortune that it was.

CHAPTER 3

Rhetorical Inclinations

"Sure, But Does He *Really* Understand What We Say?"

In the first part of this book, Sue Savage-Rumbaugh tells of a number of occasions, many of which were recorded on film, of Kanzi understanding complex sentences of spoken English. In the following passage, she describes some of those occasions.

> For example, when he heard "Would you put some grapes in the swimming pool?" he got out of the swimming pool, walked over to where a number of foods were placed on a towel, and picked up the grapes and tossed them in the water. When he knew we were playing a game of hiding surprises, and he heard a clue such as "I hid the surprise by my foot" or "Rose hid the surprise under her shirt," he immediately raced to the correct location and retrieved his surprise. When asked on a walk in the woods, "Would you please give Panbanisha an onion?" Kanzi looked around for a patch of onions and, when he found one, pulled out a bunch and took it back to Panbanisha. When he had a new ball that he wanted to take into the colony room with him when he went to visit Matata, he was told "Your ball stays here"; he placed it by the door while visiting Matata but of course retrieved it immediately after he left.
>
> One day when Kanzi was visiting Austin, he wanted some cereal that had been prepared specifically for Austin. He was told, "You can have some cereal if you give Austin your monster mask to play with." Kanzi immediately found his monster mask and handed it to Austin, then pointed to Austin's cereal. When told "Let's go to the trailer and make a water balloon," Kanzi went to the trailer, got a balloon out of the backpack, and held it under the water faucet. He needed help fitting it on the faucet and filling it with water, but he had clearly understood the sentence. (See p. 67 of this book.)

The characterizations of these scenes are given by Savage-Rumbaugh in all honesty, spontaneity, and sincerity; but—as her colleagues in the scientific community naturally want to ask—are they in fact *true?* Had Kanzi, in fact, "clearly understood" these sentences? Or, from a scientific perspective, does Savage-Rumbaugh give overhasty, loose, even subjectively biased characterizations of Kanzi's response to hearing these utterances? Do Savage-Rumbaugh's characterizations make up a true and objective representation of what had occurred? Is she in fact justified in characterizing the scenes as she does?

What is clear from these reports is that Savage-Rumbaugh and her collaborators unhesitatingly responded to Kanzi's behavior in these situations as manifesting his understanding of the utterances addressed to him. Moreover, their spontaneous responses do not appear to have been defeated by the subsequent development of the interactions. Kanzi did not go on to reveal that he really hadn't understood the request to give Panbanisha an onion (say, by continuing to hold on to the onions and waving them around in front of everybody present); or that he had not really comprehended the clue about the hidden surprise; or that he only *seemed* to grasp what was being said about going to the trailer and making water balloons (for example, by revealing that *whenever* he heard the word "water" he would run to the trailer and hold a balloon under the faucet). Savage-Rumbaugh therefore goes on to assert that, at the age when these events occurred, "Kanzi could understand language at least as well as a child two to three years old, perhaps better if the topic was of keen interest to him." Yet only a few lines later she remarks that this assertion did not meet with general acceptance in the scientific community: "[T]he belief that animals are incapable of such high-level mental activities remained so strong that few critics accepted Kanzi's responses to such sentences as evidence of the true capacity of his mind."

The scientific community, in other words, was not (and still is not) agreed that Kanzi really had understood the sentences spoken to him in the episodes just reported, or in the many other episodes like them. According to many of "the critics," even though Kanzi's behavior *seemed* to manifest his understanding to those who were interacting with him at the time, his behavioral responses should instead be explained not as instances of his understanding the semantic content of the sentences, but rather as the effect of such phenomena as contextual information, inadvertent cuing, prior training, nonlinguistic associations, or even luck (and good guesswork). He may have *acted as if* he understood the sentences, but he did not *really* understand them. The critics argued, in other words, that Kanzi's behavior only gave the illusion that he had understood what the sentences meant, just like the behavior of a pet dog gives the illusion that she understands the sentence "Go get your leash and bring it here if you want to go out for a walk."

To respond to such skepticism, Savage-Rumbaugh designed and, over a period of nine months, carried out a formal program of controlled laboratory tests. (These are discussed in chapter 1 and, at greater length, in Savage-Rumbaugh et al. [1993].) The aim of these tests was to apply rigorous methods of scientific proof to show that Kanzi really could understand the meanings of some kinds of spoken English sentences and to determine what levels and types of syntactic and semantic complexity were within his grasp. The results strongly supported Savage-Rumbaugh's assertion: Kanzi really did understand sentences as well as a two-and-a-half-year-old human child. Nevertheless, these results still met with the same sort of skepticism from within the scientific community. Although some do believe that Savage-Rumbaugh is justified in claiming that Kanzi understands spoken English sentences of certain types, there are many more who believe that she does not have that justification or who are willing to accept the authority of those who insist that she does not. What is certain is that, in spite of the effort, time, ingenuity, and money that has been expended on this and many other similar research projects, no consensus of opinion has yet emerged within the scientific community as to whether Kanzi, or any other ape, can justifiably be claimed to understand a single sentence, either of English or of any other natural or artificially constructed language. Given the lengths to which Savage-Rumbaugh has gone to demonstrate the justification of her claims for Kanzi and the other apes with which she has worked, and given the argumentative tools that remain available to any critic who wants to challenge the justification for such claims, it is far from clear how any progress will ever be made in scientific research on the communicational and cognitive abilities of apes. Indeed, as things now stand it is far from clear how any progress ever *could* be made.

Evaluating Metalinguistic Claims: Logical Prerequisites

Surely one of the most frustrating controversies in contemporary science is that, in spite of awe-inspiring successes in countless research domains, it seems beyond the capacities of scientists and scientific techniques to come up with satisfactory answers to questions such as these:

1. Can a laboratory-reared ape, such as Kanzi, really understand what a spoken English sentence means?
2. Do the signs and lexigrams that some apes have learned to produce really mean or refer to anything?
3. Are any of these apes, when producing or responding to communicational behavior, really following (even simple) linguistic rules?
4. Does any such ape know what it is doing when it produces or responds to language? That is, does it really understand, as we do, that language is for communicating thoughts and intentions to others, for speaking truly (and sometimes falsely) of the world, and for attaining particular communicational goals?

These are clearly important questions—some of the most important questions facing contemporary science. Moreover, at least at first glance, they do not appear to be particularly challenging. One might therefore be forgiven for thinking it a relatively straightforward, uncomplicated task to answer any one of them. After all, don't we determine countless times a day whether our interlocutors, for instance, understood what we said to them? Or whether, when they spoke, they were referring to that object or person over there? Surely it is therefore natural to presume that it is only a bit more complicated to find out whether, as is asked in (1), the bonobo Kanzi understood the sentences we said to him? Or, as in (2), whether Kanzi was referring to the red ball when he pressed the lexigram "ball"? Presumably, understanding is understanding and referring is referring, regardless of whether we're talking about a human or an ape. Therefore, finding out, for example, if our interlocutor has understood what we said to him or her should, in principle, be the same sort of task with ape interlocutors as that which we regularly accomplish with our human interlocutors every day.

We mustn't let ourselves lose sight of such instinctive, "commonsense" responses to questions like those listed (although, as later sections will argue, we must also be careful in how we interpret those responses). What is so often the case is that the considered, professional responses of scientists are radically different from those of "commonsense." That is, although the four questions listed have been the focus of scientific research for more than thirty years, and although many answers to them have been proposed and strongly argued for, the fact is that none of them has yet been given an answer—positive, negative, or "qualified"—that meets with general agreement in the scientific community. And, although they will not be the focus of this chapter, it is worth adding that the same is true with the related, and no less important, questions concerning the cognitive abilities and behavior of apes: that is, questions concerning the possession of concepts, the attribution of knowledge, the formation of intentions, and so on.

And yet, it is not the absence of agreed *answers* to its central questions that makes the ape language controversy so frustrating. Instead, the source of this frustration lies in the continued lack of agreed *methods of evaluation* (or justification) by which any proposed answers can be assessed. In other words, if, at the end of extensive experimental research, a reputable research team proposes a definitive answer to one of these important questions—for example, asserting that Kanzi understands spoken English sentences of particular grammatical types—there are no agreed methods by which the scientific community can determine whether that conclusion is or is not well founded. There is no agreed standard of scientific proof by which one may determine whether that conclusion deserves to be taken as a valid answer to the question posed: that is, *whether we should believe it or not.*

To put it another way, the lack of agreed answers to the first-order questions listed earlier is matched by—*or rather, is a product of*—the scientific community's inability to arrive at agreed answers to the following second-order, methodological questions:

1'. What observational or experimental evidence would be sufficient for it to be justifiably asserted that an ape understands what a spoken English sentence means?

2'. What would constitute sufficient proof that the signs/lexigrams produced by an ape really mean or refer to something?

3'. What must the researcher show to justify the claim that an ape is following a particular linguistic rule (or set of such rules)?

4'. How could one prove that an ape knows, as we humans know, that language is for communicating thoughts and intentions to others, for speaking truly (and sometimes falsely) of the world, and for attaining particular communicational goals?

Yet as long as agreed answers to these second-order questions are lacking, there will remain no grounds for optimism that consensus answers to any of the first-order questions will ever emerge. Clearly, just as we would need an agreed system of measurement if we wanted to come up with agreed measurements of spatial or temporal phenomena, we also need agreed methods of evaluation if we are to come up with agreed evaluations of the phenomena that are the subject of ape language research. We need to know what has to be shown if we are satisfactorily to justify a claim about the communicative (or cognitive) abilities or behavior of an ape.

The following analogy will help in further exploration of this dilemma. Some of us are watching a group of children play in a swimming pool below our balcony. We decide, for our own amusement, to give comparative evaluations of the behavior of each of the children in the pool, in the manner of the juries who evaluate professional skating and diving competitions. We agree on a set of five expressions by which to present our evaluations: "very poor," "poor," "good," "very good," and "excellent." And so we begin to write down our evaluations of each child's behavior. However, it quickly emerges that our evaluations are not in agreement but diverge widely. I gave a "very good" to Bobby, but you gave him a "very poor," and another friend gave him an "excellent"; I gave Henry a "very poor," you gave him an "excellent," and our other friend gave him a "good." And so on.

We ask each other to give our justifications for these evaluations. I reveal that I scored Bobby as "very good" because I thought his backstroke and crawl were surprisingly good for a child of his age and because his diving, though a bit ungainly, showed real potential. On the other hand, I gave Henry a "very poor" because his only stroke was a modified dog paddle and he hasn't yet learned to dive head first into the pool. But you explain that you gave Bobby a "very poor" because he was very rough and aggressive with the other children in the pool, he scoffed at the admonitions of the lifeguard, and he refused to wait his turn in the queue at the diving board. On the other hand, you explain that your evaluation of "excellent" for Henry was determined by his courtesy and good manners at poolside and his respectful attitude toward the adults swimming laps in the lanes. Our friend then objects that our evaluations are unjustified and explains her own as follows: Bobby received "excellent" because his imitation of a sea lion was wonderfully nuanced and lifelike, and Henry only received a "good" because his imitation of a killer whale was not particularly inspired (to put it kindly).

These attempts to justify our evaluations reveal that although we have been using the same evaluative expressions—"excellent," "very good," "good," and so on—we have been using different methods of applying those evaluative expressions to the children's behavior; and doubtless this revelation is what explains the wildly different evaluations we arrived at. It also confirms that there would be little point, for instance, in my arguing that you had made a mistake in evaluating Bobby as "very poor" because you failed to take account of his advanced skill in the backstroke, and that the correct evaluation was "very good." Similarly, it would be pointless for you to argue that it was my evaluation of "very good" for Bobby that was unjustified because I had neglected his deplorable poolside manners. For poolside manners are irrelevant according to the method by which I apply those evaluative terms, just as stroke proficiency is irrelevant to the method of evaluation you use (and both these behavioral characteristics are irrelevant to the method of evaluation our friend uses). We may be using the same ordered set of evaluative expressions, but we are still using different methods of evaluation because we apply those expressions according to different criteria. Thus, if you and I are asked to justify using, say, the expression "very good" to characterize a child's behavior, we will each refer to different aspects of the child's behavior as providing the criteria that justify our uses of that expression.

Nor, of course, can it make any sense to compare our different evaluations. Is your "excellent" a *better* evaluation of Henry's behavior than our friend's "good," given that you each used different methods of evaluation? Is my evaluation of Henry's behavior as "very poor," based solely on his stroke proficiency, comparable with your and our friend's evaluations, based as they were on poolside manners and animal-imitative skills? How could such comparisons make any sense?

Evaluating the poolside behavior of children is only a form of amusement in our community, so it really doesn't matter too much whether we ever do agree on a common method for doing so. But this is not the case with the communicative and cognitive behavior of apes and humans. If science is to make any headway in investigating the abilities of apes, we must be able to compare different scientists' uses of linguistic, behavioral, psychological, gestural, communicational, and cognitive terms, that is, what I will call the set of metaexpressions that includes the metalinguistic terms *understands*, *refers*, *means*, *sentence*, *language*, *warns*, *says*, and so on. We must also be able to compare how they use these terms when they talk about *humans* and how they use them when they talk about *apes*. Furthermore, for both comparisons, the uses of these metaexpressions must be evaluated according to the same method of evaluation: regardless of who is using those expressions or whose abilities—a human's or an ape's—they are being used to describe. Unfortunately, the fact that all the investigators of human and ape abilities draw from roughly the same set of such metaexpressions—yet without an agreed method of applying them—is highly misleading. For using the same set of metaexpressions promotes the illusion that meaningful comparisons *can* be made between one scientist's assertion that *his* bonobo "understands" a given sentence and another scientist's assertion that *her* bonobo does not or, for that matter, between one's assertion that by a certain word a chimpanzee "means x" and another's assertion that the same word "means x" to a human.

What sense, for example, are we to make of the critics' refusal to accept Savage-Rumbaugh's assertions that Kanzi understood the English sentences reported in the quoted passage that opens this chapter (or that he understood the sentences on which he was tested in the laboratory)? Are the critics using the same method of evaluation as Savage-Rumbaugh in determining whether she is justified in asserting that, in this or that particular instance, "Kanzi understood"? Furthermore, do the critics (and, for that matter, does Savage-Rumbaugh) also use that method of evaluation when determining if it is justified to assert the same thing of *a human*? Or is it merely that the same metalinguistic expressions are being used—"understood," "did not understand," and so on—yet, in each case, are being applied according to different justificational criteria?

If the critics and Savage-Rumbaugh are using the same metalinguistic expressions but are applying them according to different criteria, then (as in the poolside analogy) different methods of evaluation are in use. In this case, it would be illogical to claim that the critics are denying what Savage-Rumbaugh says, that is, denying *the very same proposition* that is asserted by Savage-Rumbaugh. (Are you denying the same proposition that our friend is asserting when she claims that Bobby's behavior at the pool is excellent and you reply that no, it's not excellent? Rather, it would appear that, because of the different methods of evaluation being used, the assertion and the denial "pass each other by.")

Similarly, if scientists use the same set of metalinguistic expressions when talking about the abilities of both apes and humans *yet apply those expressions according to different criteria when talking about apes than when talking about humans*, then, again, different methods of evaluation are in use: one for metalinguistic discourse about apes and one for metalinguistic discourse about humans. In this case it would clearly be illogical to claim that it is the same propositions that are being affirmed—or denied, or contrasted—for both humans and apes. If we have used different methods of evaluation in determining whether it is justified to say, on the one hand, of Kanzi and, on the other, of my friend Stuart that they understood the sentence "Would you put some grapes in the swimming pool?" then it would make no sense to conclude, for instance, that Stuart did but Kanzi did not understand that sentence, or for that matter that they both did or both did not.

And if one scientist's assertion does not logically make contact with the other's denial (because, as in the present case, the scientist and her critics are employing different methods of evaluation), does it even make any sense to *hope* that—by looking more closely at the data, or by reexamining the behavioral phenomena directly, or by improving the data collection techniques, and so forth—we can find out which of them is right? Without agreed methods of evaluating the use of such metaexpressions—the terms for describing, evaluating, characterizing, and comparing behaviors and abilities—a rational, responsible, *scientific* investigation of those behaviors and abilities cannot even begin.

One must instead conclude that a method of evaluation for metalinguistic claims about animals must satisfy two *logical prerequisites*: a Commonality Requirement and an Equality requirement, as follows.

Commonality Requirement: The same method of evaluation must be used by all who judge whether it is justified to assert a given metalinguistic claim.

If this requirement is not satisfied, then it makes little sense to compare how one judge (using one method) evaluates the justification of a metalinguistic claim with how another judge (using a different method) evaluates the justification of that same claim.

Equality Requirement: The same method of evaluation must be used in evaluating metalinguistic claims about both apes and humans.

If the Equality Requirement is not satisfied, then it cannot make any sense to compare how a claim was evaluated (by one method) when it was asserted about an ape with how it was evaluated (by another method) when it was asserted about a human. If we want to know whether an ape can do what we do (e.g., understand a particular sentence), then whether it is justified to claim that an ape has some communicational ability must be determined in the same way that it is determined whether it is justified to make that same claim about a human.

It is not as if the lack of an agreed evaluative method has gone unnoticed in the scientific community. Far from it. As discussed earlier, many within the scientific community have expressed great frustration at the fact that little or no progress has been made, in over three decades of research, toward the goal of forming consensus answers to first-order questions such as those numbered 1 to 4 above. Furthermore, it has long been recognized that this lack of agreement on the first-order questions has been rendered unavoidable because of the lack of agreement on the second-order, methodological questions. And recognition of this connection has naturally led to periods of increased attention to the methodological issues and to the goal of establishing agreed methods of evaluation that satisfy both the Equality and Commonality Requirements. However, in spite of all the attention these issues have received, that goal continues to remain tantalizingly beyond the reach of the scientific community.

One should not forget, of course, that it is in the interest of some schools of opinion that no agreement on a common method of evaluating such abilities should ever be reached. There are many scientists who, for one reason or another, refuse *on principle* to accept even the possibility that a nonhuman ape could share any of the communicational or cognitive abilities of a human, or less-evolved versions of them. For someone who wants dogmatically to maintain the presupposition of a fundamental, unbridgeable, categorical distinction between the communicational/cognitive abilities of humans and of apes, the continuing lack of agreement on a common method of evaluating those abilities can appear to confirm that presupposition. That lack of agreement can appear to confirm the presupposed incommensurability of ape and human abilities.

In chapter 2, Stuart Shanker examines the historical development and philosophical underpinnings of the attempts by cognitive psychologists and philosophers of mind to grapple with these methodological problems. He analyzes the concepts and arguments that these theorists have employed in their efforts to found a common metric, or method of evaluation, for the scientific community's investigations of the cognitive abilities of humans and apes. Yet Shanker reveals the existence of deep-rooted, *epistemological* presuppositions that act like hidden magnets, magically guiding those who work on these problems to the same sterile, irresolvable controversies: controversies that, because of their frustratingly perennial character, take on the appearance of fundamental *philosophical* issues. Shanker also shows how Savage-Rumbaugh's work can be seen both as shedding new light on these longstanding methodological problems and as suggesting a means of dissolving their puzzling character. In the remainder of this chapter I want to adopt a different perspective on these problems, on their epistemological presuppositions, and on the implications that Savage-Rumbaugh's work with apes has for their resolution: a perspective from which the sources of the methodological problems, as well as their solution, appear as rhetorical matters.

What do I mean by "rhetorical," and how does rhetorical analysis differ from the philosophical analysis given in the last chapter? The best way I can answer this question is by illustrative example, beginning in the next section. But the following remark from Wittgenstein's *Philosophical Investigations*, although it addresses the methodological problems plaguing not cognitive or communicational theories but the philosophy of mathematics, nevertheless gives a good idea of the kind of material a rhetorical analysis concerns: "What we 'are tempted to say' . . . is, of course, not philosophy; but it is its *raw material*. Thus, for example, what a mathematician is *inclined to say* about the objectivity and reality of mathematical facts is not a philosophy of mathematics, but something for philosophical treatment" (Wittgenstein 1953, sec. 254; emphasis added). It is in the raw material of these *rhetorical inclinations*—that is, in what, typically, "we are tempted to say" in talking about the abilities and behavior of humans and animals (and in *why* we are tempted to say it)—that one may find both the source of the scientists' frustrating inability to arrive at common methods for evaluating those abilities and behaviors and the tools with which one may begin to treat that inability.

The Commonsense Picture of Communication

To understand the methodological problems that plague scientific discourse on the communicational abilities of *apes*, one must first examine the rhetorical characteristics of scientific discourse concerning *human* communicational abilities: that is, scientific discourse that makes use of the kinds of metalinguistic expressions just discussed. Consider, for instance, the following metalinguistic remarks, which could hardly be said to be controversial.

A. We usually (but not always) understand what we say to each other.
B. To understand someone's utterance, we must understand what it means.
C. All, or at least most, of the words we use mean something.
D. In speaking we often refer to things and/or ideas.
E. The truth or falsity of what we say depends on how the things we refer to really are.
F. There are other people who speak the same language we do.

Any number of commonplace metalinguistic remarks could be added to these: remarks such as "To converse successfully with another speaker, we must use the same language"; "It is possible for two people to give different pronunciations to the same word"; "If we know a given language, we know many, perhaps all, of the ways its words may be combined into sentences"; "We use language to communicate our thoughts to others"; and so on. The highlighting of the six metalinguistic remarks listed is not intended to be significant.

Anyone who denied the truth of these remarks would typically be called a skeptic. That is, only a skeptic would maintain that:

A'. We don't usually understand what we say to each other.
B'. We don't have to understand the meaning of someone's utterance in order to understand that utterance.
C'. The words we use don't mean anything at all.
D'. We don't ever refer to things.
E'. The truth or falsity of what we say is in fact independent of how the things we refer to really are.

F'. Even though we take there to be millions of speakers of English, this is incorrect. In fact, there are not now and never have been two people who
speak the same language.

There is an internal relation between, on the one hand, the fact that someone
who denied claims like A to F would typically be characterized as a "skeptic" and,
on the other, the fact that the claims themselves would typically be characterized
as "commonsense": that is, they are like two sides of the same coin. Accordingly,
those who study human communication are inclined to treat the skeptic's denial
of such claims as controversial and to dismiss the skeptic's argument as "an assault on commonsense." (On the rhetoric of skepticism in language theory, see
Taylor [1992].)

Intrinsic to characterizing claims like A to F as "commonsense" is taking them
to be *true*. (Thus another word for a statement of commonsense is a "truism.")
Moreover, as is reflected in claim E, we are inclined to view the truth of a sentence—for example, "The Earth has only a single moon"—as determined by facts
that are independent of the utterance of that sentence: in this case, the fact that
there really is only one of the things we call "moons" revolving around our planet.
Analogously, we take the truth of the claims A to F to be determined by the fact
that things really are as those claims declare them to be. Again, only someone
who would typically be called a skeptic (or relativist) would deny this and affirm
instead that a sentence may actually be true even if things are *not* in fact as the
sentence says they are.

Take claim C as an example: "All, or at least most, of the words we use mean
something." It is surely a "truism" that *if it really were the case that the words we
use did* NOT *actually mean anything, then C would be false.* That is, the truth of C is
determined by the fact—a fact that is independent of the utterance of C—that the
words we use *really do* have meanings. Accordingly, C strikes us not just as some
groundless platitude nor as something we are just "inclined to say"; rather, we take
it as actually corresponding to "the real facts" about our words. Commonsense inclines us to the view that we don't just *say* that our words mean something; they
really do.

In other words, the distinction between a sequence of sounds meaning something
and not meaning anything is not one that we are inclined to take merely as a *de dicto*
distinction: that is, a verbal illusion that is created by—is a "construct" of—the ways
in which we metalinguistically talk about those sounds. Instead, we treat the distinction between meaning something and not meaning anything as *de re*. That is,
when we say that a sequence of vocal sounds means something or doesn't mean
anything, we take what we say to be true only if the facts of the matter are actually
as described: the sequence really does (or does not) have a meaning. By extension,
the same goes for the other statements A to F and for other similar metalinguistic
"truisms." I will use the expression "the commonsense picture of communication"
to refer to the general conception of communicational "facts" that is implied by the
taken-for-granted truth of such commonsense metalinguistic statements. This picture of the reality underlying human communicational behavior is a rhetorical legacy
of our inclination to treat such metalinguistic statements as "truisms."

On the other hand, it is no surprise that scientists of human communication typically "tinker with" or "reinterpret" some of the features inherited from this commonsense picture of communication. A communication theorist may deny that we are justified in assuming, say, that we usually understand what we say to each other (see claim A); on the contrary, she may insist that much of the time all that we really are justified in assuming is that our interlocutors do not radically *mis*-understand what we're saying. Or a sociolinguist may object that no two people really speak the very same language (see claim F); rather, the language spoken by any one of us is only more or less similar to that spoken by others in our community and is less similar to that spoken by people living at a greater social or geographical distance from us. And so on. But what is most important is that only someone whom the scientific community would typically ostracize as a "radical skeptic" would want to reject the *basic outlines* of the commonsense picture as the foundation, the core set of assumptions, from which to begin serious inquiry into human communicational phenomena. Moreover, it is quite understandable that this is how we are inclined to respond to such radical linguistic skepticism; for if we gave in to it, we would be unable to carry on.

This last point needs explaining. Imagine that, every time you and I meet, I make a point of denying (and behaving in accordance with that denial):

- That you understand anything I say
- That I understand anything you say
- That the words we are using mean or refer to anything
- That either of us knows the meanings of any of the words we're using
- That the truth of what I or you say depends on the facts
- That you and I are speaking the same language

It seems clear that if I talked and behaved in this way it would pose a serious, probably insuperable obstacle to our interactions. How could we go on—what communicational goals could we possibly achieve—if I persisted in acting thus? How could we plan to meet somewhere, explain where and how we hurt, give each other road directions, ask for help, complain about our treatment, and so on, if to everything you said I responded as if I believed that your words do not mean or refer to anything, that the truth of what you said is independent of how things really are, and that you and I are not speaking the same language? And if this were how I treated what *I* said as well? Simply trying to envisage such an interaction brings one very quickly to a frontier with the unimaginably absurd.

Now, consider if *everyone* began to act as I do, and did so *all the time*. Everyday communicational interaction—and so, human life as we know it—would collapse.

The importance of this point needs to be emphasized, for it explains our attachment to what I have called the commonsense picture of communication. It is not because we are naive, or stupid, or theoretically uninformed "folk" that we attribute the status of truism to metalinguistic remarks like A to F and that we consequently accept the general outlines of the commonsense picture projected by those truisms. The attribution of an authoritative status to such metalinguistic statements strikes us as a prerequisite to "ordinary life," as is made clear by the attempt to imagine what life would be like if we rebelled against that authority. And the acceptance of some version of the commonsense picture of communication seems to follow naturally. We are therefore strongly inclined to think that to deny that those truisms *were true*, that they gave a more or less accurate description of "the way things really are," would itself amount to challenging their authoritative status and therefore also the stability and comprehensibility of ordinary life. (For a demonstration of the kind of thing that would occur were the authority of such commonsense "truisms" challenged, see the famous experiments recounted in Garfinkel [1967, ch. 2].)

In sum, "commonsense"—here illustrated by claims A to F—provides scientific inquiry into communicational abilities with a powerful rhetorical legacy (that is, what Wittgenstein called *raw material*). This legacy takes the form of a rich, albeit vague and incomplete, picture of the reality ("the facts") underlying human communicational behavior: a reality that is populated with such things as meanings, languages, referential relations, grammatical rules, states of understanding and of misunderstanding, and so on. Those scientists who study human communication are thus strongly inclined to take for granted (at least *some version* of) this picture, along with the premise that (some as-yet-unspecified version of) the reality pictured *must* obtain. For example, it must be the case that we humans often refer to things with the words we use. This must actually *happen*; it's not just something we *talk about*. Words, at least some of them on some occasions, really do refer to things. Reference (or meaning, or languages, or understanding, etc.) are not just imaginary creations, with a purely *de dicto* existence. They are *de re*: phenomena that "exist in the world."

Animal Research and the Scarlet Letter

How does the commonsense picture of communication influence the methodological problem raised earlier: the problem of how to determine whether an ape like Kanzi understands a spoken English sentence? It is clear that the rhetoric of metalinguistic discourse about humans inclines us toward the view that the distinction between a person who does and a person who does not understand a given sentence is not merely a *de dicto* distinction. That is, that it is not a distinction that exists only in how we metalinguistically talk about those people. Instead, we are led to the view that the distinction between understanding and not understanding is *de re*. When we say P understands and Q does not understand, that verbal distinction is correctly applied *only if the facts of the matter are actually as described*: P really does and Q really does not understand. (We might use as a shorthand way of referring to the *de re* distinction: "P does *in fact* and Q does not *in fact* understand.") Furthermore, that rhetoric also inclines us toward the view that, *ceteris paribus*, we typically get it right when we say of someone that he or she understands. In other words, that ordinarily, although hardly universally, when we say that someone understands us or that we understand him or her, we truly describe what really is the case.

But what about apes? Does any ape ever really understand something said to it by another ape (via gesture, or vocalization) or, in the case of laboratory-reared apes like Kanzi, something said to it by a human? Can we justifiably ever claim of any ape that it does *in fact* understand a sentence of English? When researchers such as Savage-Rumbaugh assert that an ape understands something they've said, are such claims ever actually true?

To see why understanding-claims about apes are treated as they are, one needs first to look at the broader rhetorical differences between metalinguistic discourse about humans and metalinguistic discourse about nonhuman animals *generally*. It is hardly viewed as unusual when someone who has a pet dog makes a commonplace remark like:

G. His barking means he wants us to take him for a walk.
H. He knows what I am scolding him for.
I. He understands that we are talking about going to the vet.
J. He knows what "naughty" means.

However, the scientific community does not characterize it as "skepticism" when a scientist objects that such commonplace remarks are unwarranted, or even false. The scientific community would never treat such a scientist as a skeptic if he insisted that there is no justification in attributing meaning to the vocalizations of a dog, or in describing the dog as knowing what an utterance refers to (e.g., the puddle on the carpet), or in speaking of the dog as understanding a human sentence or word.

Indeed, not only is it perfectly acceptable—among those researchers who study the abilities and behavior of nonhuman animals—to treat with skepticism any commonplace remarks about animal communication; it is an obligation. A skeptical attitude is a rhetorical requirement for those who want to be accorded a respected status in animal research. That is, whereas human communicational inquiry eschews a skeptical attitude toward commonplace metalinguistic remarks, in animal communicational inquiry the situation is the reverse. A special ostracizing label is attached to the animal researcher who is thought to be *insufficiently* skeptical in her attitude toward commonplace remarks about animal communicational behavior. This special label—which begins, coincidentally, with the same letter as Hester Prynne's notorious brand—is the adjective "anthropomorphic."

A good scientist of animal communication is required to adopt a skeptical attitude toward commonsense remarks (such as G to J) about the communicative behavior of animals. This requirement manifests itself in the norms of primatological discourse, in the rules that are enforced by, among, and on primatologists who study communication and cognition in nonhuman primates. These rules are taught to those coming into the field. They determine what may and what may not acceptably be said, what may count as justification of a given claim, what may count as evidence, what may count as a strong argument, or a plausible hypothesis, and so on. Furthermore, it is by the use and enforcement of these norms that the decisions are made determining how research programs in primate communication are set up and directed, which proposed programs receive funding, whose papers get published in which journals, and who gets tenure. At the same time the requirement to be skeptical is manifested in the demand that Savage-Rumbaugh provide a special justification for her claims about Kanzi understanding spoken English sentences.

It is often possible to find this obligatory disciplinary skepticism hidden behind some dissembling remark in which the scientist concedes that metalinguistic claims such as G to J are indeed acceptable *in colloquial contexts*. However, the scientist continues, in the context of *serious* inquiry such claims are patently nonserious. With more than a little condescension, he corrects the speaker of G, saying something like the following:

> Well, no, actually his barking doesn't really mean anything at all. Rather, the description of the animal's behavior as having a meaning—although perfectly acceptable in colloquial speech—is strictly incorrect. It is in fact only a metaphor. Yet when we have the scientific goal of discovering and stating the truth—as opposed to displaying a sentimental affection for our pets—such a figurative description of the dog's behavior manifests a dangerous intrusion of emotion into the crucial scientific practices of empirical observation and description. Strictly speaking—and scientific inquiry obliges us to obey strict norms of language-use—there is no justification in attributing meaning to the vocalization of a nonhuman animal.

Yet it goes without saying that only someone who would be dismissed as a "crazy skeptic" would raise an analogous objection to a remark about a human's communicative behavior, such as "Barbara's comment about the lateness of the hour means she wants us to end the meeting soon."

> Well no, actually her vocalizing doesn't really mean anything at all. Rather, the description of a human's behavior as having a meaning—although perfectly acceptable in colloquial speech—is strictly incorrect. It is in fact only a metaphor. Yet when we have the scientific goal of discovering and stating the truth—as opposed to displaying a sentimental affection for our friends—such a figurative description of a woman's behavior manifests a dangerous intrusion of emotion into the crucial scientific practices of empirical observation and description. Strictly speaking— and scientific inquiry obliges us to obey strict norms of language-use—there is no justification in attributing meaning to the vocalization of a human animal.

What is the reason for such rhetorical asymmetry? Why isn't the skeptic's denial of commonsense remarks such as G to J viewed as disdainfully in the study of animal communication as is, in the study of human communication, the denial of the commonsense remarks in A to F? The answer lies in the different ways that such skepticism would fit with, on the one hand, our treatment of animals and, on the other, our treatment of our fellow human beings. It seems clear that our day-to-day interactions with and life with animals would not be severely affected by the adoption of the scientist's skepticism about the ability of animals to understand, refer, mean, deceive, intend, etc. Indeed, the converse is more likely: that is, a wholesale *rejection* of that skepticism about animal abilities—analogous to the commonsense rejection of skepticism about the ability of humans to understand, refer, mean, and so on—would not sit at all well with the ethical presuppositions of our treatment of animals as exploitable sources of food, free labor, clothing, cleaning agents, jewelry, and so on. How could we possibly believe that it had been scientifically established that an animal such as Kanzi does in fact have all the abilities that we might "loosely" speak of him as having—the ability to understand some of what we say, to have beliefs and knowledge like ours, to think thoughts like ours, to communicate something like we do—yet continue to treat him as being without rights and to act as if it is we who have the right to do with him whatever we choose?

Yet, as the skeptic's response to Barbara's remark makes clear, the situation is quite different when we turn to consider the hypothetical consequences of a whole-sale skeptical denial of our *fellow human beings'* communicative abilities. While the commonplace adoption of a skeptical attitude to everyday metalinguistic remarks about humans would constitute a dangerous threat to the metalinguistically mediated understanding of human behavior that is essential to our participation in and maintenance of social life as we know it, this is not the case for the adoption of a skeptical attitude toward everyday metalinguistic remarks about animals. It is here that one may find the source of the rhetorical asymmetry between scientific discourse about the communicational and cognitive abilities of animals and scientific discourse about human possession of those abilities.

The Epistemological Conception and Its Methodological Legacy

In the preceding sections, I have proposed a rhetorical analysis as a way of making sense of the scientific community's evident inclination, on the one hand, to adopt a skeptical attitude toward claims about the communicational abilities of animals, yet on the other, to dismiss as absurd the skeptical treatment of similar claims regarding humans. When addressing the philosophical and methodological problems raised by the study of animal cognition and communication, it is to this *raw material* that one should turn. By this means one may shed light on the source and continued vitality of those problems in order to determine how they may best be treated. The goal of this rhetorical approach is to *change* how the scientific community views those problems so that they no longer appear as insuperable obstacles standing in the way of progress in the study of animal abilities and behavior.

But how does this rhetorical analysis affect how one views the methodological problem discussed earlier—the problem of establishing, for the purposes of scientific inquiry, a common method for evaluating metalinguistic claims about apes, both human and nonhuman? How, for instance, can it help us address the second-order question 1'?

1'. What observational or experimental evidence would be sufficient for it to be justifiably asserted that an ape understands what a spoken English sentence means?

We are inclined to conceive of such questions as epistemological matters. That is, it strikes us as little more than a commonsense truism to maintain that there is a particular state of affairs that obtains (indeed *must* obtain) when it is asserted truly that someone understands a sentence: namely, the person in question understands the sentence referred to. He or she does *in fact* understand. So, for example, when we remark metalinguistically, "Stuart understands 'Would you put some grapes in the swimming pool?'" it is the fact, and only the fact, of Stuart's under-

standing that ultimately could determine whether what we metalinguistically assert is true. If that state of affairs obtains, then what we say is true; and if it does
not, then what we say is false. Again, this reasoning is hardly controversial, but
can be seen as following from the commonsense interpretation of a truism like "If
'He understands the sentence' is true, then he does *in fact* understand the sentence."
It is not only the members of the *scientific* community who would regard as per-
versely skeptical anyone who persisted in denying such an obvious truism.

Analogously, only if the planet Saturn really has seven moons is the assertion
"Saturn has seven moons" true. Commonsense tells us that what matters for the
truth of that assertion is not whether some, or even all, people feel it's all right to
say that Saturn has seven moons, but whether the state of affairs *claimed* to obtain *really does* obtain—whether there are *in fact* seven of the things called moons
circling the planet we call Saturn.

Given this reasoning, it is hardly surprising that, when a methodological question like 1' is raised, we tend to assume that what is at issue is information about
the obtaining or nonobtaining of a hypothetical state of affairs—*the ape's understanding of the spoken sentence*. What we need to know, it appears, is whether
this *de re* state of affairs does or doesn't obtain: whether the ape does or doesn't
in fact understand the sentence (not just whether people *feel it's all right to say* he
does, but whether *he really does*). For as commonsense unambiguously confirms,
only the obtaining of that state of affairs can justify the assertion that the ape understands the sentence. Only then is the assertion *true*.

Consequently, we naturally take question 1' as asking how much and what kind
of evidence we need in order to determine whether that hypothetical state of affairs does in fact obtain. (Compare: How much and what kind of evidence do we
need in order to determine whether Saturn does in fact have seven, and only seven,
moons?) It is by these rhetorical means that we are inclined toward what I have
called an *epistemological conception* of methodological questions like 1'. We
conceive of such questions—that is to say, we treat them—*as matters of knowledge about hypothetical states of affairs*: here, about an ape's understanding of a
sentence. We may not be able to observe directly whether that state of affairs
obtains, but we can gather evidence to help us determine whether it does: that is,
to determine whether the ape does *in fact* understand.

This is what an epistemological interpretation takes to be at issue in question 1'.
And so naturally this is also how the scientific community is inclined to conceive of
the problem of formulating a common method of evaluation for metalinguistic
claims. In other words, it is felt necessary to impose an essential requirement on
any attempt to formulate such a method of evaluation. *Any proposed method must
be based on one particular kind of justificational criterion: the provision of sufficient evidence to establish that the hypothetical state of affairs that the metalinguistic
statement is about does in fact obtain.* A method of evaluation must evaluate as
justified only those metalinguistic claims that satisfy this criterion. Thus, for example, any method of evaluation that determines that it is justified to assert that Kanzi
understands a particular English sentence must base that determination on evidence
showing that Kanzi does *in fact* understand that sentence. Again, this requirement
is nothing more than commonsense: Would it not be absurd to deny that if an

assertion is to be confirmed as true, then the state of affairs asserted to obtain must actually be shown to obtain?

Still, how much evidence, and of what kind, is required for us to know whether the ape does *in fact* understand? (Not merely whether the ape *acts like* he understands, or whether people who observe him *feel it's okay* to say he understands; but whether he does *in fact* understand.) In other words, exactly how should we formulate the criterion for the method of evaluating claims about the communicational abilities of animals? Exactly what type or types of observational evidence should be accepted as sufficient to justify the claim that, for example:

- An ape understands the spoken sentence "Would you put some grapes in the swimming pool?"
- An ape follows the grammatical rule requiring subjects to be placed before verbs?
- An ape knows what "easy" means, or that it is the antonym of "difficult"?
- An ape uses symbols to refer to things?

And there is a corollary to this requirement: the criterion must be applied equally to apes and to humans. If it is not, then—as I showed earlier—different methods of evaluation are being used, so the Equality Requirement is not satisfied. The consequence in turn would be that metalinguistic assertions about an ape (evaluated by one method) cannot be compared with similar assertions (evaluated by a different method) about a human, even though the same metalinguistic terms are being used. That is, it would be illogical to maintain that what was being affirmed of the human was the same thing that was being affirmed (or denied) of the ape— that the ape and the human both understand the meaning of the word "please"; or that the human can, but the ape cannot refer to past events. *For such comparisons to have any sense, the same methods of evaluation must be applied.*

After all, what the scientific community wants to know is whether any ape does or can be taught to do *the same* (communicational) things that we humans do: understand sentences, grasp the meanings of words, use language to refer to objects and events, follow grammatical rules, and so on. To answer these questions (positively or negatively), a method of evaluation that satisfies the Equality Requirement must be used. Otherwise, the answers given will only be pseudoanswers.

It is of course here that the opinion of the scientific community divides into many opposing schools and subschools of thought, with the result that no method currently in use yet satisfies the Commonality Requirement. However, it is essential to recognize that underlying these frustrating divisions over methodology, and the consequent pessimistic outlook for research on the communicational abilities of animals, is a shared rhetorical premise: the *epistemological conception* of the problem of formulating a method of evaluation for metalinguistic claims about animals. For it is by presenting the problem as a matter of knowledge, of sufficient evidence, and of the states of affairs for which evidence is required, that the epistemological conception sows the rhetorical seeds of that discord. In other words, the frustrating methodological divisions—and so the obstacle to progress in the study of animal communicational abilities—are a rhetorical legacy of the epistemological conception of the problem of an evaluative method. (*"Qui sème le vent récolte la tempête.*") If the problem were conceived differently, that disagreement simply could not arise. In the following sections I will attempt to make these last points clear by means of illustrative examples.

But first, it is perhaps worth recalling why the methodological problem of evaluating understanding-claims about apes does not independently arise for understanding-claims about humans: that is, independent of science's attempt to determine if animals have any of the communicational abilities (such as understanding) that we humans have. For, *prima facie*, one might think that having to justify the claim that Kanzi understands "Would you put some grapes in the swimming pool?" is no different from having to justify the claim that a human understands that sentence. After all, it is certainly possible that either of them might *act like* they understand yet not really do so, or that common opinion might *take it to be acceptable* to describe them as understanding although in fact they really do not. For each of them, the same state of affairs has to be shown to obtain—it has to be shown that the ape or the human does *in fact* understand. Therefore, determining what kind and how much evidence is sufficient to justify either claim should, at least in principle, present the same sorts of methodological problems and offer the same room for disagreement and division. However, this is clearly not the case; and that is because rhetorically the two claims, and so also the two justificational tasks, are quite different. In other words, we "are inclined" to see them differently, as follows.

As I showed earlier, it is a cornerstone of commonsense that, all things being equal, people usually understand sentences spoken to them in a language that they themselves speak. Only someone who would naturally be deemed a skeptic would maintain that usually people do *not* understand sentences spoken to them in their language. Therefore—again, all things being equal—my English-speaking friend Stuart can be expected to understand the sentence "Would you put some grapes in the swimming pool?" (Of course, things might not "be equal." For instance, Stuart might never have seen a grape before, or he may not have heard me clearly. And so on. But we are here making the a priori assumption that all things *are* equal.) Consequently, if Stuart acts like he understands that sentence when it is spoken to him (e.g., he gets right up and puts the grapes in the swimming pool), the onus is naturally placed on the skeptic to establish *her* claim that, in spite of appearances, Stuart does not really understand. And we may go one step further. For if we are rhetorically entitled to assume from his behavior that he understands the sentence, then we may infer that the relevant state of affairs does in fact obtain: that is, the state of affairs that, according to the commonsense picture, *must* obtain *if* he really understands the sentence. In other words, the rhetoric of metalinguistic discourse places the onus *on the skeptic* to establish that someone who acts like he understands a sentence does not *in fact* understand it.

However, for the reasons already discussed, rhetoric inclines us differently when the subject is not a human but an ape. In this case, it is "anthropomorphic" to assume that Kanzi, or any ape, *can* understand an English sentence. Therefore, we cannot assume—as we could with Stuart—that, all things being equal, Kanzi will understand the sentence "Would you put some grapes in the swimming pool?" That is, even if Kanzi acts like he understands it (e.g., behaving just as Stuart did), the onus is placed not on the skeptic, but rather *on the ape language researcher* to establish that he does *in fact* understand it. Thus arises the problem of formulating a method by which such claims may be established and which, at the same time, satisfies the Equality Requirement.

Methodological Reductivism

According to the epistemological conception, metalinguistic claims are matters of knowledge about the obtaining of *de re* states of affairs. Moreover, we already *know* that we humans understand, mean, refer, and so on. But do we know that any ape does or can be taught to do these things? As I have shown, we are led by the epistemological conception to require *any method of evaluating such claims to be based on one justificational criterion: the provision of sufficient evidence to establish that the hypothetical state of affairs that the metalinguistic statement is about does in fact obtain.* However, the criterion is no more precise than this. As such, it leaves open two crucial matters.

To put it another way, the required justificational criterion incorporates two structural "variables": an Epistemic Object variable and an Epistemic Conviction variable. Each of these variables can be expressed as a question.

1. Epistemic Object variable: What is the hypothetical state of affairs that the metalinguistic statement is about and that must be shown to obtain?
2. Epistemic Conviction variable: What counts as sufficient evidence to establish that the state of affairs in (1) obtains?

These two variables provide the locus for the superficially radical divisions between theoretical schools on how to formulate a method of evaluation for metalinguistic claims about animals. (Those divisions are only *superficially* radical because there remains the underlying epistemological conception.) The divisions may be traced to the different "values" that different schools give to these "variables": what they count as "sufficient evidence" and what they take to be "the hypothetical state of affairs" that has to obtain for the metalinguistic claim to be true. The choices for these "values" foreground the rhetorical relationship between the method of evaluation and the commonsense picture of communication.

Put in this way, it becomes possible to see why the methods that have been proposed for evaluating metalinguistic claims about animals fall into two general types, which are distinguished by their opposite choices of values for the two structural variables. One type of method is characterized by the choice, as Epistemic Object, of a *de re* state of affairs, the obtaining or nonobtaining of which is relatively simple to establish. Such a reductive method of evaluation is typically adopted in those forms of communicational research that are based on what are usually called "behaviorist" principles.

A reductive method of evaluation for a claim such as "She or he understands S" might determine a subject's understanding sentence S to consist in the subject making one of a particular set of bodily movements in response to hearing S. For example, an experimenter might determine the subject's understanding of the sentence "Press the red button" to consist in the subject pressing the red button in re-sponse to hearing that sentence. In other words, this act is what the metalinguistic claim "The subject understands 'Press the red button'" is deemed *to be about*: the Epistemic Object. It is this, and only this, *de re* state of affairs that must obtain for the metalinguistic claim to be true; and it is therefore this state of affairs that must be *shown* to obtain if the method of evaluation is to evaluate the claim as justified.

What this example brings into relief is the rhetorical relationship between the Epistemic Object and Epistemic Conviction variables. In particular, it reveals how, by defining the Epistemic Object in this reductive manner, the problem of Epistemic Conviction is greatly simplified. For it is a relatively straightforward matter to col-lect evidence to see whether the subject presses the red button in response to hear-ing the sentence "Press the red button." Therefore, *if* behaving thus has been de-fined as the state of affairs that the metalinguistic statement is about (i.e., as the Epistemic Object), then it is just that simple to produce evidence sufficient to estab-lish whether that state of affairs does or does not obtain. In other words, *given this type of broadly reductivist method of evaluation*, the researcher can much more easily establish whether a metalinguistic hypothesis—such as "The subject understands 'Press the red button'"—is true. Consequently, if such a method of evaluation for metalinguistic statements about apes were commonly accepted in the scientific com-munity, it would be much easier to reach widespread agreement on the answers to a host of modern science's most puzzling metalinguistic questions, such as ques-tions 1 to 4 posed earlier. If each communicational ability that we wanted to know about could be given such a behavioral definition, then the search for those answers would be a relatively simple matter of seeing whether the ape produced that behav-ior in the appropriate conditions.

There is no doubt that this reductive approach to the problem of formulating a method of evaluation for metalinguistic claims offers certain procedural benefits to scientists studying the communicational abilities of apes. As I have shown, science wants to determine whether an ape has or can acquire some of the very same communicational abilities that we humans have, as opposed to fundamen-tally distinct abilities that we—perhaps misleadingly—characterize by the same metalinguistic expressions. So if we are to make any sense of metalinguistic claims affirming or denying that an ape possesses one or more of the communicational abilities typically associated with humans, those claims must be evaluated accord-ing to the same method of evaluation as is applied to the affirmation or denial of the same metalinguistic claims of a human: the Equality Requirement must apply. This means that if this reductivist type of method of evaluation is employed in determining whether it is justified to affirm *or deny* a particular communicational ability *of an ape*, then the same method of evaluation must also be employed to determine if it is justified to affirm or deny that same ability *of a human*. Here is the problem.

Of course, it is perfectly *possible* to choose particular behavioral states or events as Epistemic Objects for most metalinguistic claims typically made about humans: for example, to identify the act of pressing the red button as the state of affairs that the metalinguistic claim "She or he understands 'Press the red button'" is about. If we make this methodological choice, then only if the human subject presses the red button on hearing "Press the red button" will that metalinguistic claim be evaluated as justified. It is as feasible to choose a behavioral Epistemic Object for a metalinguistic claim about a human as it is to do so for a metalinguistic claim about an ape. But whether it will seem to us to make much sense is another matter.

But why should this be? For, as I have shown, commonsense inclines us to the view that, all things being equal, someone who *acts* like they understand a sentence, does *in fact* understand it. And, in parallel fashion, if someone *acts* like they do *not* understand the sentence, we are inclined to accept that, in fact, they do not understand it. So a reductive method of evaluation would appear to sit well with our commonsense inclinations.

However, "all things" might not "be equal." Commonsense also inclines us to leave open the *possibility* that although someone acts like she understands, she may not in fact really understand. And we take it also to be *possible* for her to act like she does *not* understand, even though she really does. In other words, we are inclined to preserve a distinction between *acting as if* one understands a sentence (or means such-and-such by what one says, or is referring to a particular object, or is following the rule R) and *actually doing so*. We make room for the possibility that even though Barbara did not press the red button on hearing "Press the red button," she may still have understood the sentence perfectly correctly. But a reductive method of evaluating metalinguistic statements abolishes this distinction, and so this possibility, by fiat.

Would it not indeed strike us as absurd if someone insisted on the absence of any distinction here? Imagine if I tell Charlie that even though Barbara acted like she understood his request to leave the dog in the car, she didn't really understand what he said; and to justify this superficially skeptical remark, I point out that Barbara had had her Walkman on quite loud when Charlie spoke and that she always leaves the dog in the car anyway. But Charlie objects to my claim as nonsense: for according to him, the fact that Barbara acted as if she understood the request logically guarantees that she did in fact understand it. She *cannot possibly* have failed to understand it, for her understanding is nothing more and nothing less than her behavioral response. Or imagine the opposite scenario: I tell Charlie that even though Barbara acted like she hadn't understood his request to leave the dog in the car, she had in fact understood what he said perfectly well. To justify my claim, I point out that she is quite angry with him and so was doubtless doing the opposite of what he requested "just to spite him." But then Charlie objects that, no, Barbara's acting as if she hadn't understood makes it *impossible* for her actually to have understood. For her lack of understanding *consisted in* her behavioral response.

It is hard to imagine what the effect would be on everyday life if everyone ordinarily argued for and acted in accord with the positions that Charlie here supports. No one would act as if there were any distinction between talking about communicational behavior and talking about the communicational states and processes (e.g., understanding, meaning, referring, following rules, intending, etc.) that—in the real world—we typically speak of as underlying or motivating that behavior. If everyone were to act this way, then there would no longer be any sense to our everyday talk about reasons for someone's behavior, what someone really thinks, justifications for someone's actions by reference to their understanding of the situation, and so on. What is clear is that "everyday life as we know it"—or rather, the variety of practices by which we reflexively make sense of our lives to ourselves and to each other—does rely on that distinction; hence its status as "commonsense." Have we not often had the experience of finding out that someone who acted like he understood what we said did not really do so? Or that someone who acted like she was referring to one object was in fact referring to another? Or that someone who behaved as if he were following a particular rule was really following another (or no rule at all)? Making sense of these experiences requires the very distinction that is abolished by a reductive method of evaluating metalinguistic claims.

However, we must not confuse two different issues here. Commonsense does indeed incline us to place the *rhetorical onus* on skeptics to establish their case: that is, to show that someone who acts as if she understands does not actually do so. Yet we are also commonsensically inclined to preserve a distinction between *acting as if* one understands and *actually doing so*. In fact, these two issues do not conflict. On the contrary, if it is to make any sense to place the rhetorical onus on the skeptic to establish his claim that someone who acted as if she understood did not really, then we cannot do away with the metalinguistic distinction between acting as if one understands and actually doing so. For the sense of the former practice logically requires the latter distinction. It is essential to our commonsense concepts of understanding, meaning, referring, and so on (i.e., all those things that science wants to know if an ape can do) that acting as if one is doing one of these things is logically distinct from actually doing it. But a reductive method of evaluation does away with this commonsense distinction by decree.

At the same time, commonsense also inclines members of the scientific community to put the rhetorical onus on the *animal researcher* to prove that an animal who acts as if it understands a particular sentence does in fact do so. Remember the reaction of the scientific community to Savage-Rumbaugh's claims that Kanzi understood the English sentences in the episodes reported in the passage quoted at the opening of this chapter. To Savage-Rumbaugh's critics, the fact that Kanzi *acted as if* he understood the sentences only promotes the *illusion* of his linguistic competence. But, the critics insist, there are other possible explanations for that behavior: contextual information, inadvertant cuing, prior training, nonlinguistic associations, and so forth. What is still required is proof that he *really* understood the sentences.

A reductive method of evaluation invalidates this requirement; for if the animal acts as if it understands, then there simply is no possibility that it does not. If Kanzi pushes the red button in response to the sentence "Press the red button," then *ipso facto* the metalinguistic claim that he understood the sentence is true, for, according to a reductive method of evaluation, his understanding consists in nothing more and nothing less than that behavioral response. The same is true of his behavioral responses to "Would you put some grapes in the swimming pool?" or "Rose hid the surprise under her shirt" or "Would you please give Panbanisha an onion?" or other sentences mentioned earlier. A reductive method of evaluation can therefore appear paradoxically anthropomorphic; for it leaves no logical room for skepticism regarding a metalinguistic claim about an animal. While it satisfactorily fulfills the requirements imposed by the epistemological conception of metalinguistic discourse, still, because of how it *challenges* our inclinations toward metalinguistic claims about both animals and humans, a reductive method of evaluation clashes with commonsense.

At this point the proponent of a reductive method of evaluation might say "Okay, so reductivism clashes with commonsense, in particular by abolishing the distinction between acting as if one understands and really understanding. But is commonsense necessarily *right*? Maybe it's *wrong* to make such a distinction? After all, science has a long and distinguished history of correcting mistaken concepts and distinctions that commonsense had long inclined us to adhere to."

But what determines "right" and "wrong" here? What might make it *right* (or, for that matter, wrong) for a method of evaluation to take the metalinguistic claim "She understands S" to be about someone's behavioral response to the sentence S but *wrong* (or right) for it to take that claim to be about a state of affairs that is distinct from the behavioral response? According to what standard are we to judge how to apply the terms "right" and "wrong" to a method of evaluation, and why should we accept that standard *itself* as right?

As I have shown, the theorist of communication is free to establish any method of evaluation that she or he chooses: for instance, a method according to which it would be judged "wrong" to draw a distinction between "acting as if one understands" and "really understanding" and "right" not to do so (or vice versa). However, one does not succeed in grounding that choice by appealing to another super- or metamethod: that is, a method that would determine whether that choice of method of evaluation was itself "right" or "wrong." For such a metamethod would also stand in need of justification. Consider the analogy: nothing could make it inherently right to apply metric rather than British standard conventions in measuring lengths. That choice could only be judged right by reference to another set of conventions. So, it is right to apply metric conventions in France, where social and governmental conventions require the use of the metric system. But what makes *those* conventions right? What *could* make them right, except another set of meta-metaconventions: for example, a United Nations convention enforcing the use of metrical conventions on all member governments? But again, what, except another set of conventions, could make that convention right? What matters is that there is nothing in the nature of lengths or in acts of measurement that could possibly make using the metric system inherently right; for "right" is a normative term whose use can only be grounded within a normative practice.

Similarly, although one may freely choose to apply a reductive method in evaluating metalinguistic claims, nothing could determine that the choice of that method is "right"—*or* that it is "wrong"—except another method (i.e., meta-method) of evaluation. So, according to the conventions—perhaps of some scientific association—one might be required to use only reductive methods of evaluation; any other method would be automatically judged "wrong". But then that metamethod would itself stand in need of evaluation as the "right" meta-method to apply. (Why should that scientific association's conventions be judged the "right" conventions?) And so on, *ad infinitum*.

Ultimately, what is demanded of a method of evaluating metalinguistic claims is that it enable the scientific community to determine whether it is justified to claim that an ape can do some or all of the communicational things that commonsense inclines us to believe that we humans do. Seen from this perspective, a reductive method of evaluation appears only to *pretend* to tackle this important assignment. That is, what a reductive method seems in fact to be doing is

1. Determining whether it is justified to claim that an ape can produce some of the same *behaviors* that we humans typically produce and then
2. *Rebaptizing those behaviors with metalinguistic labels, such as "understanding," "referring," "meaning," "following rules," and so on.*
3. The result is that it looks as if what had been determined, in (1), was that it was (or was not) justified to claim that an ape can do one or more of the communicational things that we humans can do—things that we typically call "understanding," "referring," "meaning," "following rules," and so on.

From the perspective of the commonsense picture of communication, a reductive method of evaluation thus seems to accomplish its assigned task by means of a rhetorical trick: amounting to something like pulling a metaphysical rabbit out of a behavioral hat. Analogously, it is not our use of the same evaluative terms that determines whether the evaluations you and I make of the children's swimming behavior is logically comparable. For we might be applying those terms according to different criteria. That is, we might be using different methods of evaluation. But, even if we were using different methods, it would still be relatively easy to deceive an onlooker to our judging ceremony, making him think, for instance, that the fact that you and I both give "very good" to Peter and "very poor" to Jim means that we agree in our evaluations of the children's behavior.

Similarly, the reductive method makes use of the same set of metalinguistic expressions as does commensense metalinguistic discourse; so it *appears* to produce metalinguistic claims that are comparable to the metalinguistic claims that we make in everyday discourse: for example, a claim that some person understands what was said or that she is referring to what happened yesterday. Both sets of claims appear to be about the same things and to assess them according to the same method of evaluation. But, because the reductive method applies those expressions according to different criteria from those applied in commonsense discourse (e.g., abolishing any distinction between acting as if one understands and actually understanding), different methods of evaluation are therefore in use. In this case, the claims produced by applying a reductive method cannot sensibly be compared with those to which we are inclined by commonsense. Because different methods of evaluation are being applied, different things are being talked about. A reductive method cannot tell us whether an ape or a human "understands the sentence," as we typically take that metalinguistic expression to mean (i.e., as we apply it) in everyday discourse. But this is what we want to know: to find out whether, like we humans, an ape can understand a sentence. Yet a reductive method can only tell us whether an ape or a human behaves in a certain way, although it will go on to characterize that behavior with the same metalinguistic expression "understands the sentence." Consequently, it is difficult to resist the impulse to affirm that, while such a method can establish whether apes and humans can *behave* alike, nevertheless the scientifically important questions—those about communicational abilities that the method was asked to solve—are all left unanswered.

However, this conclusion does *not* amount to the nonsensical claim that a reductive method of evaluating metalinguistic claims is wrong. For there is nothing inherently wrong about applying expressions differently from how they are applied in everyday discourse. There is nothing inherently wrong in studying the production of behavioral acts and then referring to those acts with metalinguistic terms whose use is differently evaluated in everyday discourse. But what this conclusion does mean is that a reductive method cannot easily satisfy the Commonality Requirement. To the extent that any method of evaluation shifts away from the commonsense picture of human communicational abilities, the scientific community—whose approach to communicational research, as I have shown, is rhetorically derived from that picture—will be comparatively less inclined to be persuaded that that method or any of its evaluative conclusions make sense. And so, also, the scientific community will be less inclined to adopt that method as a standard evaluative metric in communicational research. This tendency may well be reflected in the fact that while behavioristic methods are used frequently in the study of animal behavior, there has been and continues to be strong resistance to their use in the study of human abilities.

Methodological Operationalism

As I have shown, two structural variables are generated by an epistemological conception of what is required of any method for evaluating metalinguistic claims about apes. What I called the Epistemic Object variable is the focus of the rhetorical strategy underlying a reductive method of evaluation. The rhetorical strategy motivating the other main method of evaluation focuses instead on what I called the Epistemic Conviction variable. This strategy is directed at the question of what should count as sufficient evidence to establish the obtaining of the state of affairs that the metalinguistic claim is about.

I have argued that the Epistemic Conviction variable is a straightforward matter for a reductive method of evaluation. For a reductive method chooses as the Epistemic Object a *de re* state of affairs, the obtaining of which may be shown relatively simply. That is, it is comparatively easy to find "hard" empirical evidence to show that that *de re* state of affairs obtains—evidence that would be deemed sufficient, even according to the most rigorous scientific standards. Nevertheless, while a reductive method simplifies the matter of Epistemic Conviction, the cost incurred by this strategy is paid for in its clash with commonsense over the choice of Epistemic Object.

The rhetorically opposite strategy to reductivism is "operationalism," for an operational method of evaluation eschews any conflict with commonsense over the choice of Epistemic Object: the choice of the state of affairs that must be shown to obtain if a metalinguistic claim is to be evaluated as true. For instance, if an operational method is to evaluate as true the metalinguistic claim "Kanzi understands

'Would you put some grapes in the swimming pool?'", then it will not in principle be sufficient merely to establish that Kanzi *acts as if* he understands that request. According to an operational method, if that claim is true, then he must *in fact* understand the request, regardless of how he behaves. And so this is what an operational method requires to be established if the metalinguistic claim is to be evaluated as true. In other words, an operational definition of "understanding a sentence" preserves, and even draws on, the commonsense distinction between acting as if one understands and actually understanding. Similarly, it conforms with our inclination to distinguish between acting as if one is referring to an object, acting as if one means what one says, acting as if one is following a given rule, acting as if one knows what language is for, and so on, and *actually doing so*.

However, by rejecting a reductive "solution" to the problem generated by the epistemological conception, an operational method is left with the thorny matter of Epistemic Conviction: *What should a method of evaluation count as sufficient evidence to justify a claim that the state of affairs that must obtain for the metalinguistic claim to be true, does in fact obtain?* In particular, how much and what sort of evidence is *sufficient* to establish such a claim? Clearly, this question is made especially difficult by the distinction between acting as if one understands and actually understanding. Finding sufficient evidence for the former is one thing; for the latter, the task is more daunting. To this problem must be added the fact, as I have already shown, that the rhetorical onus is on she who *affirms* a communicative ability of an ape: the truth of that affirmation must be established beyond the reach of skeptical doubt. Given this further requirement, the task of determining how much and what kind of evidence is sufficient may well appear impossible.

Faced with this challenge, the operationalist makes a crucial preliminary move: he changes the question. The orientation of the question is reversed, so that it poses not an *inductive-evidential* problem but a *deductive-explanatory* one. In other words, instead of asking how much of what sort of evidence would be sufficient to establish inductively that the required state of affairs obtains, the operational strategy asks: *Given that a certain behavioral act (or pattern of acts) occurs, the obtaining of what state of affairs would best explain that occurrence?* But how can answering this question provide a means of accomplishing the task set by the Epistemic Conviction variable? How can it help determine what evidence should be taken as sufficient to establish the claim that a given communicational state obtains?

Suppose that current theory holds that the occurrence of behavioral act (or pattern of acts) B is best explained by the metalinguistic claim that communicational state C obtains. For example, every time Stuart is given the request "Press the red button," he is observed to respond by pressing the red button in front of him (act B); on these grounds, the theory concludes that the best explanation for Stuart's behavior is that he understands the request (i.e., communicational state C obtains). It should be clear how this kind of approach simplifies the problem of Epistemic Conviction. For, given the theory's conclusion and the grounds on which it is based, the production of act B will constitute powerful evidence for the claim that state C obtains. If the fact that C obtains is what will best explain an occurrence of B, then doesn't it follow to take the occurrence of B as strong evidence of the obtaining of C?

"Strong" and "powerful" evidence, yes; but not logically conclusive. So the question would seem to remain: Is the evidence *sufficient*? Consider the following illustrative example, excerpted from Cheney and Seyfarth's influential *How Monkeys See the World* (1990). They begin by noting that the vervet monkeys that they and others studied "certainly seemed to be using (alarm) calls to denote external referents"—that is, to refer to the predators in the surrounding area (1990, 104). They cite Struhsaker (1967) to support this observation. They note, furthermore, that "in human language . . . the referential function of signals is not in doubt" (1990, 109). But can the same thing justifiably be said of a vervet's signal? Do the vervets' alarms *really* function in this way as well? Do their signals really denote external referents (the approaching predators), in the manner *we know* human signals do?

More to the point, *how do you tell* if vervets' alarms really denote external referents? How can it be established whether such a communicational state obtains: that is, the communicational state that must obtain if the metalinguistic claim "Vervet alarm calls denote external referents" is true? In an experimental test you might be able to determine that a particular vervet *acts as if* the alarms have a referential function; but how much of what sort of evidence would be sufficient to establish—in the face of skeptical doubts—that that is what is *actually* the case?

To answer this difficult metalinguistic question, Cheney and Seyfarth (1990, 9) apply a method they describe as "operationally" based. That is, they transform the question from an evidential issue into an explanatory one (106): How can we best explain the way a vervet behaves when she hears an alarm call? Accordingly, they designed a test of various explanatory hypotheses by means of playback experiments. In these experiments, the authors artificially reproduced the alarm calls in order to see "how variation in a call's acoustic features and variation in other contextual events affected the monkey's responses to a particular vocalization" (106). The authors then examined the experiments' results to see which of the explanatory hypotheses best fit the monkeys' behavioral responses. Only one of the four hypotheses put forward, that which I have italicized in the quoted passage that follows, explains the alarms as having a referential function. According to Cheney and Seyfarth's theory of reference, if alarm calls denote particular external referents, then each such alarm will elicit a consistent set of responses, with each such set being solely a function of the vocalization's acoustic form.

> Playback experiments allowed us to test these alternative explanations. . . . If vervet alarm calls were simply general alerting signals, the monkeys should have responded in similar ways to all of the acoustically different calls. If call meaning was determined primarily by context, then the response to each alarm should have varied depending on the context in which it was presented. By contrast, *if each call's meaning was determined largely by its acoustic features, a given call type (leopard, eagle, or snake alarm) should have elicited a functionally consistent set of responses regardless of the context in which it was presented.* Finally, if calls conveyed information primarily about the emotional state of the caller and only secondarily about the type of predator that had been seen, it should have been possible to blur the distinction among responses to the different call types by varying acoustic features associated with a signaler's level of excitement. (106–7)

After describing the playback experiments used to test these hypotheses on the vervets, Cheney and Seyfarth report their results. Predictions of the third explanatory hypothesis are borne out: "each type of alarm call . . . elicited a distinct set of responses" (1990, 107). They conclude by explaining these results as follows: "Each type of alarm call refers to, or denotes, a particular type of predator. Different types of alarms are distinguished by their different acoustic properties and convey a meaning that is relatively independent of the context in which they are given" (110).

Let us return to the general question. Even if we grant Cheney and Seyfarth's argument that the best way to explain how the vervets behave is to attribute a referential function to their calls, the question still remains: Is that behavior sufficient evidence to establish the claim that the vervets' alarms do *in fact* refer to types of predators?

At the very least, we must recognize that there are two quite different questions here:

1. The question whether the claim that communicational state C obtains (e.g., that vervet calls have a referential function) is *the best explanation* for behavioral pattern B (e.g., the behavior observed in the playback experiments)
2. The question whether B is *sufficient to establish the truth* of the claim that C obtains.

Particular kinds of evaluative techniques are applied to the issue of determining which of all candidate explanations is *the best* for a given set of behavioral data. According to this "language game" of behavioral explanation, whether we can justify that one explanation is the best explanation for behavioral pattern B will typically depend on such matters as: how that explanation accords with current theoretical opinion; whether any other explanations have been proposed for B; whether there are any means of experimentally falsifying the proposed explanation or its competitors; and what one counts as an explanation (as compared to a description, or a reformulation, or an interpretation, etc.). At the limit, the explanation may qualify as "the best" merely by default because no alternative explanation has been proposed.

Given these evaluative techniques, it is understandable that Cheney and Seyfarth might be taken to have confirmed that their explanation of the vervets' observed behavioral patterns is indeed "the best": that is, their metalinguistic claim that the vervets' alarm calls have a referential function. Be that as it may; nevertheless, it remains the case that the observation of those behavioral patterns does not guarantee the truth of that claim. For, as the excerpts quoted reveal, the argument supporting that explanation contains two components. There is, first, the following conditional hypothesis, linking communicational state C with the production of behavioral pattern B:

> If the calls have a referential function (C), then each call will elicit a functionally consistent set of responses from the vervets (B).

Second, there is the observation, in the playback experiments, of the vervets' production of a functionally consistent set of responses to each call—the observation of B.

Yet, even if we grant the truth of that conditional hypothesis and accept the results of the playback experiments—which, together, would typically be taken to establish the explanatory claim—nevertheless, the observation of behavior B cannot logically guarantee the truth of the claim that C obtains. For the hypothesis does not state that B can *only* be produced when C obtains. *If C, then B* does not imply *If B, then C*. Nor has the latter been shown. (It's difficult to imagine how it could be shown, unless the obtaining of communicational state C could be independently identified; but in this case there would be no need of a method of metalinguistic evaluation.) The possibility is therefore left open that *B is the effect of some other cause*. The vervets may behave as they do for some reason other than that claimed by Seyfarth and Cheney: that is, their claim that vervet calls denote external referents. They may *act as if* their calls denote external referents, even though this is not *in fact* the case. Neither the truth of the conditional hypothesis nor of the experimental results is sufficient—singly or jointly—to establish the truth of the claim that the vervets' calls have a referential function. Yet what is needed, under an epistemological conception, for a method of evaluating metalinguistic claims is *sufficient evidence* to establish the truth of such claims.

In this case, one must reconsider the question already raised. How can the operational strategy of converting a question about evidence into one about explanation determine what evidence should be taken as sufficient to establish the claim that a given communicational state obtains? How can it accomplish the rhetorical task set by the Epistemic Conviction variable?

The answer is that, by converting a question about evidence into an explanatory question, *the operational strategy makes it possible to shift the onus of proof from the ape language researcher*—who affirms the metalinguistic claim—*to the skeptic*, who denies that that affirmation is justified. As we have seen with the Cheney and Seyfarth example, the metalinguistic claim that C obtains (i.e., vervet calls have a referential function) at least provides *a* coherent explanation of the production of the act B (i.e., the vervets' responses to those calls). And it is an explanation, moreover, that has been judged "the best," according to the kinds of evaluative techniques just discussed. Were we simply to accept a skeptical appraisal of that metalinguistic claim, the judgment reached by the application of these techniques would be invalidated, and we would no longer have any similarly validated explanation of why B occurred at all. Indeed, those very evaluative techniques—and any other conclusions they have led us to—would themselves be put into question.

Therefore, within the "language game" of behavioral evaluation, any explanation that has been validated by that language game's evaluative techniques will always be rhetorically preferred to no explanation at all. And the onus will be on he who denies that explanation to demonstrate that another one should be evaluated as "even better." "Sure, it's possible to criticize this explanation and the strength of its evidential support. For every explanation is open to some skeptical criticism. But until you come up with a better explanation of your own to replace it, it cannot be overturned." In other words, unless the skeptic can come up with a "better" (according to the evaluative techniques of the language game) explanation for B's occurrence—that is, an explanation that does *not* affirm the obtaining of C—

the metalinguistic claim that C obtains will retain its rhetorical validation. And this validation will be extended to the behavioral evidence supporting that claim. Given this reasoning, if the skeptic wants to argue that that evidence is not in fact sufficient to establish the metalinguistic claim, the onus is on her first to provide a "better" explanation of the behavior which that claim is taken to explain.

So, how specifically would an operational approach help us formulate a method for evaluating a metalinguistic claim about an ape? Suppose one wants to formulate a method of evaluation to determine whether it is justified to claim that Kanzi really understands the request "Press the red button" or whether, as the critics insist, he is merely behaving *as if* he understands it (that is, whether, as Steven Pinker insists, Kanzi "just doesn't get it" [Pinker 1994, 340]). According to the epistemological conception, we have to determine what behavioral evidence would be sufficient to justify the claim. Suppose, furthermore, that current theory tells us that the kind of behavior that the metalinguistic claim "She or he understands 'Press the red button'" *would be the best explanation for* is the following: on hearing the request, the addressee presses a red button. Given these imaginary circumstances, an operational approach would lead us to choose the occurrence of that behavioral response as sufficient evidence to justify the claim. And, if Kanzi did indeed respond to the request by pressing the red button, our method of evaluation would determine that the metalinguistic claim is justified. At least until a "better" explanation could be found.

As the last remark suggests, an operational method of evaluating metalinguistic claims about apes remains vulnerable to a particular kind of rhetorical strategy: a strategy that has been used to great effect in generative linguistic critiques of ape language research. Suppose that an operational method takes the production of act B to be sufficient to establish the claim that communicational state C obtains, and that it does so because the claim that C obtains has been shown to be the best way to explain why B occurs. However, imagine a critic objects that if communicational state C really obtains, then not only will it be possible to observe act B being produced, but also acts D and E. For example, if someone really understands the request "Press the red button," then not only will she press the red button when requested to do so (act B), she will also point to the red button when asked "Where is the red button?" (act D) and will refrain from pushing the red button when requested "Don't press the red button" (act E).

Does an ape do these things too, the critic asks? For *any human* who understands the request to "Press the red button" will also be able to perform these two acts D and E as well. What if the ape cannot? Isn't that a good reason to question whether "He understands the request" really is the best explanation for his behavior? Wouldn't a *better theory* of understanding than the one we have been operating with so far tell us that "He understands the request" is the best explanation of behavior B *only if* the subject produces behaviors D and E as well? In this case, it would be more parsimonious—and, for this reason, "better"—to replace that explanation with one that explains what the ape does as something short of *full* understanding: call it "quunderstanding" (by analogy to what Kripke [1982] calls "quaddition," an arithmetical function similar to "real" addition). Quunderstanding would be a communicational state of affairs that is somewhat similar to real understanding, except that it does not enable the subject to respond to sentences in the two further ways described. If all an ape has been shown to do is quunderstand a sentence, then we still really do not know whether he can actually *understand* a sentence as we humans do.

Criticism of this rhetorical type has in fact been addressed to Savage-Rumbaugh's claims about Kanzi's ability to understand sentences. For example, in his article "Can an ape understand a sentence?" Tomasello (1994) accepts that Savage-Rumbaugh et al. (1993) have made a strong case for the claim that Kanzi can understand certain kinds of spoken English sentences. However, he maintains that, for various reasons, a *better explanation* of Kanzi's responses to test sentences would be to say that he achieves something short of the full understanding that we humans eventually develop. He argues that Kanzi does not seem able to make sense of sentences including recursive structures and, even more significantly, does not "have control over . . . the grammatical category of the verb" (384).

> He has something like a grammatical category of noun allowing him to comprehend (and perhaps produce) newly learned object labels in the same sentence frames in which previously learned object labels have been used. He has yet to form any class of verbs or subclass thereof, however, that would license word order or other grammatical generalizations across events. (384)

It is clear that underlying Tomasello's argument is the premise that these are things we humans *do* and that they make up an important, ineliminable component of what understanding a sentence consists in for us. Therefore, if Kanzi doesn't appear to grasp recursive structures or construct grammatical generalizations, then what he is doing is *better explained as something other than what we do* when we understand a sentence: quunderstanding.

I mention this example not because Tomasello (1994) is one of the more trenchant critiques of Savage-Rumbaugh's metalinguistic claims about Kanzi; for, on the contrary, he concurs with many of her most important findings. Instead, its function here is to indicate the slippery rhetorical slope down which Tomasello's criticism takes the first hesitant steps and which linguistic critics have turned into something like an Olympic bobsled run. Tomasello indicates just two kinds of behavioral responses that, he feels, Kanzi ought to be able to produce if the behavioral responses that he *does* produce (e.g., putting some grapes in the swimming pool) are to be best explained by claiming that "he understands the sentence." For when we humans understand a sentence, we *can* produce the former two responses.

But why should we stop at two? Any human who understands the request "Would you put some grapes in the swimming pool?" can do a lot more than simply respond to it by putting some grapes in the swimming pool. He can point to the grapes and to the swimming pool. He can respond appropriately to "Would you put a grape in the swimming pool?" and "Would you please *not* put any grapes in the swimming pool?" and "Would you put the grapes that are in the box in the bottom of the refrigerator into the swimming pool?" He can explain what "swimming pool" means and determine whether the original request means the same thing as "Go to the swimming pool and put in some grapes." He can probably tell you how many words are in that request and maybe even something about how they each relate to the others in the sentence. And so on.

So, if these are the kinds of things that any human who understands that sentence can do, doesn't it make sense for a method of evaluation to require that an ape be able to do those things too: that is, if that method is to evaluate as justified the claim "He understands the sentence"? And, if the ape cannot do all these things, would it not appear that the claim that he understands is an inappropriate explanation of his reponse and that it would be better explained by something like "quunderstanding"? For example, it is in this vein that Tomasello argues that instead of applying generalized grammatical categories—as we humans apparently do when we understand a sentence—a better explanation of what Kanzi does is something that falls short of that. Naturally, Tomasello doesn't use the expression "quunderstanding." Instead, he suggests that what he calls the "the Verb Island hypothesis" is what Kanzi applies when he hears a verb in a sentence, instead of applying the generalized grammatical categories that we adult humans apply when we understand (Tomasello 1994, 383). Seeing how easily this game is played, linguist critics have upped the ante a great deal higher.

In other words, there is nothing to prevent the linguistic critic from availing herself of the possibilities inherent in the operational approach. She can go so far as to demand that *if it is to be justified to affirm of an ape any* ONE *of the metalinguistic claims that are typically affirmed of humans*, then it must also be justified to affirm ALL, or at least all those which this or that linguistic theory represents as implicationally related. To see how much sense this makes within linguistics, one need only consider the perspectives of the two dominent theoretical schools of this century. For instance, according to Saussure's structuralist linguistics, the meaning of any sign is structurally defined by its relation to every other sign in the language. So it would not be possible to understand one word, or for that matter a single sentence, without knowing the whole language.

Or, if we turn to Noam Chomsky's school of generative linguistics, we find that—at least according to one its most prominent members—to understand a given sentence one's brain has first to "parse" it (Pinker 1994, 196). And this can only be done if one possesses an internalized generative grammar, with all its attendant principles, parameters, rules, lexical and phrasal categories, dictionary entries, cases, and traces, as well as the mental parsing program for teasing out all these and other structural features in the sentence's grammatical and semantic organization (196–201). Can Kanzi do all this? Does he possess all this mental paraphernalia? If not then, according to generative theory, *he cannot possibly understand a sentence.* So doesn't it make sense, if we want a rigorous means of determining whether Kanzi really understands any sentences, to require that he be *shown* to do and possess each and every one of the things that are apparently *necessary* to the ability to understand a sentence (and all of which, the theory tells us, we humans do and possess)? For, if any one of them is absent, then the best explanation of Kanzi's response to the sentence cannot really be that he understands it, but rather that the communicational state that actually obtains is something like quunderstanding.

Thus, a linguist who—for one reason or another—is troubled by Savage-Rumbaugh's claim that Kanzi understands the request to put some grapes in the swimming pool and who wants to formulate an operational method of evaluation that reflects this worry, can insist that that claim ought to be evaluated as the "best" explanation of Kanzi's response *only if* it can be shown that it is justified to attribute to Kanzi more or less all the communicational abilities that this or that theory of language attributes to an adult human. For we human speakers of English, who easily understand such requests, have countless other communicational abilities as well; and, according to most of the dominant linguistic theories of the age, these abilities all form a complex implicational web. And these theories, and the implicational links they draw, have deep roots in the commonsense picture of communication. After all, can someone really be said to understand a sentence if he cannot understand each of its words? But can he really understand a word if he cannot *say* what it means? Can he understand grammatical relations if he doesn't understand the words thus related? And how can he grasp any of the meanings conveyed in human language if he doesn't understand any of the words, and so any of the sentences, and so any of its grammar?

Adopting an operationalist method of evaluating metalinguistic claims has the advantage of avoiding a clash with commonsense over what such claims are conceived to be about. But it has the disadvantage of making it methodologically plausible for the critic of primate research to demand that, for a metalinguistic claim about an ape to be evaluated as justified, *the ape must be proven to be a human.*

Metalanguage as Cultural Technique

To understand a sentence means to understand a language. To understand a language means to be master of a technique.
Wittgenstein, *Philosophical Investigations*, section 199

This chapter began by arguing that no progress will be made in answering metalinguistic questions like 1 to 4, repeated here, until there is agreement in the scientific community on common methods by which hypothetical answers to such questions are to be evaluated.

1. Can a laboratory-reared ape, such as Kanzi, really understand what a spoken English sentence means?
2. Do the signs and lexigrams that some apes have learned to produce really mean or refer to anything?
3. Are any of these apes, when producing or responding to communicational behavior, really following (even simple) linguistic rules?
4. Does any such ape know what it is doing when it produces or responds to language? That is, does it really understand, as we do, that language is for communicating thoughts and intentions to others, for speaking truly (and sometimes falsely) of the world, and for attaining particular communicational goals?

As I have shown, any method of evaluating a metalinguistic claim about an ape must satisfy two *logical* requirements. First, scientists must use the same method of evaluation if a comparison between their evaluations is to make any sense. Second, that method must be applied equally to both apes and humans; for what we want to know is whether an ape possesses any of the communicational abilities *that we know we humans possess*. Consequently, any metalinguistic claim about an ape must be evaluated by the same method as is applied to a comparable claim about a human—otherwise, the claims are *not* comparable. If this Equality Requirement is not satisfied, then comparing a claim commonly made about a human with one asserted about an ape will not be a matter of comparing "like with like." Instead, it would be like comparing my evaluation of Bobby's behavior in the swimming pool with your evaluation of Henry's behavior, when each of us is using a different method of evaluation. Such a comparison can only produce nonsense. And the same is true if the Commonality Requirement is not satisfied. If a generative linguist and a behaviorist psychologist each assert something about Kanzi's communicational abilities, it can only make sense to compare their assertions if each assertion is "measured" by the same method of evaluation.

In addition to these two logical requirements, further *rhetorical* requirements are typically imposed on the task of formulating a method for evaluating a claim about an ape's communicational abilities. These rhetorical requirements are derived from what Wittgenstein calls the *raw material*: in other words, what we are commonsensically *inclined to say* in discourse about communicational behavior and abilities. For it is these discursive inclinations—which are illustrated in what I have been calling the commonsense picture of communication—that lead us, by a fairly direct route, to the epistemological conception of what a method of metalinguistic evaluation *must* do and, equally significantly, to the conviction that that conception is the *only* way to make sense of that task.

Of course, the epistemological conception is far from being a controversial way of looking at the task of evaluating metalinguistic or, for that matter, cognitive claims. The modern scientific study of language is founded on it. The cognitive theories examined by Shanker in the previous chapter *all* incorporate an epistemological conception. And it is hardly surprising, for the steps by which one gets from "commonsense" to the epistemological conception are all patently obvious. After all, it is surely nothing more than commonsense to expect that a method of evaluation will require any claim to establish that *that which it claims is in fact true*. (Surely we expect such a method only to evaluate the claim as justified if it is really true?) Nor is it a strain on commonsense to interpret that requirement as demanding that the state of affairs that must obtain, if the claim is true, actually *be shown to obtain*. (Again, we must surely expect that if a metalinguistic claim is to be judged true, then it must be shown that that which it *says* is a fact—e.g., Kanzi understands this sentence, this keyboard symbol refers to that toy, Kanzi interprets sentences using the Verb Island hypothesis, etc.—*actually* is *a fact*!) Finally, wouldn't it be absurd to object to interpreting this last demand in terms of a rule prescribing that *enough evidence, of the right kind*, be provided to establish that that state of affairs does in fact obtain? And this is, after all, nothing more and nothing less than what the epistemological conception requires.

At the same time, one should keep in mind that it is perfectly understandable that we should have these commonsense inclinations—the *raw material* of the rhetorical patterns here analyzed. For they are not arbitrary, or even reasoned, options that—in order to avoid their methodological consequences—we could just as easily free ourselves of. On the contrary, their roots are deeply embedded in the habitual soil of our everyday lives: in our routine, intuitive ways of interacting with each other and making sense of those interactions, both to ourselves and to others (see Taylor 1997, chap. 1). Were we to abandon these commonsense ways of talking and thinking about our communicational acts and abilities, about the relationship between these acts and abilities and the physical, social, and cultural world around us, and—at a further reflexive level—about these very ways of talking and thinking, we would lose all that we know ordinary life to be. We are "inclined" to the commonsense picture of communication—and so also to an epistemological conception of metalinguistic evaluation—because we feel unable to imagine any other possibility.

However, while on the one hand, we are powerfully inclined to the epistemological conception of what a method of metalinguistic (or cognitive) evaluation must do, on the other hand, *the central argument of this book is that it is the epistemological conception of that task that bears primary responsibility for the frustrating inability of the scientific community to come up with a common evaluative method.* And without a common method of metalinguistic evaluation it will be impossible to make real progress on any questions about the communicational (or cognitive) abilities of apes (and other nonhuman animals).

I have presented an analysis of the two main types of rhetorical strategy being used today by those who are trying to develop such a method: reductivism and operationalism. These analyses were intended to present paradigmatic illustrations of the two contrasting types of rhetorical possibilities made available by an epistemological conception of metalinguistic evaluation. However, as Stuart Shanker shows in his analysis of the historical and contemporary patterns of thought in cognitive science, most methods of metalinguistic and cognitive evaluation are supported by arguments that *combine* both these strategies. For example, in the published texts of most animal language researchers, one will find both operationalist and reductivist arguments employed to motivate the author's methodological claims; and which of these is employed at any one moment seems to be a function not of rhetorical consistency but of the characteristics of the particular metalinguistic issue at hand. To the extent that a method of evaluation employs a reductivist strategy, it solves the problem of Epistemic Conviction by reducing to observable behavior the state of affairs that must obtain if the metalinguistic claim is to be evaluated as true. Still, because it can tell us nothing about that which commonsense inclines us to call understanding, meaning, referring, and so on, its strategic "solution" to that methodological problem amounts only to a rhetorical illusion. To take the result of applying such a method as providing answers to the questions motivating scientific research—for example, whether, like us, apes can understand, refer, mean, and so on—would amount to illogical nonsense.

Operationalism, on the other hand, does not clash with commonsense in this way. Instead, by transforming the problem of Epistemic Conviction from an evidential to an explanatory matter, an operationalist strategy imposes on any method of metalinguistic evaluation the requirement to prove that the explanatory theory justifying its evaluations is the "best" theory available. The search for sufficient evidence is thus recast as a quest for "the best theory" of communicational abilities. The rhetorical consequence is that a specific question about an ape's communicational ability—asking, for example, whether Kanzi understands or Austin refers or Panbanisha means what she says—is a matter to be addressed no longer by practices of empirical observation but rather within the language games of theoretical argument. And to the extent that a given explanatory theory of communicational abilities represents any one such ability as implicationally related to any others, that theory requires a method that evaluates the attribution of that ability to an ape to establish that the ape in fact possesses them *all*.

The conclusion of the analyses given in the last two sections should therefore be clear: *Each of these rhetorical strategies is a street leading to a methodological cul-de-sac.* Yet what keeps luring us down these same dead end streets, again and again, is the epistemological conception. For reductivism and operationalism are strategies designed to address particular *kinds* of methodological problems, and these kinds of problems only arise under an epistemological conception of the task of metalinguistic evaluation. The epistemological conception represents understanding a sentence, referring to someone, performing a particular speech act, knowing a language, and so on, as states of affairs: those that must obtain if the claims about them are true. And it represents the behavior that we observe as *evidence* for or against such claims. Given these conceptual presuppositions, it is only natural that we expect a method for evaluating metalinguistic claims to determine *if that evidence is sufficient to establish that those states of affairs do in fact obtain.* Reductivism and operationalism are two strategies specifically designed to respond to this (rhetorically generated) expectation.

And yet again—because it cannot be repeated too often—the rhetorical roots of the epistemological conception run deep into our "raw," intuitive inclinations in everyday, practical metalinguistic discourse and, indeed, into the foundational role which that discourse plays in the taken-for-granted ways in which we participate in and make sense of even the most routine events in everyday life. But if this is true, then what hope can we have to break the conceptual spell of the epistemological conception? As the analysis of its rhetorical consequences shows, *break it we must.* But how? How could we possibly keep ourselves from succumbing to its allure? And how could we learn to resist the temptation—when we consider questions like 1 to 4 stated earlier or like those discussed by Shanker in chapter 2—to walk headlong yet again into the methodological dead end of giving those questions an epistemological interpretation? The experience of the last 350 years of Western thinking on the cognitive and communicational issues will hardly give one any grounds for optimism.

Nevertheless, at least in principle, the answer to our dilemma is obvious. We need to see metalinguistic questions differently; we need to respond to them with different inclinations, different compulsions. For the source of our dilemma, the *raw material,* is a compulsion: a rhetorical compulsion. When, as scientists of communication and cognition, we read Savage-Rumbaugh's description of an occasion when Kanzi understood something she said, we feel *compelled* to reply "Yes, but does he *really*?" And, taking a confident step into the cul-de-sac, we feel compelled to see our skeptical question as raising epistemological issues and, so, to address it accordingly. Yet, while it is essential that we acknowledge this compulsion, we do not *have to* give in to it. We do not *have to* respond to this commonsense compulsion to impose an epistemological interpretation on the kind of metalinguistic description that Savage-Rumbaugh provides in chapter 1. Nothing *forces* us down this road. On the contrary, some compulsions, as we all know, have to be resisted; and most of us are more or less good at doing so. There are well-known methods designed to help us do so. And, equally important, we all already have plenty of experience responding to metalinguistic claims in ways that do *not* treat them as raising epistemological matters: that is, when those claims are about our fellow humans. Of course, we may occasionally reply to such a claim with "Yes, but does s/he *really*?" But, as I have argued, such a response is not and, significantly, *could not be* the norm. And going one step further, by interpreting and treating that response epistemologically, would be an absurdity.

At the very least, reflecting on our everyday experiences of metalinguistic claims should help us to appreciate the following. *If*—against the rhetorical grain of these "commonsense" inclinations—someone *does* feel inclined, as Savage-Rumbaugh and others undoubtedly do, to speak of an ape like Kanzi, in certain circumstances, using the same metalinguistic terms as those that we ordinarily employ in speaking of a fellow human in similar circumstances, then it would make little sense to respond to (treat, evaluate, criticize) the resultant metalinguistic claim as if it existed *sui generis*. For, as Savage-Rumbaugh's narratives make palpably clear—and as our experiences of everyday understanding-claims should confirm—such a claim exists not as an autonomous, empirically based hypothesis, but as a functional component of our lives with the ape or humans concerned. As an instance of practical metalinguistic discourse, it is integrated within our form of life, which is in turn made up of routine, interactional techniques by which we cooperate with the apes or humans concerned, contend with them, try to bend them to our will, depend on their reactions to accomplish joint interactional tasks, express our pleasure or displeasure at their actions, treat them as moral agents, and so on. That is, speaking of our neighbor or of Kanzi in metalinguistic (or, for that matter, cognitive) terms is consequential for how we can "live with" them in these sorts of ways; just as how we "live with" them has consequences for our inclination to speak of them in certain ways (see Smith 1988, ch. 7). Speaking of them thus is a functional component of the interactional techniques that constitute our form of life.

However, when we take one such metalinguistic (or cognitive) remark out of this practical context-of-occurrence and evaluate it epistemologically—asking *what* it is true of and whether *that state of affairs obtains*—we treat that remark as if it existed *sui generis*: as if it had an identity (in this case, an epistemological identity) that is independent of that context-of-occurrence. In so doing, we extract it from the cultural soil of life, from which it draws its nourishment and to whose ecology it makes an essential contribution. No wonder that the result of such an extraction is to effect an immediate and paralyzing halt in the growth of knowledge and understanding.

Looking at Savage-Rumbaugh's metalinguistic claims from this perspective may give us the means to mount some resistance against our rhetorical compulsion to conceive, and so treat them, epistemologically. For it would be a non sequitur to extract one of her claims from the natural, interactional context of which it forms an integral part and treat it instead as if it were a "primitive" empirical hypothesis to which an epistemologically conceived method of evaluation should be applied. While this might satisfy the kind of rhetorical compulsion discussed above, it would also lead to at least two unwelcome effects. First, it would take the first step down the road into the kind of rhetorical cul-de-sacs mapped out above. But more fundamentally, it would treat Savage-Rumbaugh's claim as if it were something which it is not. In other words, if in order to subject it to an epistemologically conceived evaluation, one extracted her claim from the interactional techniques of which it is an integral part, the effect would be to change the identity of the claim. The result would not be a more rigorous or more objective evaluation of that claim; *it would be the evaluation of a different claim.* Analogously, if you evaluate my assertion "Bobby's swimming pool behavior is very good" by reference not to my own method of evaluation but to yours, the claim that you evaluate—although misleadingly formulated with the same expressions—will not be that which I had asserted. That is to say, you will fail to evaluate my claim.

This argument has a parallel in discussions of attributions of *value*. We can imagine a set of circumstances in which attributing a value of twenty thousand dollars to a chair—that is, saying something like "This is worth twenty thousand dollars"—fits perfectly. In order to make better sense of this imaginary scene we would have to fill it out with such details as the age of the chair, its period style, its maker, what current opinion in the art world says about the chair or ones like it, who is selling it, who is considering buying it, their financial circumstances, where the discussion is taking place, how much other interest in the chair has been expressed, how much other chairs of its type have recently sold for, how many others of its type are known to exist, and so on. The attribution of a value of twenty thousand dollars *can* only be seen to make sense if it is taken as "embedded" in a context characterized by details of this and similar kinds. As such, the identity of that attribution—what is actually being said—is inseparable from its function *as an integrated component of* that context (see Harris 1995, ch. 2).

But what sense could we make of the attribution if we extracted it from that context and treated it instead as having a *sui generis* identity and validity? In other words, if we completely ignore all the kinds of details just mentioned, how can we possibly evaluate the justification of such an attribution of value to the chair? Or of *any* attribution of value? Would it not be absurd to think that value inheres in a material object completely independently of all such contextual features and that, therefore, to justify an attribution of value one must demonstrate that the state of affairs in which that inherent value consists must be shown to obtain? (To see this absurdity, one need only imagine a Samuel Beckett play in which there is a nuclear holocaust, leaving nothing in the world except this chair and the two people dickering over its price. In what sense could they even be conceived as talking about the same thing as the buyer and seller just evoked?) An epistemological method of evaluating attributions of value would clearly be absurd (which is not to say that it hasn't frequently been proposed or that it will not be again). Why, in the analogy that Smith (1988) draws attention to, should we not see the same absurdity in giving a similarly *sui generis* treatment to a metalinguistic claim?

An appropriate method of evaluating the actual claims made by Savage-Rumbaugh must be one that takes into account—to the extent possible—the integration of those metalinguistic and cognitive claims into particular kinds of interactional techniques and contexts: particular kinds of "language games" and the forms of life to which they contribute. It is for this reason that this book begins with Savage-Rumbaugh's extended narrative of Kanzi's upbringing as well as many interactional episodes from her life with Kanzi. For the claims she makes about Kanzi's behavior and abilities must be seen—if we are to make sense of them—as emergent properties of the lived story that is partially recounted in that narrative: not as *sui generis* propositional atoms. And it is as the former rather than the latter that those statements must be evaluated, if their sense is to be grasped and assessed accordingly. One way of putting this might be to say that coming to an appropriate evaluation of those claims—learning how to evaluate those claims sensibly—involves coming to know Kanzi. The appropriate method of evaluation is one that becomes, to the extent possible, a part of that process.

Of course, an argument like this *might* be taken to imply the conclusion that only Savage-Rumbaugh (and a few of her colleagues) can really know if Kanzi understands what she says to him (or whether his words refer, or whether he knows what language is for, etc.). And this reasoning might suggest that the foundations of one of her metalinguistic claims about Kanzi are necessarily different from those that could support a superficially similar claim that I or anyone else in the scientific community might make about Kanzi—or, for that matter, about a fellow human being. For after all, while I have observed Kanzi in person and on tape for many hours, this is nothing compared to the years that Savage-Rumbaugh has spent living in close company and interacting with Kanzi. As the narrative in chapter 1 shows, they are accustomed to participating together in using a great number of interactional techniques; they share, in this respect, a common form of life. Kanzi and I do not. In this case it might be concluded that, if the foundations for her claims about Kanzi's communicational abilities inhere in these shared techniques and common form of life, then any metalinguistic claim that *I* might make about Kanzi could not possibly have the same foundations. The reasons why *she* is justified in speaking of Kanzi as understanding something she said, it would seem, cannot be *my* reasons. And the same would go, of course, for the reasons of the rest of the members of the scientific community.

However, how is this situation different from those in which we evaluate claims made about the communicational behavior and abilities of many of our fellow humans? Imagine, for instance, that you told me that a man I have never met—call him John—had understood a particular remark that you made? Here, also, I have no firsthand experience on the basis of which to evaluate your claim. Imagine also that, for some reason, I am prevented from obtaining any: say, John recently died. Of course, I would typically be inclined to take the accuracy of your opinion for granted. That would only be commonsense. But we are ruling that out here for the sake of the comparison with Savage-Rumbaugh and Kanzi, where commonsense inclines us in a different direction. So what would I do? I would doubtless listen very closely to your description of John's response to what you had said; I would consider how well you had known him and how often and how successfully you had interacted with him. I would consider whether the way that you explained the justification for your claim matched my own expectations. And so on. In other words, I would do the best I could with the methods available: that is, with the practical methods by which we ordinarily determine if someone understands what we or someone else says. But the point is that it would be illogical to abandon those practical methods and substitute another in their place, simply because there were obstacles to their normal application. If the problem is to get more of something that we are lacking—for example, the kind of firsthand experience just described—it would be absurd to think that the way that problem must be solved is by obtaining *something else in its place.*

It is clear that no one except Savage-Rumbaugh herself (and perhaps a few of her colleagues) can ever have had her firsthand experience of interacting with Kanzi as he grew up: the developing form of life in which her claims about his communicational abilities are founded. But the solution to the *practical* problem that this raises for the task of evaluating those claims is not to commit the *logical* non sequitur of shifting to another, theoretically conceived method of evaluation. Instead, it is the record of those experiences that we in the scientific community should examine if we want to see the justification for those claims. We should study her narrative descriptions, as well as those of her colleagues and of others who have observed her interacting with Kanzi. If possible, we should attempt to observe their interactions ourselves, or at least view the many videotapes of those interactions that are currently available. By means like these we should gradually be able to make better sense of the justification for her claims about Kanzi's abilities. The obstacles that such a method might encounter would be of a practical nature and would be more or less surmountable depending on the equally practical circumstances. But, in contrast, the rhetorical obstacles that an epistemologically conceived method of evaluation would encounter, as I have shown, are insurmountable *in principle.*

These methodological recommendations might be thought to amount to a conclusion that many in the scientific community would perceive as disappointing: that is, the conclusion that unlike the claims made in many other scientific fields, metalinguistic and cognitive claims about apes and other nonhuman animals cannot be evaluated according to the scientific method. Of course, whether such a conclusion is appropriate would obviously depend on what one's conception is of the scientific method. All the same, it remains that *if* this is the appropriate conclusion to draw for metalinguistic claims about apes and other nonhuman animals, then it cannot be any less appropriate for metalinguistic claims about *humans.* And why should that be so disturbing? Would such a conclusion mean that we would be any less sure that we typically understand what others say to us, that they typically understand what we say to them, that we speak the English language, or that the expression "The White House" refers to a particular building in Washington, D.C.? Would the fact that these claims could not be subjected to the scientific method mean that *we could not therefore be sure whether they were true*? Would this mean that it is possible that everyone is wrong and that "The White House" really refers to some other building?

Scientific method or no scientific method, if the comparison of evaluations is to make any sense, logic demands equality of evaluative method. So, if this familiar kind of practical certainty is not—*in principle*—enough for our ordinary metalinguistic claims about each other, then nor is it in principle enough for our claims about Kanzi. But, on the other hand, if it *is* sufficient for our claims about each other, then we can only conclude that it is also sufficient for our claims about Kanzi. The practical matter, then, is whether we can attain that degree of certainty in making a metalinguistic claim about an ape like Kanzi. But that practical matter cannot be wished away by changing its conceptual definition; *it must be addressed with practical methods.*

Progress in scientific research on the cognitive and communicative abilities of apes is stalled because we misconceive the role that cognitive and communicational claims about our fellow humans play in our everyday, cultural lives. The rhetorical inclinations of "commonsense" blind us to the practical foundation of such claims: that is, *to their functional integration into the interactional techniques that make up our cultural forms of life.* Instead, we are led to the assumption that those claims require an epistemological foundation. Furthermore, because commonsense also tells us that we humans ordinarily understand each other, refer to objects, have beliefs, make reasoned choices, and so on, we take it for granted that typically those claims do in fact have that foundation when we affirm them of our fellow humans. By means of this conceptual illusion, we are thereby led to place an impossible rhetorical requirement on ape research. We demand that, when such cognitive and metalinguistic claims are applied to apes, they also be epistemologically grounded.

In her article "Eating Meat and Eating People," the philosopher Cora Diamond discusses the closely related issue of arguments against the practice of eating animals. She shows that those animal-rights philosophers who attempt to found such arguments on "reasons which are reasons for anyone" are making a rhetorical mistake. For such a strategy is based on a misconception of our own inclination not to eat *our fellow humans*: as if that inclination were itself founded in rational argument and that therefore the same must be established for the vegetarian's inclination not to eat animals. "The moral expectations of other human beings demand something of me as other than an animal; and we do something like imaginatively read into animals something like such expectations when we think of vegetarianism as enabling us to meet a cow's eyes. There is nothing wrong with that; there *is* something wrong with trying to keep that response and destroy its foundations" (Diamond 1991, 333). Analogously, we might say that the moral expectations of our fellow humans demand that, all things being equal, we typically treat them as understanding what we say to them. We do something like imaginatively read into an ape such expectations when we think that, by treating it as understanding what we say, we make it possible to interact with it in a more productive, coordinated fashion. There is nothing wrong with that; there is something wrong with trying to keep, or to reject, that response by replacing its foundations with others that are epistemologically conceived. Another way of saying this, and one of the main points we are trying to convey in this book, is that the following equivalence runs both ways: "[O]ur *hearing* the moral appeal of an animal is our hearing it speak—as it were—the language of our fellow human beings" (333–34).

Perhaps the conclusion that we must come to is that the rhetorical obstacle to progress in gaining scientific knowledge about the cognitive and communicational abilities of apes is only a side effect of the other, more daunting, practical obstacles that prevent us from living more harmoniously in their company and so from participating in the kind of fine-grained interactional techniques that would go into sharing with them a form of cultural life. Sue Savage-Rumbaugh has had astonishing success in overcoming many of those practical obstacles; and her descriptions of the cognitive and communicational abilities of Kanzi are some of the more valuable fruits of that success. But the more general, methodological point that we must take away from her work also promises much. We must learn to resist the illusory conception of those practical obstacles as having an epistemological foundation and, therefore, as requiring epistemologically conceived solutions. In so doing, we will facilitate the achievement of real progress in research on the cognitive and communicational abilities of apes. And we will gain the added benefit of eliminating that illusory conception from the armory of rhetorical weapons that are regularly employed in defending the refusal to hear the moral appeal of any other species but our own.

CHAPTER 4

Beyond Speciesism

Apes Have Language: So What?

Do apes really have an intellect that encompasses what we would call language? And even if one were bold enough to conclude that they do, why should we think that the utterances of apes will tell us anything about human language, or the formation of the human mind? Why, for that matter, should someone be interested in the question of whether or not apes have language? If language is innate—part of the "human birthright"—then what of import is to be found in ape language research? Even more to the point: Isn't the idea that another species should learn a human language anthropocentric? Shouldn't we learn their "language" if we want to understand them? These are the questions that will be addressed in this concluding chapter.

It is our belief that the epistemological biases and presuppositions that we have examined in this book have prevented scholars from recognizing the full implications of the basic behavioral and cognitive similarities that extend, in various forms, throughout the primate order. The linguistic competencies displayed by Kanzi and Panbanisha potentially undermine the assumptions that undergird much of modern linguistics, psychology, and philosophy. This is the reason why a large part of the "ape language debate" has centered around whether or not the capacities of the ape subjects are being represented in an accurate manner (Wallman 1992). Rarely, in science, has the presentation of data been subject to so much dispute or discrediting. Generally, it is the interpretation of data that serves as the focus for debate. But in the case of ape language, almost any interpretation of the data leads inevitably to a redefinition of man and the sciences that study man. Hence, those scientists who are not yet ready to entertain the possibility that a group of animals may be proficient in the capacities of language and reasoned thought have made the data itself the focus of concern.

Our Shared Heritage

When considering data from ape language studies, we would do well to recall that our species (*Homo sapiens*) offers but one among many solutions to the problems of survival as a social primate. Evolution is about surviving, and the anatomy and the capacity to discern what one should and can do with the anatomy inherited from ones' forebearers are the parameters of survival. It is often assumed that animals simply respond mechanically to their environment, and that any "learning" that they might require in order to survive is of a very different order than that required by man (Bickerton 1990; Lieberman 1991). This assumption is mistaken. Animals raised in an artificial environment can rarely survive if returned to their natural habitat unless they have a "mentor" who teaches them what is safe to eat, how to locate food, how to avoid predators, and how to establish the sorts of relationships with other animals that are necessary for survival and reproduction. Other primates, like man, spend most of their infancy and juvenile periods of life acquiring and refining these skills (Chevalier-Skolnikoff and Poirier 1977; King 1994).

Each anatomical plan provided by natural selection sets certain constraints on its inhabitants (Goldfield 1995). Once constraints are set, the sorts of solutions to problems of survival that a species can adopt are limited. For example, if a forest habitat becomes dryer and the food rarer, the solutions—both anatomical and behavioral—that are adopted by primates will surely be different from those adopted by elephants or large cats. It is also true that any anatomical solution must be preceded by a behavioral one. For example, early hominids may have become efficient bipeds in order to cope with a decrease in the area of the rain forest. But if this was the case, then before there were any changes in their anatomy that made this possible, there had to have been changes in their behavior: that is, nonefficient bipeds were trying to make their way across the savanna. The solution to move out onto the savanna and to adapt a different way of life came first and in turn forced a solution on anatomy. Anatomy is always, in a sense, playing catch-up with the more flexible brain.

The important anatomical parameters of the primate solution to survival include hands that have the ability to grasp; eyes that have the ability to see color and depth; and brains that enable the inhabitant to develop extensive social matrices based on individual recognition, kinship, and previous social encounters (Bramblett 1985; Hinde 1983; Schultz 1969). Their large brains also enable primates to recall food resources across decades and variable seasons; to coordinate social cooperation toward commonly recognized goals; and to communicate their desires and intentions to one another (Nishida et al. 1992). Human politics are basically primate politics elaborated and altered to deal with existence in the modern city-state, in which most inhabitants no longer know each other as individuals (de Waal 1989).

The genus *Homo* shares the basic primate survival plan, with a few important additions. Our brains are larger relative to the size of our bodies, and our shoulder girdle is uniquely adapted to permit hand-over-hand movement in the trees. Together these adaptations produce the ability—developed to a high degree only by man—to propel objects rapidly through space (Klein 1989). There are three more unique physical constraints that differentiate *Homo* from the rest of the primate order. Our hips have become wide and more horizontally angled, so that they are able to support the weight of a continually erect spine. Our infants have lost all ability to support themselves by clinging. And we have become endowed with small teeth that cannot shred or pierce (Feder and Park

1989). Of these changes, it is the need to carry infants that differentiates us most from the rest of the mammalian order (Savage-Rumbaugh 1994).[1] All other mammals either cache their helpless infants in a nest, or the infant is able to cling to its mother's body. Our infants cannot be left alone, and they are unable to cling. Therefore it is up to the human mother to keep the infant with her constantly, without assistance from the infant itself. It is from the needs provoked by these fundamental anatomical facts that the peculiar way of life of the human species has arisen.

The appearance of these physical differences was, we now know, of relatively recent origin: beginning perhaps no more than four to six million years ago and completed in only the last million years. The needs for survival that gave rise to man prior to that time are identical to those that gave rise to the four other ape species. For reasons that are unclear, apes appear to have changed far less from the last common ancestor that hominids shared with them than we have (Schick and Toth 1993). Although some hypotheses have been offered, we do not yet fully understand why we are bipedal, why our infants do not cling, why our teeth are so small, or why our brains are so large. But whatever the reasons, we can be certain that they reflect the outcome of behavioral decisions that pushed the anatomy toward a new use that was not easily accommodated at first.

However, regardless of the reasons why humans diverged from apes, it is nonetheless a fact that we shared the same body plan and the same environmental pressures for millions of years. Indeed, for more than 99 percent of our evolutionary journey we were one creature. Thus, if we wish to understand ourselves in a manner that is not totally confined by the experience of being human, we need to learn as much as we can about the capacities that we shared with apes before we diverged on our separate journey. Human beings have changed so fast that it is all too easy to assume that our closest living relatives, the apes, are so distant and primitive that we have little to learn from them about ourselves. Certainly, if we consider modern technological society as the inevitable result of human intelligence, then it is difficult to see any but the faintest semblance of a link between apes and ourselves. However, the fact is that technology is not the inevitable result of human intelligence.

Primal Man

Many hunting and gathering communities existed until the end of the nineteenth century with lifestyles that differed little from that of apes, apart from the possession of a few extremely primitive stone tools and fire (Service 1962; Weyer 1959). Such societies would probably still be extant were it not for the advent of long-distance air travel, which has brought the "fruits" of the modern world to virtually every stone age culture. Even the remotest of peoples now sport T-shirts that have somehow made their way through thousands of miles of trackless forest, along with a few metal pans, knives, and machetes.

Nonetheless, there are still human groups that live by daily hunting and gathering in remote areas of New Guinea, South America, and Africa. In some parts of Africa, many of the foods these hunting and gathering groups consume are the same as those eaten by apes living in close proximity (Kano 1992). Indeed, there is little difference in their lifestyles, apart from the humans' use of fire, and weapons for hunting. In this situation, man's bipedal stride means that he must hunt on the ground, and his knowledge of fire enables him to cook his meat (perhaps a necessity brought about by his small teeth). His dwellings are constructed on the ground, but they are temporary, and in many cases only slightly more elaborate than the tree nests of his ape cousins.

It is primarily because stone age peoples have language that we think of them in quite different terms from apes. From their language we have learned that they have a complex kinship structure, an organized cosmology, and many sets of rituals and rules for social conduct. Because we learn these things by talking to such peoples, we naturally assume that language itself not only is a vehicle for communicating the existence of a complex mental life, but is the agent responsible for generating that complex mental life: that without it there would be no such cognitive capacities (Bickerton 1995). But this assumption rests on an anthropocentric view of human uniqueness. We have concluded that we are different from all other living creatures as regards the capacity for reason and morality simply because other creatures have not been able to tell us, in a language that we recognize, of such things. But had we looked solely at the behavior of stone age hunting and gathering human groups, we might still regard these peoples as little more than apes who had developed primitive tools and mastered fire, and who specialized in the hunting of meat.

We know much more about such people simply because we have talked with them. When an anthropologist sets about to study a remote human group, the first step he/she takes is to learn the language of the people through the assistance of an informant. The second step is to interview individuals in order to ascertain the kinship structure and the cosmology of that group. In sharp contrast, the first step of an anthropologist setting about to study apes is to follow them about at a distance, not reacting with them in any way, in order to habituate them to his/her presence. Imagine what would happen if an anthropologist adopted such a strategy with a human group! Any person who constantly followed the group about without interacting or speaking with them would be regarded as crazy and would not be tolerated.

Apes may not think the anthropologist crazy, but they do appear to resent the constant stare of persons who remain outside the group. Sometimes they make friendly overtures and at other times they display aggressively. Once a group becomes "habituated," they find it difficult to avoid researchers without going out of their way to hide for long periods, or by traveling on other than their accustomed routes. Since they no longer fear being shot, they find it easier to tolerate the observers than to avoid them. Moreover, apes themselves join other groups by hanging around on the periphery and slowly making friends. Thus it may not seem all that odd to them when a lone researcher begins to hang about on the perimeter of the group. However, when a small army approaches with notebooks, cameras, and so on, and does nothing but stare at them, this surely must be disconcerting.

Since there are no ape informants, and since we assume at the outset of all investigations of ape behavior that one should not attempt to integrate oneself into the group, we are destined to arrive at a picture of apes that differs to an extraordinary degree from the picture we paint of hunting and gathering peoples. Our very techniques of research lock us into the odd position of claiming that all animals—even our closest relatives—possess a way of life and a mental existence that is completely dissimilar to our own (Bennett 1991; Lieberman 1984; Pinker 1994; Wanner and Gleitman 1982). We make this assertion despite the fact that, before the last four million years—a mere blink on the evolutionary calendar—we lived as one species; or that apes' brains, bodies, behavior, facial expressions, and emotions are nearly identical to our own; or that their child-rearing patterns are similar and that their infants go through many of the same developmental phases as do our own offspring. Moreover, the wealth of evidence we now possess from captive research shows us that apes are not dimwitted creatures who lack the ability to think creatively, to plan ahead, or to organize a structured set of patterned actions and interactions (Wrangham et al. 1994; Tuttle 1986). Why do we ignore the self-evident commonalities between apes and ourselves?

We humans desire a means of relating to other animals on the mental plane. It is not enough for us to know that another species looks like us, or even that their lives are like ours. We need, it seems, to make a mental connection—whatever that may be. Is this possible? Is it somehow possible to learn whether our long common history of shared body and brain extends in any way to the realm of the mind?

There have been two separate sorts of attempts to understand apes. One has been to observe them in the wild, and the other has been to study their language and other cognitive capacities in captivity. It is often asserted that the only "real data" regarding nonhuman primates must come from field observations (Reynolds and Reynolds 1995). This assertion is like insisting that the only "real data" about man must come from locating the few remaining remote tribes that are untouched by modern influence in the Amazon or the highlands of New Guinea. Certainly, we need to know far more about such peoples, for they offer unique perspectives on what it is to be human. But no matter how much we learn about small groups of human beings in remote areas, nothing we find from such studies could ever prepare us to predict the behaviors and the inventions of modern man. How could we discern, from studying stone age cultures, man's potential for the development of mathematics, the discovery of electricity, or the technologies that allow words and pictures to be distributed worldwide in a matter of seconds?

Discussions with any such technologically primitive group would quickly reveal that they were capable of imagining worlds that they could not see; of understanding and constructing abstract relationships between dissonant categories of things; of acquiring basic mathematical skills; and of learning other languages. Through such intercourse we could assure ourselves that technologically primitive man could come to live in, and possibly even adapt to, the modern world. But we would find no basis on which to predict that stone age man could have, or would have, if given sufficient time, created this world that we now inhabit. Indeed, if we did not know that the world of modern man existed, our studies of stone age man would surely cause us to conclude that a society whose inhabitants willingly packed themselves together into towering concrete structures, and who were able to communicate with each other across oceans by nearly instantaneous invisible waves, was another species whose intelligence greatly transcended stone age man. Indeed, members of remote hunting and gathering groups readily assert, on hearing stories and seeing videos of what the "outer" world is like, that these other people are fundamentally different from themselves, and that they could never attain such competencies.

We know that man has the potential to create the modern world only because it exists. We assume that it could be created by the mind that typifies individuals living in extant hunting and gathering groups, even though these groups have not made significant indigenous inventions in their cultures for thousands of years. We assume this not because of anything we see in the behavior or the culture of such peoples, but because individual members of such groups speak to us in a way that reveals that their mental worlds are populated with the same sort of concerns and flights of fancy that we ourselves manifest. It is this "mental connection," made possible through language, that permits us to declare that these stone age peoples are every bit as "human" as ourselves. The conviction that the mental lives of apes are devoid of such concerns and flights of fancy is based on the presupposition that discussions with apes are impossible. The fact that simple conversations do occur with captive apes who have acquired language is discarded as "irrelevant," because it is said that the behavior of such creatures is not genuinely linguistic, or even that it is somehow "unnatural" for the species (Pinker 1994; Sebeok and Rosenthal 1981; Wallman 1992).

Those who take such a stance fail to recognize that apes, like human beings, must be studied under a wide range of conditions before it is possible to begin to understand what it means to be an ape. Their behavior, like ours, is highly adaptive, versatile, and flexible; but these traits do not readily show themselves in the wild, where life appears to follow the same rhythm day after day. It is only under "tight conditions," where pressure is suddenly put on the group from many different but often invisible sources, that the remarkable ingenuity and creativity of the nonhuman primate mind manifests itself in a way we can easily grasp. Short of these conditions, the primate mind—including our own—is a rather lazy sort of apparatus, able to do infinitely more than is demanded of it on a given day. And so the observer of apes in the wild can easily be fooled into thinking that they live a life of relative ease, never bothering or able to better themselves (Byrne 1995).

Indeed, it has often been observed that although apes have a far larger brain than monkeys relative to their body size, they often seem to do much less in the wild. Surely the brain of early man, which was considerably larger than that of an ape, would equally puzzle any field primatologist able to peek in on a free-living troop of *Homo erectus*. Apart from spending some time smashing rocks together to make extremely crude tool flakes, the daily life of *Homo erectus* would not require, in any obvious way, a brain the size of which filled his calvarium. Apes in the wild sometimes spend hours a day smashing rocks together in order to open nuts (Boesch and Boesch 1983; McGrew 1992). Smashing rocks to create a sharp edge does not, on the face of it, require vastly greater intelligence than that demonstrated by apes who crack nuts using a stone anvil and hammer-stone (Schick and Toth 1993). Certainly there is nothing about producing a flake of rock that would indicate the existence of an intelligence which would eventually lead to the concertos of Mozart, the theory of relativity, or the understanding of electromagnetic fields.[2]

The trouble is that neither the existence of intelligence nor its potential manifestation is necessarily self-evident from observing behavior in "natural circumstances."

Wholistic Intelligence

It was the predictability of food resources brought about by the domestication of plants that meant that man no longer had to follow a nomadic way of life, forever moving about in search of food as the resources in one place dwindled and those in another became abundant. Apes, and a few small human groups, are still moving in lockstep with changing food cycles, trying to predict them efficiently, rather than trying to control them as modern man does. It takes intelligence—a great deal of it—to predict what nature is going to provide, and when, in quantities large enough to feed forty to sixty individuals. It also takes intelligence to coordinate the movements of all the members of the group. Such social behavior cannot be random but must be constantly organized in a manner that keeps the group integrated and well fed. Nature is not eminently predictable: her cycles change from year to year, across decades, and over even larger spans of time. If it were not easier to predict the availability of food by growing crops, man surely would not have done so, since it is certainly more work to tend crops than it is to simply pick those that nature provides. It is also less pleasant to be bound to a field than it is to wander freely about in the forest.

The kind of intelligence required to survive well off what nature provides is no longer obvious to modern man, as he himself is never required to do so. Instead, the kind of intelligence that controls crops, animals, objects, and inventions is the kind that is of value to modern man. This object-oriented, hierarchically structured intelligence is what we now prize most; and because we prize it so, we look for it when we attempt to study ourselves and the manner in which we manifest intelligence (Lakoff 1987; Mervis 1987; Rosch 1973). Any structure that can be characterized as "hierarchically organized" is viewed as a good and marvelous manifestation of the human mind (Chomsky 1957; Posner 1989).

Of course, not all that we do can be interpreted through the lenses of hierarchy and category. Some forms of intelligence, which have been termed wholistic or Gestalt, result from an organization of the parts that is neither hierarchically structured nor dissociable. That is, one cannot break wholistic or Gestalt constructions into subcomponents while preserving any sense of the whole; nor can one systematically build the whole from the subcomponents. The subcomponents seem to arrange themselves into an alignment that has no partlike existence, other than the whole they form. Thus it is sometimes said that the whole is greater than the sum of its parts. But such a characterization is inaccurate, for the parts really exist in the mind as "parts" only by virtue of the whole having already been "seen" by the mind. If the whole had never been seen, the parts themselves would not exist in our perception (Shipley 1995). Many perceptual figures have such characteristics, but so do integrative theories and great works of art. In these realms intelligence is organized at a synthetic level that focuses on what is achieved rather than the process of the achievement.

It is this sort of intelligence that is required to live within nature, to adapt to her ever-changing environment and food supply, and to learn the things that one needs in order to survive each day. In the rain forest, food must be located by new and nonobvious means each day. It is this sort of intelligence that allowed man to cope with life before he learned how to make his world increasingly predictable by the domestication of crops and animals, and before the invention of a calendar and the subdividing of "units of time."

The kind of intelligence that accepts whatever nature offers from one moment to the next, and tries only to predict what is the most efficient thing to do given the current situation, is what the brain of *Homo* evolved to do for the entirety of our existence on the planet prior to the domestication of plants and animals. Only in last twelve thousand to fifteen thousand years have we begun to try to conquer nature (Jones, Martin, and Pilbeam 1992).[3] Now, just as it seems we are about to "conquer Nature," we are beginning to realize that our success in this endeavor may be only an illusion. We are starting to see that the by-products of our actions—such as the exhausts of the fuels we use to subdue nature—can so alter the planetary balance of atmospheric and oceanic transport mechanisms that it may become impossible for our species to continue to exist, much less carry on as we have been doing (Vig and Kraft 1994).

As enamored as we are of the hierarchical intelligence that has generated our modern technological advances, it is useful to recognize that this sort of intelligence is a relative latecomer on the scene, and that it may have a limited sort of usefulness. We need to view hierarchical intelligence as a subset of a more global intelligence: a subset that is highly developed in modern man because of our constant emphasis on the manifestation of category and structure in all aspects of our lives.

Hierarchical Intelligence

The nervous system, being a very plastic sort of affair, can be extensively restructured in response to events that take place shortly after birth. For example, when a sense organ is destroyed during infancy, the portion of the brain originally programmed to process information from that organ becomes preempted by nearby structures. When this happens the motor and sensory areas of the preempting structure become far larger than they are in normal individuals (Churchland 1986). It is frequently the case that hypertrophied skill goes along with this increased space. Thus feet can become able to type efficiently, or, for a person lacking sight, sound localization and kinesthesia can become so astute that they nonetheless are able to learn to ski.

Similarly, just as limbs or sensory systems can grab extra space, it is reasonable to suppose that one form of intelligent information-processing could take over large portions of brain function, to the detriment or even elimination of other forms of intelligent processes. Taking such a perspective, it becomes possible to conceive of man as an ape who, by virtue of his relatively recent emphasis on hierarchical intelligence, has altered his behavior and consequently the functioning capacity of his nervous system to such an extent that he now exhibits a hypertrophied intelligence of a particular sort. This hierarchical intelligence has become extraordinarily adept at designing buildings, computers, and other artifacts of modern society, but it also now makes it difficult for humans to recognize intelligence that manifests itself in nonhierarchical thought. In the most extreme form of brain specialization, some individuals become "autistic savants." These persons exhibit intelligences that are capable of "superhuman" feats of calculating dates or mathematical sums, or exhibiting extraordinary talents in art or music, while at the same time displaying almost no capacity for the social intelligence required in daily life. The existence of such individuals suggests that the brain has a remarkable capacity to specialize or focus on a single sort of information-processing ability to the exclusion of all others. It is as though a single function or topic has so usurped the entire brain that the individual cannot do other than become an expert in that one area while simultaneously neglecting self-development in all others.

When an autistic savant answers a math question in a few seconds that none of us could calculate in several minutes, even with pen and paper, we are inclined to think that some sort of "higher-order" intelligence is operating, even if the person is socially inept in all other aspects of life. However, when an ape convinces forty other apes that it would be wise to travel to location A, a trip of three hours travel time, because fruit should be ripe there, we are likely to dismiss this feat as the execution of a simple "instinct." Even more troubling is the fact that anything an animal does that receives the label "instinct" is deemed at once to be a form of behavior that has no reasoned premise. Such is the power of words that a complex act of our own species can be seen as intelligent even in an individual known to be deficient by all normal standards of human behavior. But complex behavior in our ape relatives can be termed "instinctive" and dismissed without further ado.

What results is a tautology of sorts. If a behavior is said to be "innate" in an animal, then we must assume that the animal carried out those actions without reflection as to their consequences, and lacking advance planning. All that occurred was that some stimulus presented itself in the environment and the animal proceeded to mate, or display, or hide, or engage in whatever action was innately linked to the environmental stimulus. When a human behavior is said to be "innate," it means that the propensity to learn a complex skill was already present in the human being prior to being shown how to do the task at hand. Thus we find "human being" to be another word for "cognitive ability," and "animal" to be another word for "innate stimulus-driven actions"; and we see the category boundaries between humans and animals as immutable and preordained.

Language and Mind

Only by getting some insight into the mental world of animals can we break down these conceptual boundaries that we ourselves have erected. While we may eventually discover many ways of doing this, right now we have only one—and that is language. We need to talk to the apes, and we need to listen when they talk back. Since it is not likely that we are going to meet an ape on the street with whom we can exchange pleasantries—if we want to determine whether or not they are capable of language and thought, we are going to have to depend on the reports of those who do talk with them. At least we are going to have to do this until we become more proficient at recognizing intelligence by other means.

Certainly, in the case of modern hunters and gatherers, we discern intelligence by talking to them. Talking—for us human beings—is the manner in which we come to convey what we call our "intentions." Since we believe that "intentions" undergird all our conscious actions as well as the actions of other human beings, we often find it difficult to relate to animals because we cannot understand their "intentions" or indeed, even if they have intentions (Dennett 1983). Talking is also the way in which we human beings convey our "thoughts" to one another. Knowing some of the thoughts of people in other cultures, we have come to conclude that they share a wealth of mental experiences that are similar to our own. So it would seem to follow that if we want to understand apes, we would do well to talk with them, if such is possible, since talking seems to be our human means of getting to understand other entities.

Since apes, like stone age peoples, do not live across the street or appear in universities, we shall have to rely on the reports of those who have attempted to cross the species barrier and establish communication with apes, just as we rely on anthropologists to travel to New Guinea and bring back reports of the lives and capacities of those peoples. Many linguists, philosophers, and psychologists are unwilling to accept these reports, however. At first this hesitancy was based on the fact that language, as employed by apes, was taught by techniques of conditioning and molding, leaving little reason to assume that apes either understood what they were saying or what was being said to them (Terrace 1985). However, it has been clear since the mid-1980s that apes can learn language without being taught and that their comprehension of what is said to them far exceeds their ability to speak (Savage-Rumbaugh, Sevcik, Rumbaugh, and Rubert 1985). This limitation is not because of any cognitive deficit, but simply because they lack a human larynx and diaphragm. They lack voluntary control over the regulated exhalation of air, and they lack the glottal stop capacities needed to form consonants. Thus, when they do try to speak, the sounds come out in brief unmodulated bursts that lack phonemic distinctiveness (Crelin 1987). But they do try to speak; they even try to speak clearly. Yet, like many retarded or autistic persons or persons born with speech defects, apes simply cannot speak. Those apes that do learn to comprehend language remain, like retarded or autistic persons, locked in a body that cannot express what the mind can understand and conjure. By all observations and accounts, this appears to be a very frustrating affair for such apes.

However, the fact that apes like Kanzi, Panbanisha, Mulika, and Panzee have learned to comprehend and produce simple language when raised in an environment where they are spoken to and treated as competent communicative partners has not had the impact on the fields of linguistics, philosophy, psychology, and behavior that such findings would have had if the results had been accepted as legitimate accounts of ape behavior (Savage-Rumbaugh, Murphy, Sevcik, Brakke, Williams and Rumbaugh 1993). The reports of those who talk to such apes are accused of being produced by persons who are "too close" to the apes. Closeness to animals, it is assumed, biases one's thoughts and one's data (Sebeok and Rosenthal 1981).

Similar closeness to human beings is *not* assumed to unduly bias one's thoughts or one's data. Even though anthropologists working in a New Guinea tribe become close to their informants, and even though Piaget became close to his children, such reports were never deemed "suspect." By contrast, any report of something Kanzi has said is immediately classed as "suspicious," regardless of the nature of the evidence. Two observers might have seen the utterance, it could have been filmed, it could have been repeated or expanded on—but all these "confirming facts" will be overlooked if the utterance occurs as part of a two-way relationship between an ape and a person. Because the conversations are reported by a human partner, it is suggested that somehow they are tainted. Of course, the logical outcome of this position is that the things that apes say cannot be accepted as serious science unless the apes are able to engage in the reporting of scholarly data on other apes. Obviously, if such criteria continue to be held by large numbers of the academic community, it will be some time before any insight is gained into the mental lives of apes or other nonhuman creatures.

Relationships are an inevitable part of real linguistic communications. Normal execution of linguistic exchanges takes place not in a vacuum but rather between two or more individuals who are attempting to coordinate their actions by exchanging information about their intentions, goals, plans, and desires. Language in children emerges in the same sort of crucible; indeed, children are indoctrinated into a culture through the vehicle of language. By learning language they acquire the formal, nonstated, and unconscious ways of their society. Language becomes the glue that binds the individual into the matrix of social expectancies, responsibilities, and moral principles.

Language is, in a sense, the abstracted portion of the culture, the part that can be lifted from the ongoing stream of action and discussed at the level of "meta-action." In this sense, language is behavior about behavior. It is used to determine what "we" are going to do next, in a constantly changing stream of events that are only partially predictable. Without language, any single individual can determine autonomously what he or she will do next, and if the behaviors of individuals do not need to be coordinated, the decisions of single individuals are sufficient. However, whenever behaviors must be coordinated—and they must when any two individuals are going to interact by exchanging patterns of action—communication about this coordination must take place before the intertwined actions themselves occur, unless these patterns are completely predetermined.

Linguistics and the Innateness Conundrum

Linguistics has achieved a modicum of success in its drive to produce a hierarchical analysis of language by lifting language out of the stream of interaction and studying it only as meta-action. The function of this meta-action, in the arena from which it emerged and in which it continues to operate daily, is declared to be unimportant to the understanding of language itself. In other words, language is assumed to have become such a complete system of meta-action and such a complete reflection of the cultural expectancies that generate it that it can be properly studied of its own accord (Newmeyer 1986; Wasow 1989).

Before the advent of written language, it would have seemed odd to attempt to study language as a phenomenon that existed apart from situations that included the intentions of the speakers and the effectiveness of the utterances (Olson 1994). However, the existence of written language made it clear that communication of some form could occur in a nonsocial setting. The sentences that emanate from the mind of a writer are generally more carefully thought out than is his or her speech. They are more grammatically complete and correct, since writing permits one the luxury of reviewing, editing, and changing a statement after it has been made. In real-life exchanges, such luxury is absent.

By assuming that the intentions, goals, and desires of the speaker were irrelevant to the analysis of language, linguistics attempted to permit itself to formalize the study of the patterns of language in a manner that did not depend on any sort of "meaning" inherent in the content of the utterance itself. It strove to achieve the formalism inherent in mathematics, where relationships between symbolic quantities can be shown to hold regardless of the specific numbers that are used to compute the equation. Through such formalizations linguists strive to specify the underlying principles of language, in the same manner that mathematical physics strives to specify the nature of the physical parameters of the universe. Linguists also seek to discover constants, equivalent to pi or the speed of light, that can be utilized within the formalisms to demonstrate the applicability of their formalistic approaches across all languages.

Students of mathematical physics have historically ignored minor fluctuations in their equations caused by variables that are difficult to compute in fact, but easily understood in principle. For example, the wind resistance determines how far a golf ball will travel and where it will land, just as does its original mass, its weight, and the force and direction of the blow that sets it on its course. However, wind resistance on any given day varies from moment to moment and is more difficult to compute than the other factors, which themselves determine the basic trajectory and distance traveled and which always direct the ball to the same spot in an ideal system. Therefore, while wind resistance is viewed as a real factor, it is not taken into account by formulas of classical physics that attempt to predict the behavior of objects of a specific mass, under the influence of gravity, when acted upon by a certain force. It is assumed that the essence of the way in which the physical world operates can best be understood by focusing on principles that undergird that operation in a constant manner while ignoring things such as wind resistance that can, on a given day, vary moment by moment.

Thus, just as the formulas of classical physics can determine the trajectory and landing position of a golf ball, linguistics seeks similar formalisms in language. But rather than searching for invariant relationship between numbers, linguists search for invariant relationships between categories of words, where the categories themselves, such as verb and noun, are devoid of semantic content. By understanding the formalisms that are assumed to underlie the relationships between such syntactical categories, linguists hope to write the mathematics of language. They assume that the formalisms operate in a manner similar to that of mathematical equations in physics. Once the correct mapping rules have been deduced, language can be reduced to mapping the semantic meaning of words onto the rules, just as physicists can plug numbers into equations. It is the equations that give the general relationship; the numbers only compute a specific one. Similarly, the underlying formalisms of language are thought to embody the patterns of human thought—words give forms to the patterns, but do not alter them.

Linguists anticipate that once they achieve their goal, just as the laws of classical physics permit us to compute the trajectories and landing positions of balls of any size, struck at any location on earth, the formal rules of language will permit us to interpret any sentence in any language. Difficulties in so doing will reflect not inadequacies in the rules but minor cultural factors that operate in a manner analogous to air resistance.

A corollary of such a linguistic perspective is the view that the formalisms that underlie grammatical competency must be inherent in the human brain, just as the formalisms that underlie classical physics are thought to be inherent in the physical world. And just as no one "teaches" a golf ball where to go once it is acted upon by physical forces, so, it is thought, no one teaches a child the formalisms that undergird language. Indeed, the relationship between these underlying formalisms and the speaker's external language is assumed to be dependent on more than just innate mechanisms for structuring linguistic utterances. It is assumed that these mechanisms form the basis for all human thought. They are, so to speak, the inherent mathematics of our brains. Without the presence of such algorithms, human beings would be completely unable to carry out the basic parameters of human thought, because thought itself is held to be the forming of various systematic relationships between different classes of events.

The goal of linguistics, then, is seen as none other than the discovery of the mathematics of human thought, where the term "mathematics" is used to imply the logical formalisms that are presumed to underlie all complex hierarchically organized thought. And, most important for our purposes, it is also assumed that none of these formal mechanisms that are said to underlie thinking are present in any species other than humans (Chomsky 1957; Pinker 1984).

These formalisms are viewed as a set of equations locked within our brains that permit us to interpret and produce novel sentences. Lacking them, it is assumed that all we would be capable of is the learning of simple associative response chains between external events and actions on our part that had been rewarded in the past. With them, however, we are suddenly provided with the capacity for self-reflexive thought. Because of them the "I" versus "you" distinction emerges, and reasoning man (and woman) is born.

Certainly this view of language is attractive and has much to offer to all who wish to simplify the study of language. If such an important aspect of our existence can be reduced to basic equations, we can build computers that will readily and easily translate one language into another. We could even ask them to do such tasks for us as read complex text and render it into simpler form or to take transcripts of real-life conversations and sort through the "words" to find the underlying dynamic of the exchange.

The Problem Posed by Kanzi and Alternative Resolutions

Of course, the inherent attractiveness of a given perspective and the degree of truth with which it maps to the reality of language are not necessarily one and the same. Kanzi's ability to comprehend complex language throws a very large wrench into the engine of linguistic thought (Savage-Rumbaugh and Lewin 1994). It can accommodate this intrusion in only a limited number of ways.

One is to discredit the data that Kanzi and other apes provide. This was the initial approach, and it is still taken by many; however, it is becoming increasingly less plausible with every new accomplishment by Kanzi or other apes. Another approach is to accept the data but to extend the formal capacity for reflexive thought to apes as well. The main problem with this strategy is that currently there are no reports of language in the wild. If apes are capable of the formalisms of reflexive thought, the idea that they would not be utilizing this capacity in conditions of nature seems (to scholars who assume that self-reflexive thought is what generates the emergence of mind) too appalling to contemplate.

A third approach would be to grant the data, but to assume that the formalisms that account for this behavior on the part of the ape are different from those that account for human behavior. This approach would have the advantage of granting humans cognitive uniqueness, while still allowing that something more than conditioned associations is possible in other animals. The problem with this approach is that no one knows what other sorts of formalisms to postulate if not ones based on syntactical structure, or at least a logic structure that takes as its starting point the same sort of hierarchial/sequential intelligence that manifests itself as syntax in language (Langer 1986, 1993; Greenfield 1991). Our current models of learning offer only two choices: conditioned associations or reasoned hierarchical thought structures generated by the equations of language.

A fourth approach is to grant the data and the apes' capacity for formalisms, but to abandon the view that such formalisms are innate in man or ape (Shanks 1994; Reber 1989; Brooks and Vokey 1991; Vokey and Brooks 1992) . This view assumes that the formalisms of language are constructed anew by each individual in the process of becoming a competent social being who engages in communication with other social beings for the purpose of coordinating complex patterns of behavior. This approach is the one taken by this book. It was the one taken when the decision was made to raise Kanzi without attempting to teach him language. It is our view that the fourth approach is the one that is closest to the real truth of language and the only one that will lead to a clearer understanding of how we, as human beings, construct human minds through the vehicle of language.

The difficulty with this approach is that if it is the one closest to the truth, it means that we cannot learn about the rules and regularities of language by lifting language out of context and studying it as meta-action apart from behavior. We must study it in the messy real world that it naturally inhabits. It also means that if these formalisms are constructed anew by each language participant, we cannot rely on biology to pass them along effortlessly from generation to generation. If we value the sort of linguistic edifice we have constructed as a species, we may actually have to work to keep it going. This is such a shocking thought in itself that many scientists elect to abandon the fourth approach for this reason alone. Those who can bring themselves to go beyond this difficulty find that their attempts at research become bogged down in the multitude of variables that make up what we call real life.

Psychologists and linguists have never been able to study real life—the problem has been that they do not control real life. The paradigms of research that we have inherited from classical physics insist that we must attempt to gain knowledge by controlling one parameter at time. Some might feel that newer statistical techniques like multivariant analysis and factor analysis will enable us to overcome this obstacle, since this permits us to deal with more than one parameter at a time and, hopefully, to sort out the "variance" in our data due to a number of different parameters. Still, these new methods only accomplish this feat by controlling one parameter at a time while looking across all others. They do not neglect the classical concept of control, they merely rotate it across variables.

The formalisms of linguistics have achieved great popularity precisely because they have lifted language out of the context of real life and reified it in a manner analogous to the reification of basic forces achieved by classical physics. This reification is based on the seemingly viable assumption that language can be set apart from the realm of the social relationships in which it is embedded. The justification for this assumption arises from the fact that, in a literate society, language does indeed exist in a sphere that is nonsocial. One can, as I am doing now, write down one's "thoughts" without another party present in form or corporal being at all. The "other party" in such a case is only the "imaginary reader." However, aside from the use of written language (a skill that appeared only about six thousand years ago and still is absent in many of the world's languages), language is embedded in the spoken relationships between people (Piggott 1961; Olson 1994).

The Issue of Intentionality

By reifying language in this manner, linguists have almost managed to do away with the issue of intentionality. That is, the intent of the speaker, in producing the utterance, does not need to be taken into account in the formulation of rules that govern utterances. Again, this method follows that of classical physics. The intent of the golfer who hits the golf ball need not be taken into account in the computation of the ball's trajectory or where it will land. It is sufficient that we know the direction and force of the blow; this, along with our knowledge of the mass of the ball, will enable us to predict where it lands. The fact the person who hit the ball "wants" it to land somewhere else is irrelevant; the forces of the physical world are such that they need not take into account "desires" that underlie the cause of action, nor do they need to deal with the cause itself in any direct manner. It is sufficient that they predict the relationship between the initial application of force and its consequent effect.

By the same token, linguists assert that the intention of the speaker need not be taken into account when attempting to understand the formalisms that underlie all utterances. It is sufficient that these formalisms make it possible to generate, and to interpret, all potentially possible utterances. If the intent of the speaker is not met, he or she, like the golfer who can hit another ball, can utter another sentence. On the face of it, this seems a simple enough solution. However, this seemingly simple solution harbors a great difficulty that is hidden in the apparently appropriate analogy between evaluating the trajectory of a golf ball and the appropriateness of an utterance.

The golfer, whose ball lands in the rough, does not conclude (most of the time, anyway) that the forces of natured "wanted" his ball to land in the rough. He simply concludes that he hit it improperly, and he makes another attempt to direct the ball where he wants it to go. However the speaker of a language is in quite a different situation. Any sentence directed toward another party may not have the intended effect—for any number of reasons that have little, if anything, to do with the manner in which the original sentence was uttered. The other party might not have heard it, she might have heard only part of it, she might have heard all of it and not understood it, she might have understood something quite different from what the utterer intended, she might think that she understood and thus act as though she did when she did not, and so on. The problem is that the speaker never knows exactly where any given utterance has landed in the same sense that he knows precisely where his golf ball has landed. Utterances do not have a direct effect on a listener in the same sense that actions do. They are meta-action.

This fact becomes quite clear if one takes a simple example like "pushing." When party A actually pushes party B, A can observe whether or not B really moves. A may just be trying to push B over so that there is room on the bench for both, or A may be pushing B off a cliff. Whatever the intent of A, the results of his actions toward B will be self-evident (including, of course, the fact the B may well push back far more forcefully than A anticipates).

However, once we move out of the realm of direct action and into that of indirect or meta-action through the hand of language, the methods by which we evaluate the effects of our behavior are drastically altered. Suppose, for purposes of example, we find that professor A is trying to "push" professor B into accepting her view of the importance of viewing autistic persons as unable to form a "Theory of Mind." The ability of A to evaluate the effect of her utterances becomes a very different sort of affair. Some of the utterances of A may actually speak to facts about known deficits in social capacities in autistic individuals. Other utterances may reference the names of well-known individuals or granting organizations interested in this phenomena. Others may describe individual personal experiences with autistic patients, and so on. A may also attempt to "push" B not only by talking to him but by talking to other parties with the intent that they then talk to B on her behalf. But how will A know if she has succeeded?

The only means A has of evaluating her effectiveness is some change in the utterances of B. B may begin to talk "like" A, saying the same sorts of things about the causes of autism. However, it is quite possible to talk like A without adopting A's views. A knows this and so will monitor B for other clues as to whether her efforts have achieved the desired ends. Does B cite her work on autism, does B approve her grant requests, and so on. B, on the other hand, will be trying to interpret the "intent" behind A's utterances. Is A pressing him to adopt a view known not to be compatible with his own hypothesis of autism as a sensory disorder because A needs his support, or is it because A does not really understand that he is working on the problem at a more fundamental level? Why is A so concerned that B does not cite her work when it clearly is not relevant to what B is doing? Of course, such an example can be continued and elaborated in far greater detail. The simple point is that A and B's inferences regarding the intent of each other's utterances become the focal point for determining the effect of language.

Utterance interpretation is composed of three variables: the words (and syntax) that are used; the inferred intent of the speaker; and the immediate physical context surrounding the utterances that is taken as common knowledge by both speakers. These variables are not equally weighted in all circumstances. In most cases the inferred intent carries far more interpretive weight than the words. To take a simple example, suppose two guys are sitting at a table, and as two attractive women walk past one looks up and says, "Let's go fishing." It is not likely that the other one will assume that the next thing they should do is drive home and begin to look for their fishing poles. It is also not likely that any formal analysis of language structure that is lifted from the context will provide an interpretive account of the utterance.

The simple fact is that most of our exchanges place a great deal of weight on the interpretive variable. Once we are in an exchange, we cannot, as can the golfer, simply hit our ball over again. Every previous utterance affects the interpretation of our current utterance. Consequently, utterances are not independent events as are shots from the tee. The interpreted intent that engulfs each utterance guides the effect of each utterance as surely as the angle of the blow guides the ball through space. The difficulty with this set of events is that we currently have no means of externalizing, objectifying, and measuring "intentionality." Nonetheless, it is relatively easy to see that lifting language out of the medium of use is not going to give us the rules for predicting the effects of utterances, because the effects are not determined by the formalisms of structure alone. Even more important are the inferences made regarding the intent of the utterance. These inferences are so influential that they can easily override the ordinary interpretion of both syntactical rules as well as that of semantic content. Thus the meaning of an utterance such as "go fishing" need have little to do with the content or structure of the utterance itself.

The simple fact of the matter is that words can mean what ever we elect them to mean, and we can change meanings extremely rapidly, even at times within the same sentence. The idea that there is a dictionary that allows us to look up the meanings of words confuses us. It makes us think that the meaning of a given word is in the dictionary—in some way oddly inherent in the word itself. But it is not, it is only in the usage; this is why a word such as "fish" can so rapidly change its meaning. How is it then, if words have no stable meanings, that we can interpret the intent of the speaker, and how is it that children, much less Kanzi, learn what words mean, if their referents are indeterminate to any significant degree?

Social Constructionism

To answer these questions, we must take the fourth approach to the language problem. We must begin by assuming that the ability to think and reason as a cultural and linguistic being in a given society is constructed anew by each individual during the process of coming to behave as a competent member of that society. This approach is not new. It has roots in the social constructionism of John Shotter (1990, 1993), in the language as a guided reinvention perspective of Andrew Lock, in the "making-sense" through acquisition of shared meaning stance of Katherine Nelson (1985), in the joint attention framework of Jerome Bruner (1983), and in the language games of Wittgenstein (1953) and protolanguage games of Canfield (1995). All these approaches use slightly different terms to get at a common theme. The common underlying theme is a social account of how language comes to map onto, to regulate, and to guide both action and thought.

Language is seen first and foremost as an inherently social process, one whereby the nature of interaction between a mother and her child leads naturally, spontaneously, and in a sense effortlessly, to the acquisition of structured thought, manifest first in structured patterns of interactions that are mutually understood and anticipated by both participants. The second manifestation of the same process appears on the linguistic plane and is marked first by the use of language to coordinate interaction, second by the use of language to control the actions of the others, third by the use of language to proscribe and plan the actions of others, and fourth by the use of language to alter the linguistic expression of the opinions of others. Each of these levels of language use builds on the former.

There is, however, a singular difference between the theoretical perspectives formulated by those working with normal human children and the perspective that has resulted from the capacities demonstrated by Kanzi and now confirmed by three other apes. The perspectives just offered are limited to human beings. They concentrate, for the most part, on the interaction between a mother and a child, and they illustrate the ways in which the perception of the caretaker both structures and refines the actions and utterances of the child as the caretaker seeks to encourage the child to take an increasingly greater role in their joint interaction. The caretaker is presented as having a very fine knowledge of the infant's perceptions as well as of its abilities. This knowledge permits the caretaker to structure the world around the child at a level that is only slightly beyond the child's current capacity to deal with things on its own. Certainly it is true that most middle-class American mothers behave in this manner. And in America, we have parenting classes for those mothers who do not know how to accomplish the feat of "interacting with their children at the appropriate level."

Yet somehow mothers who have no such classes manage to raise remarkably healthy and socially competent infants; and studies that have attempted to find a link between maternal scaffolding abilities and linguistic competency continue to come up empty-handed. Indeed, short of severe neglect, it has proven difficult to demonstrate that anything done during the period of language acquisition has a profound affect on a child's speech or quality of learning. While such negative findings should not be taken to imply that the social acquisition account of language is incorrect, it is nonetheless difficult to understand why caretakers who appear to be more efficient at scaffolding do not, in effect, have children whose language is more advanced, if indeed the development of language is dependent on such scaffolding.

The Perspective Shift Driven by Kanzi

A perspective shift becomes inevitable when one attempts to look at the processes of language acquisition and enculturation in a developing organism that is an ape rather than a child. Not only is Kanzi an ape, the first two and a half years of his life were spent in the constant company of his natural ape mother. Since the life span of apes is equivalent to two-thirds of that of a human child, Kanzi was raised by Matata to the human equivalent of 3.1 years of age, or throughout the critical developmental period for language acquisition. Matata did no language scaffolding for him and very little behavioral scaffolding. Nor did the human caretakers fill the gap, as they were focused not on scaffolding language for Kanzi but rather on training Matata. Their goal was to teach her to select the proper symbol in order to be vended a specific food. She experienced great difficulty learning to discriminate between the geometric patterns of the symbols themselves. The first ten months of her training were devoted to teaching her to recognize a single pattern from among many others, when all patterns were relocated at every trial. The remaining ten months were devoted to teaching her to associate one of each of the six patterns that she recognized with a specific food. She was required to search through ten patterns that were relocated at each trial and select the one that corresponded to the piece of food in a vending machine just outside the room. The food changed every few trials.

Such training, which is hardly akin to the scaffolding processes of the human mother, cannot account for Kanzi's progress, since he did not participate. Although he had adequate opportunity to watch what his mother did, the fact that he never seemed to do so is perhaps misleading. It is common for parents to report that their children picked up things to which they appeared to be paying no attention. Indeed, most parents assert that this happens all the time. However, even if Kanzi was secretly watching, the discrete trial training that Matata received cannot alone account for why Kanzi was easily able to discriminate lexigrams and to associate them with specific foods and events. Kanzi's younger siblings, Panbanisha and Mulika, never observed such training sessions, yet they had no difficulty discriminating lexigrams, and they came to comprehend spoken language just as did Kanzi.

Yet the many studies of joint attention, scaffolding, acquisition of shared meaning, and guided reinvention all place heavy emphasis on the role of the caretaker in the "passing on" of the culture and language. This role is not just that of modeling appropriate behaviors but also that of fitting oneself into the child's actions in a manner that is designed to promote increasing competency on the part of the child. This "teaching role" of the parent is even regularly asserted to be one of the most important distinguishing traits of the human species, and it is often assumed that without such efforts our offspring would not become competent adults (Greenfield forthcoming; Tomasello, Kruger, and Ratner 1993). It is of more than passing interest that in a society that places considerable emphasis on the role of the parent, the role of the parent is being handed over to other caretakers with increasing frequency (Clarke-Stewart 1989). These caretakers are no longer part of the extended family, as was the case during the majority of our evolutionary history, but trained "specialists" in the art of child care. We tend to view it as increasingly important that such specialists understand their role in coordinating their behaviors with those of the child in their care.

Not having been trained in the art of scaffolding, Matata let Kanzi do pretty much whatever he wanted. Because the experimenter working with Matata was focusing on training Matata, she also let Kanzi do pretty much whatever he wanted. Kanzi kept himself extremely busy playing with a variety of toys and practicing his acrobatics on ropes hung up for that purpose. Somehow he still managed to learn to tell one geometric pattern from another, to differentiate the speech sounds that his caretakers were using, to match these speech sounds to different geometric symbols, to associate both the sound and the symbol with specific foods, objects, and events, and to use these symbols, in combination with each other, as well as with gestures, to announce his own desires. These skills went far beyond those he observed in his mother. One is reminded of the manner in which children who learn a pidgin language develop it into a creole in one generation, even though they have no model for a creole. This fact is often cited as evidence for the fact that language is innate (Bickerton 1984). If one were to follow this sort of logic, then, given the fact that Kanzi's understanding and use of lexical symbols went far beyond anything demonstrated by his parent, one would have to conclude that lexical symbols are innate in apes.

Of course we know that this cannot be the case, just as we know that written language and mathematics are not innate competencies of the human being. We know these things because we know that the systems of writing, mathematics, and lexigrams are recent inventions and just like ideas such as the telephone or bow and arrow—they cannot be innate. The point remains, however, that the logic by which many have reached the conclusion that language is innate could be employed with equal appropriateness toward many other skills known not to be innate. If such an argument would produce a misleading conclusion about the innateness of lexigrams for Kanzi, it can clearly lead to incorrect conclusions regarding the innateness of language in our own species.

Since it is reasonable to assume that neither lexigrams nor spoken English would be "innate" in a bonobo, and since neither Kanzi's mother nor the experimenters working with her scaffolded Kanzi's rapid development of lexical production and English comprehension skills—how did Kanzi learn? And how can anything that he did be said to be due to some sort of social construction of behavior between him and his caretakers?

Quine's Dilemma and Locke's Puzzle

Before embarking on an attempt to answer these questions, it is necessary to consider the pitfalls encountered by previous attempts to explain the puzzle of language acquisition. There are two pivotal questions underlying many of the current theories and discussions regarding the acquisition and function of language. The first is that often referred to as Quine's dilemma (Quine 1960). This question asks: How is that children come to know the referent of any communication directed toward them without already knowing the structure of the language and/or the meaning of the words that are used? After all, if one points to a field containing horses and cows of various colors doing various things, grasses of various sorts, along with bugs, odors, sounds, and wind, how is the child to know what the adult means when he says, "Oh, look at the cow eating some grass"? The second question, often termed Locke's puzzle (Taylor 1984), asks how it is that language can ever be adequate to convey the thoughts of the mind of one speaker to that of another, since all words are imperfect representations themselves of what is in the mind of the speaker. Taylor (1984) puts the problem as follows: "As the hearer cannot know the thoughts of the speaker, he cannot be sure what the words of the latter signify. That is, the words you utter express your own ideas; but when I hear those words, I can only interpret them as the signs of my own idea. Thus language fails to perform its required task of providing an intersubjective conduit between our minds" (209).

These two problems are related in that both revolve around the issue of reference, yet they remain distinct. With regard to the dilemma as posed by Quine, we assume that *if* one knew the referents of words and *if* one knew the syntactical structure of the sentence, one would then be able to know the speaker's true intent. The problem for Quine is how these two sets of knowledge get put into language in the first place, for if both semantics and syntax depend on the other for their existence, there seems to be no way in which language could ever be initially acquired. The puzzle as posed by Locke, however, does not accept the fact that reference can be clear, even when the semantics and syntax are given capacities of the both speakers. The problem revolves around how it is that reference can ever be determined, since "the same words have in different mouths, and often in the same, very different meanings" (Condillac 1798, 1:762).

The problem of how it is that a child can deduce the meaning of "Oh, the cow is eating some grass" seems to be resolved, in a manner of speaking, by Chomsky's assertion that the rules for decoding syntactical structure are innately given. Thus if the child can deduce (through an innate application of the appropriate rules) that the word "cow" is the subject of the sentence and that subjects, when linked to transitive verbs like "is eating," are generally agents, and that agents are generally animate living beings, then the child will understand that the word "cow" must apply to an animate thing in the field. Furthermore, if the child also understands that the word "grass," which follows the transitive verb, specifies the thing that the subject acts upon, then the child will know to look for an animate being acting upon an object. Finally, if there are not too many other agents in the field acting on things, then the child can deduce that the adult must be referring to the cow that is acting on the grass. Because the child can see that the cow is ingesting the grass, he or she can therefore deduce the meaning of "eat."

Thus, according to this account, all that is needed for the emergence of a proper understanding of language follows from the correct application and understanding of the principles of syntactical structure. Clearly, however, such accomplishments are not simple. How do children manage them? Parents have not been observed to instruct their children in how to interpret sentences like "The cow is eating some grass," therefore linguists have concluded that this capacity must be innate (Marcus 1993). They assume that the child is born in possession of an innately given capacity (generally termed a LAD) that easily permits the child, indeed compels the child in a manner not under the child's own volition, to appropriately decompose the sentence and thereby deduce the intent of the speaker (Pinker 1994).

The difficulty posed by Locke is not so easily explained, however. If we grant that a LAD can explain how the child understands a sentence linked to physical entities of the real world, we nonetheless remain at a loss to explain how it is that an adult understands more abstract concepts. Let us take a sentence such as "It might appear that one would not know how to make use of conventional signs if one were not already capable of sufficient reflection to chose them and attach them to ideas: how then, it might be objected, can the exercise of reflection only be acquired by the use of signs?"

Knowing that the subject of this sentence is the word "It" does little to tell us exactly what the referent of "it" might be. The word "it" is used again after the semicolon, but here "it" has a different referent, which is equally vague. Being able to look up the dictionary meaning of the word "appears" and knowing that it functions as a verb in this sentence also tells us very little. What is the "it" that "appears," and where can it possibly appear, except in the mind of the reader? It seems that the more we try to use semantics and syntax to unravel the meaning of this sentence, the more the meaning vanishes—yet syntax and semantics are said to be the tools through which we generate meaning. What is wrong here? And how is that we understand this sentence at all? This is Locke's puzzle and it forces us to see that while syntactical and semantic explanations help us to understand the process of language in some cases, what we refer to as "meaning" goes far beyond these simple parametric levels of explanation. Indeed, if we were to rely solely on them, it is doubtful that we would be able to hold meaningful conversations with one another.

Many of those who would attempt to answer this question have realized that its roots must lie hidden somewhere in the origins of language. Condillac (1798) espoused the view that it is man's innate ability to reason that distinguishes him from all animals and that initially sets him on the path to language acquisition and use. It is also this power to reason that permits him to reflect on his own actions and to develop a language whose referential powers go beyond the meanings assigned to given words to be able to intuit the intent of the speaker. Thus, in contrast to Chomsky, Condillac asserts that reason is the engine that makes language possible and that it is reason that is innate, rather than the other way around. For Condillac, it was the emergence of the intention to communicate that set man apart from the animals and on the path to language. Syntax is simply a fallout of that set of events. Due to the complexity of language that man began to use, he needed some means of ordering the rapid flow of his words so as not to confuse his listener.

According to Taylor:

> Condillac believed the use of conventional signs to have originated in natural expressions of emotion. A cry of fear upon seeing a lion, for example, is a natural, context-determined response. It is important that such a response is context-determined. Even a complex "vocabulary" of such responses (expression of pain, of fear, of joy, etc.) would not constitute a "true" language from Condillac's perspective because the production of any one such vocal response would not be under the control of the speaker. It would depend on the occurrence of the appropriate context-stimulus. Mastery of such a vocabulary, then, would not allow man to exercise control over his mind for it would not yet even constitute control over the use of the vocalizations themselves.
>
> An important step would be taken when man came to live in society with other men. For he would then hear the same vocalizations produced by those around him and would recognize them as (natural) signs of the emotions felt by the producer. By this stage, then, the emotional cry is not simply a response to felt emotion; it also acquires a use, albeit as yet an uncontrolled and unintentional one. That is, it now also serves as an intersubjective link informing others of the speaker's emotions. But the most crucial stage is passed when man comes to use such natural signs, not simply in uncontrolled response to emotion, but with an intention to communicate. For instance, from a high tree I might see a lion creeping up on you; I would then use the "fear vocalization" to warn you of that danger, even though I do not myself feel threatened by the lion. Thus, my production of this natural sign would have been the expression of my intention to warn you, rather than a simple uncontrolled reaction of fear.
>
> This is an important step because, for the first time, the stimulus which triggers the fear-vocalization is, in a sense, self-generated by the intention to warn. (Condillac makes no mention of where such an intention might have "come from." We can only assume that it is a natural endowment.) . . . the key to Condillac's argument lies in his "demonstration" that the source of the artificiality of "true" language-using lies in its originally being an imitation of a natural behavior pattern, viz. the natural behavioral response to emotional stimuli. Thus, the guarantee that we all use language in the same way inheres in the fact that the ability to use language is based on a more primitive, shared, natural stimulus-response system. (1984, 215)

Taylor summarizes Condillac's position on the origin and use of language by stating that it encompasses three crucial factors: a natural stimulus-response system, intentionality, and a social-cooperative system. Thus Condillac may be said to be, in a sense, the first thinker to argue about language and reason from a social-constructionist perspective.

Jerome Bruner is the modern thinker who has done the most to elaborate on such a perspective. Bruner does not deny Chomsky's assertion that innate syntactic rules exist; however, he asserts that the child could never become able to even apply the rules if many other abilities were not already in place, some of which are learned through social interaction and others of which are said to be innate as well. On the "innate" side, Bruner credits the child with the innate intentions to refer, to deny, to request, to seek mutual attention, and to query, as well as an innate ability to follow a point and to follow the gaze of a cointeractant. Of course, it is not that Chomsky believes such skills are learned—he does not care whether they are learned or not, as he is not interested in anything other than grammatical analyzers. This is not to say that he assumes such skills are unimportant, only that they are irrelevant to the development of language. For Chomsky, any portion of language that must be learned is an uninteresting portion.

To Bruner, a psychologist, it is unthinkable that something as complicated as a LAD could operate if the child did not already understand the basic pragmatics of communication—which, for Bruner, entails an understanding of the topics to be communicated, the intentionality of the communicative process, and its general referential nature. Unlike Chomsky, Bruner recognizes both the critical nature of these abilities and their complexity. For him, the child's acquisition of intentionality and reference are as mysterious as the grammer module is for Chomsky. Consequently, he reaches the conclusion that these abilities must be innate as well.

Thus it seems, as Taylor points out, that no matter how we get at the matter of language, we are left with the problem that as long as we are attempting to specify what portion of language is innate and what portion is learned, we shall find that "innate" is simply another word for the part of language that we cannot explain. Of course, the same issue holds if we attempt to explain reason or consciousness. The centrality of language with regard to the innateness issue is critical only to the degree that one holds (as do Chomsky and Pinker) that it is language that permits reason and consciousness to operate. Is such an assumption valid? It has been deemed valid as long as humans have been thought to be the only animal that uses language. It has been easy to see that other animals do not speak as we do. It has been far more difficult to determine whether or not they have reasoning abilities and whether or not they are conscious. To the degree that we limit our acceptance of the existence of reason and consciousness to their expression via language, we can remain comfortable in asserting that other animals can neither reason nor experience consciousness in the same manner that we can.

If, however, we hold that reason and consciousness, especially self-reflection, are a priori capacities that underlie language and that they can exist independently of language, then we must at once conclude that animals have both the possibility of reason and consciousness, but that we do not recognize these processes in them because they cannot express them by means of language.

Prior to the initiation of ape language studies, these issues were generally of interest only to scholars of linguistics and philosophy who considered them in the hypothetical sense. Since no animal exhibited language, it made sense to consider reasoning, consciousness, and language as expressions of some underlying competency on the part of man. Exactly which of these skills came first, and how it happened, were matters for speculation, but not much more. With the first reports that an ape named Washoe was learning signs, centuries of Western thought regarding the nature of mind were challenged (Gardner and Gardner 1971). But Washoe was not like a child, in that she did not reason her way into language but rather was taught "words" through the presentation of an object followed by the molding of her hands into the sign for that object. No one knew whether this was really language or not. At first it was thought that Washoe might not be able to generalize to objects other than the specific one that was held up, but she quickly did this without difficulty. Then it was thought that Washoe might not be able to combine her signs but only be able to use them for single objects. This, too, she was able to do without difficulty. Did Washoe really have semantics and syntax? And if she did, how did she acquire them simply by having her hands modeled when an object was held up? Did this mean that she had a LAD as well, and that apes in the wild all had LADs but were not using them? This puzzle was clearly as profound as Locke's original one.

But the closer one looked at Washoe's utterances, the less they looked like language. The first problem was that she did not evidence clear comprehension when others signed to her (Savage-Rumbaugh, Rumbaugh, and Boysen, 1980). She seemed much better at expressing her needs than she was at listening to and complying with the needs of others. Was this just the result of her egocentric personality, or was Washoe only aware of what it was that language achieved for her rather than its general representational capacity? A second problem was the repetitiveness of her utterances. Sentences like "You me hurry, Me you food hurry, Food hurry me you, Hurry hurry, Food hurry?" were commonplace. Why did Washoe use so many words over and over, and why were signs like "you" and "me" a part of so many utterances?

The third problem was the most significant: Washoe did not seem to learn signs unless she was taught them. Often it took hundreds of trials or more for her to learn a new sign, and even then the new sign would be confused with other recently learned signs for some time. There were many signs that Washoe did not spontaneously produce unless someone held up or pointed to an object, as though the "stimulus" was needed to be present to induce the sign. In short, Washoe's ability was startling, but was it language? Washoe knew what to do with her signs, but did she really understand what the signs themselves did in terms of her communications with others? It was not clear that Washoe's language possessed a syntax or that she fully understood the representational power of language (Savage-Rumbaugh 1984). It was clear that she understood what the use of signs could achieve for her, and, in a sense, this understanding was a simple form of reason (Gardner, Gardner, and Van Comfort 1989). It was not evident that she could use language in the service of reason or that she understood or produced syntactically structured utterances; however, it did seem abundantly clear that Washoe was conscious and that she was intending to communicate.

Nonetheless, linguists and philosophers could continue to ignore the claims being made on Washoe's behalf as long as Washoe was being taught language. In itself, on the very face of it, the fact that Washoe had to be taught signs made it possible to dismiss her abilities as a number of higher-order conditioned responses that readily generalized across training exemplars. Real language learning was a feat that children accomplished quite readily on their own, and the ability to reason one's way through a maze of complex speech to an understanding of language was viewed as quite a different process from being taught to pair hand motions and objects (Leiber 1984; Sebeok and Rosenthal 1981).

Why Kanzi Could Not Be Ignored

It was more difficult to ignore the fact that Kanzi began to comprehend speech and to learn symbols without any training. Kanzi's language skills were clearly not situation specific, and the range of novel sentences that he understood was unlimited. His symbol use was generally spontaneous and nonrepetitive. Kanzi made it increasingly difficult to draw any sort of line between humans and apes that was based on language alone. Certainly, most humans understand more complex language than does Kanzi, but there no longer can be said to exist any real differences between the way Kanzi learns and employs language and the way we do the same thing. Of course, it remains possible to impugn the validity of the data and the honesty of the experimenters, and such continues to be frequently done (Pinker 1994). Yet Kanzi continues to demonstrate that these abilities are real, as does his sister Panbanisha. Given the overwhelming weight of the evidence, the conclusion that apes have a capacity for language can no longer be evaded.

Once we have accepted this conclusion, it can quickly be seen that none of the explanations of language as an "innate" capacity remain adequate. It really does not matter whether we are asking how Chomsky's LAD becomes activated so as to permit grammatical competence to emerge, how Bruner's Language Acquisition Support System (LASS) becomes activated so as to permit the prelinguistic suit of skills that include intentionality, reference, the ability to follow gazes and points, denial, and so on, how Condillac's pure reason leads to the invention of language, or how Lock's mothers unwittingly guide their children to reinvent language. It does not seem reasonable to suppose that Kanzi had a latent LAD or LASS, nor did his mother guide him to reinvent language. These are simple facts. They are not complicated in any way, nor are they the result of some statistical anomaly. Kanzi's sister Panbanisha has shown that Kanzi is not unique. If more bonobos were raised with early exposure to a much wider variety of symbols from birth, there is every reason to believe that their language skills would be far more gramatical and complex than those of Kanzi and Panbanisha. These simple facts mean that our current explanations regarding the manner in which our species acquires and passes on language have to be incorrect—not just partly, but completely incorrect.

So how *did* Kanzi learn? With what do we replace the current theories of language acquisition? Before offering an explanatory account, it is important to recall the explicit things that Kanzi and Panbanisha are able to do, and the circumstances under which these capacities have made themselves manifest.

1. They have learned to differentiate English phonemes, and they understand combinations of these phonemes to be words (Savage-Rumbaugh 1988).
2. They understand words spoken rapidly and in the sentential contexts, where the use/meaning of the word differs from sentence to sentence and depends not only on the rest of the words in that sentence, but also on previously uttered sentences, the ongoing social and physical context of the sentence, and the historical context that is common to themselves and to their listener (Savage-Rumbaugh 1988; Savage-Rumbaugh 1990).
3. They know the written symbol that corresponds to many of the spoken words. They can use this symbol to communicate even though they cannot speak (Savage-Rumbaugh et al. 1986).
4. They comprehend the syntactic aspects of utterances. They understand that pronouns such as "it" refer to previous sentences. They understand that word order can be used to signal a different sort of relationship so that Kanzi biting Sue is not the same thing as Sue biting Kanzi. They understand pronouns of possession such as "mine" and "yours." They understand expressions relating to time, such as "now" or "later." They understand qualifications of state such as "hot" and "cold." They understand that one clause within a sentence can modify another portion of the same sentence, for example, "Get the ball that is outdoors, not the one that is here" (Savage-Rumbaugh et al. 1993).
5. They follow the thread of conversations that they hear around them, even if they are not participating in such conversations.
6. They can make stone tools—by observing others do the same.

All these capacities appeared without special training on the part of the experimenters. Kanzi and Panbanisha were treated as though they could come to understand what was being said to them, and they were expected to try. If they failed, attempts to make the communication clear proceeded at the level of actions.

Having clarified what Kanzi and Panbanisha are able to do, it is equally important to note what they have not done.

1. They have not produced any speech that is readily interpretable as an English word, though they do attempt to do so.
2. They have not progressed in the development of language skills at the extremely rapid pace shown by normal human children.
3. They have not gone as far as normal human beings.
4. Their short-term memory capacity is less than that of normal human children, making it more difficult for them to imitate sequences of utterances or actions with only minimal exposure.
5. They have not become integrated into a human community as a full social member, with both rights and responsibilities.

None of these deficits, however, cause the abilities of Kanzi and Panbanisha to stand outside the realm of what we usually think of when we apply the term "language" to behavior.

The Malleability of the Nervous System

Any attempt to "explain" how Kanzi and Panbanisha achieved these skills will have to rely, to some extent, on some biological endowment, some "innate" component. Kanzi and Panbanisha are, after all, biological entities that bring to the task a specific anatomy. So at the outset, we have no alternative but to set out those components of the behavior that we cannot otherwise explain. Kanzi and Panbanisha brought to the task of language learning a visual-auditory processing system that was able to separate the speech stream into components that they could perceive as words. They also were able to resolve the visual world of symbols into lexigrams that, to them, appeared distinctly different and to which they could match sounds. We do not know how they did this. We do know that the age of their exposure to the sounds of speech and to the geometric configuration of the lexigrams was important. Three other bonobos who were not exposed to spoken language and visual symbols during infancy (Matata and her offspring Tamuli and Neema) remain unable to differentiate speech sounds reliably or to match sounds with lexigrams. Similarly, they have great difficult visually resolving the differences between the lexigrams, though with extensive training, this visual skill can slowly emerge after the age of three. However, if exposure occurs before the age of three, it proceeds rapidly and becomes a highly developed ability without any special training.

The perceptual problems in forming sound discriminations from the ongoing speech stream are underappreciated, probably because this happens at such a young age that none of us recalls the process. Furthermore, during infancy there is no obvious clue that it is or is not happening. This is why autism is typically not diagnosed until it is clear that a child is not speaking language. However, long before the time of speech, the processing of the units of the spoken language is proceeding at several different levels. The child is learning to segment the speech stream into its components of phrases, words, and phonemes (Kuhl 1986). The fact that the child is able to make the appropriate segmentations of the speech stream is more of a mystery than is the later appearance of syntax (Peters 1983). These differentiations, made as the child listens, not as it speaks, are in no way given or obvious.

One has only to attempt to study the vocalizations of another species to immediately realize the difficulties in separating a stream of sound into some sort of meaningful units. If there is no way to tell where words start and stop, there is also no way to decompose them further into their morphological units. Given such a problem, each sound that one hears is as different from the preceding sound as one sentence is from another. Imagine attempting to determine the meaning of a sentence if all you ever heard were different sentences, not the words within the sentence. No two sentences that are exactly alike in intonation and pattern would ever be heard. Without any recurrent patterns, how would you ever crack the code? If one could not break a sentence down into patterns that themselves are identified as being patterns one has heard or seen before, it would be impossible to understand a new sentence. For we do not recognize a sentence purely on its physical basis, but rather by breaking it down into units, units that we have encountered before and thus are able to classify at the level of words or sometimes at the level of phrases.

While we do not know how Kanzi and Panbanisha began to identify individual words, it seems quite probable that the process of pointing to specific words as they were spoken aided the development of this ability. By pointing to a visual symbol and speaking slowly, the speech stream was altered so as to give reliable visual and auditory "breaks" between at least the words that were on the keyboard. Still, there were no phonemic pauses in the speech, so the ability to separate speech sounds at this level remains a mystery. The capacity of human infants to do this has also been recognized as inexplicable and has been attributed to an "innate phonemic parser" by some accounts and to the motor theory of speech by others (Liberman et al. 1967; Lieberman 1975).

Kanzi's ability to understand different speakers, even those with an accent, as well as synthesized speech, means that this capacity cannot be due either to an "innate component" of sound processing ability found only in humans or to the motoric ability to produce speech. The quite surprising fact that, in bonobos, there seems to be a critical age for exposure to speech, even though they do not normally speak, implies that the developing brain has an extraordinary capacity to process patterns of incoming stimuli. Such a pattern-analyzing mechanism must search to extract reliable subcomponents of information. The fact that bonobos have a critical period for the understanding of human language reveals that language patterns, as they become analyzed, in some manner imprint themselves on the brain, making it possible to analyze similar patterns again in the future by rapidly identifying incoming stimuli as similar to a previously encountered pattern. The more rapidly new patterns can be identified, the more quickly additional information can be taken in. The abilities that we have thought were "innate" in human beings can now be seen as the result of the early structuring of the brain, by the brain, as it responds to stimuli within the environment that are important to the organism.

The fact that we learn to identify speech sounds at such an early age, and that we are not aware that we are even doing so, causes us to underestimate the complexity of such a skill. Thus, many people do not think it unusual that an ape should be able to understand speech. Indeed, the capacity to do so is attributed to dogs, elephants, and other animals as well. So little study of the abilities of such animals has been made that it is not known whether these animals have learned the individual sound patterns of each word, or whether they have extracted the phonemic patterns as well and can understand words even if they are spoken by speakers of different ages, by a person with an accent, or by a voice synthesizer. We also do not know if they can extract a word when used in a speech stream, if they can extract more than one word from the speech stream, or if they can relate words in the speech stream to one another.

The fact that Kanzi and Panbanisha can do so means that the brains of other animals may have this capacity as well if they are exposed to the speech stream at an early age, in a situation where it is an important part of their daily surroundings as well as affectively motivating. We do not fully understand how the developing brain determines which stimuli are sufficiently important to merit the devotion of a dedicated and intense pattern-analyzing process. This is an important decision, one that will affect the potential capacities of the organism throughout the rest of its life. The fact that the brain is sufficiently plastic to orient itself toward analyzing many different sorts of stimuli suggests that the organism comes prepared to cope with a wide variety of environments—and that any seeming similarity within a given species may be due to all individuals within that species making similar decisions about how to allocate their pattern-analyzing capacities at a very early age, rather than a fundamental, unalterable biological given.

The development of what is loosely termed the emotional system of the brain (including the basal ganglia, the amygdala, the thalamus, and the hippocampus) plays an important role in orienting the attention of the organism. The different rearing experiences of the various bonobos in our projects speak directly to this issue. Both Kanzi and Panbanisha developed an easy facility with human speech, while Matata, Tamuli, and Neema have not done so. Language training efforts began with Matata when she was approximately six years old. They continued for two years and were renewed after the birth of Kanzi, when they continued daily for another two and a half years. During the entirety of this time, Matata was in the company of experimenters who engaged her in social interactions throughout the day that were of interest to her. They also used the keyboard when speaking to her, and they encouraged her use it. Matata showed no capacity to differentiate individual words, though she did listen and respond to intonational pattern.

During the second training period, Kanzi was with her at all times, so that any speech the caretakers utilized was heard by Kanzi as well as by Matata. Kanzi, however, learned to process this speech input as words, while Matata did not. Kanzi's primary emotional attachment was to Matata, but he quickly became attached to the human experimenters as well. They carried him for many hours each day at his request, and with Matata's approval.

In contrast, Neema and Tamuli, two other infants born to Matata, did not develop as strong an attachment to experimenters at such an early age. They did hear speech, however, used around them throughout the day. The difference was that the speech that Kanzi heard was directed toward him by "socially significant others," that is, persons who interacted in a direct physical manner with both him and his mother. Such persons groomed Matata, often held and carried Kanzi, and tickled and play-bit both of them. When Neema and Tamuli were small, caretakers typically interacted with Matata only through the cage wire. They spoke to her and sometimes interacted with her physically, but always at a distance because of the wire. Such interactions are not as sensitive, it is never essential to get along with an ape that is in a cage—one can walk away if things do not appear to be going well—but it is essential to develop and constantly maintain a social rapport with an ape that is not in a cage. With young apes this is not especially difficult, but with adults who have infants, such rapport comes only through the development and maintenance of close and affectionate bonds.

Thus, both Kanzi and Panbanisha experienced apes and humans as "socially significant others" at an early age, while Neema and Tamuli experienced them, at the same early age, as caretakers who brought food and played with them through the wire. Out of this differential social importance attached to human beings during the first three years of life emerged these capacities: the ability to parse speech sounds into words, and to understand the referential aspect of speech; the knowledge that spoken words corresponded in a one-to-one manner to lexigrams; the ability to attend to and discriminate the visual lexical components of the communication system that accompanied speech; and the ability to pair sounds and visual symbols as equivalent communicators, first in the mode of comprehension and then in production. All these skills emerged in Kanzi and Panbanisha prior to three years of age.

Matata, Neema, and Tamuli were all exposed to conditions in which humans became "socially significant others," but *after* the critical period for the development of such capacities. None of them became able to parse the speech stream into words or evidence any understanding that specific words were linked to specific lexigrams. They did understand that the keyboard, and sound, functioned as an indicative communicative system, and they attempted to use both. However, they selected any lexigram to convey their intent, just as Panbanisha did around one year of age, when they first begin to view the keyboard as a communicative tool. Their understanding could be expressed as "touch this special board and people will read your mind and do what you wish them to do." However, Panbanisha soon went on to the develop the concept that each individual lexigram could be used to convey different sorts of things and thus became highly selective in her use of the keyboard. Matata, Neema, and Tamuli did not. More important, Panbanisha retained the concept of specific symbol-object relationships even when touching a specific symbol resulted in other than the desired action (for example, when requests were denied or when other alternatives were suggested).

It is a well-known fact that during this early period, brain structures are rapidly forming, and the direction and degree of development is dependent on the experiences that the organism receives while this development is occurring. Schore (1994) has specifically proposed that there is "a critical period of synaptic growth and differentiation of an affect regulating limbic structure in the prefrontal cortex . . . and that this development process is significantly influenced by the stimulation embedded in the infant's socio-affective transactions with the primary caregiver" (13). In Schore's view, if the proper sort of affective environment and social exchange does not occur during this preprogrammed period of neuronal growth and myelination, the connections that are programmed to form between the limbic system and the prefrontal cortex never mature—that is, the prefrontal system never gains the ability to properly control and modulate the emotional and attentional systems of the brain. The prefrontal ability to do so is critical because the prefrontal area receives input from the visual, auditory, and somatasensory cortices—where information from the outside world is taken in and analyzed. In order to properly evaluate and focus on this information, the brain needs input to and from its emotional and attentional system. This process is what takes place in the frontal cortex. It is therefore critical that the cortical-limbic pathways become adequately developed and differentiated.

The differences in ability to process both speech and visual lexical information that appear in apes during this critical period implies that the development of the socioaffective attachment systems and the attentional systems are closely interlinked. Certainly both those apes who experienced humans as "socially significant others" (i.e., Kanzi and Panbanisha) and those apes who experienced them merely as "significant others" (i.e., Matata, Neema, and Tamuli) had sufficient and proper stimulation to permit the development of the frontal cortex and the maturation of the limbic system. All the animals display the normal social reportoire of behaviors that are characteristic of bonobos. None show evidence of being socially stunted. They do not avoid others, they have no stereotypies, they engage in frequent play and grooming, and they are interested in objects. Thus there is no reason to suspect that the neuronal differentiation and myelination has not proceeded apace in all of them. However, what distinguishes them is their differential capacities to process both visual and auditory stimuli of one particular type, that is, the visual and auditory stimuli that are particularly representative of the communication system used by the human experimenters who became "socially significant others" during a critical period of Kanzi and Panbanisha's development.

These facts indicate that Schore's hypothesis regarding the development of the brain regions regulating socioaffective development is perhaps too limited. Given the broad cortico-cortical interconnections between the frontal lobes and the visual and auditory centers of the brain, it seems likely that the limbic attention-orienting system is operating, through the mediation of the frontal lobes, on these regions as well. The considerably expanded ability of Kanzi and Panbanisha to process and extract information from stimuli that are particularly associated with the communication system of "socially significant others" reveals that the brain, during development, has a unique potential for structuring itself in a manner that makes it possible to rapidly extract increasingly complex pieces of information from the patterning of behavior of "socially significant others."

The extracting and processing of such information is apparently characterized, through the mediation of the frontal lobes, as intrinsically rewarding—probably because it results in increased coordination of the social interaction, which in itself is rewarding, for it is the coordination of social interaction that permits social interaction to be sustainable. Uncoordinated interaction becomes too difficult for the infant to manage, and retreat from the social interaction becomes the prominent means of coping. Coordinated social interaction provides the constant level of maximal arousal that is sustainable. Well-coordinated social exchanges themselves are driven to become more complex in nature to maintain the same level of maximal arousal.

While initial coordination may be with the mother, the infant is soon driven to move beyond coordinating its social arousal with hers; and by adding other individuals, the level of stimulation is increased, as long as there remains coordination of exchange. Of course, it is not only the infant that must find the social exchange maximally arousing within the limits of coordination, the mother and other individuals must similarly find the exchange mutually arousing and satisfying.

While the neurological underpinnings that developed and guided the differentiation of Kanzi and Panbanisha's nervous systems remain to be determined, it is nonetheless the case that these two bonobos, by virtue of the context of their interactive exposure to speech, came to understand language with a competence that rivals that of human children. They also came to communicate by linking the sounds of words they knew to symbols printed on a board. The three bonobos reared without exposure to speech in an interactive environment failed to do these things. The skills that Kanzi and Panbanisha acquired developed even though their main social ties were with other apes.

They learned our language. They can understand it much better than they can speak it, but their inability to speak is a physical limitation only. Kanzi and Panbanisha acquired these skills because they organized their perception of human speech in a manner functionally different from that of their siblings who did not interact with people during a critical period of development. Once the stream of speech was decoded into "word units," the process of language learning followed by Kanzi and Panbanisha differed little from that of a normal child—with two exceptions: (1) it was much slower, and (2) they could not actually speak.

What these facts reveal, in a rather unequivocal manner, is that language is not innate in any meaningful sense of the word "innate." What they do not do is reveal how this feat was accomplished by the bonobo's nervous system. We don't know precisely the critical age or precisely the critical experiences, and we don't know how the brain "decides" which sort of incoming information to organize in such a high-level manner; nor do we know how it accomplishes that organization. What we do know is that once the ape brain has developed beyond three to four years of age, it can no longer "decide" to process speech information.

The fact that Kanzi and Panbanisha can process such information tells us no more about how it is accomplished than does the fact that we human beings are able to do this same thing. Lieberman 1984 points out that although we are unable to produce speech sounds at rates that exceed seven to nine items per second, we somehow understand speech that is transmitted at a rate of fifteen to twenty per second. He attributes our ability to do so to "specialized anatomy and brain mechanisms [that] allow us to make these speech sounds, and a set of brain mechanisms [that] allow us to "decode" speech signals in a very very special way" (38). Clearly, we can no longer appeal to a special brain mechanism evolved solely for the purpose of processing speech. If bonobos can develop the ability to process speech sounds, it is probable that we ourselves develop this ability. How we, or they, do so is still not understood, but the rapidity of speech comprehension relative to the speed of the nervous system suggests that an evaluation of speech comprehension theories is needed.

The organization of the visual and auditory cortex is a fact of nature that remains something of a mystery. As neuro-imaging techniques become more rapid and refined, we may begin to understand the link between brain maturation and experience and even be able to vary certain biological parameters via behavioral alterations. A tantalizing clue exists in the fact that the only brain of a language-competent ape yet to have been measured was 528 grams, completely beyond the scale of all previously recorded chimpanzee brain weights.

The organization process itself is likely to remain more of a mystery. Indeed, it is one of those mysteries that is likely to grow, the better we understand it—just as is the mystery of the thing we call gravity. We understand how gravity operates in increasingly greater detail, but this is different from knowing what it is—we do not yet know this. We probably will learn what emerges in the brain and the experiences that sometimes assist the organization processes; but to truly learn how a complex self-organizing process develops—this may remain an elusive goal.

The Achievement of Meaning—with Language

Nonetheless, given that Kanzi and Panbanisha somehow achieved the organization of the world of human sound into "word" units, we can address the question of how they then came to realize that these word units stood for various items and events, as well as why they began to attend to relationships between these word units. We can address this process because language acquisition is essentially a social process derived from the interaction between two or more individuals. Thus it can be "externalized by behavior" in a way that the perception of the visual and auditory sound stream cannot.

The central question regarding the acquisition of language at the level of meaning is that of how it comes to be lifted partially out of the here and now of behavioral action, so that it achieves some sort of independent level or metalevel of existence. After all, a word can "mean" something only in the context of an interaction, not really in the context of a dictionary. And "meaning" can only be constructed out of the whole cloth of interactions between individuals. Something about our behavior is said to mean something to A. Our words change, in some manner, the mental state of A, or at least we infer that they do. Generally, we make this inference because A says that our words did change his mental state.

Of course, unless A's future behavior changes as well, we do not know whether his mental state has changed or not. And indeed, even if his future behavior does change, and we attribute this change to an alteration of his mental state, we still do not know that this is an accurate reflection of events, for all we can observe in A is a change in his behavior, not his mental state. We make, in our culture, the assumption that behavior reflects mental state and that mental state drives behavior. Thus we put ourselves in the difficult position of believing that we must change how someone thinks before we can change how it is that he behaves, as we believe that mental state drives behavior. However, on reflection, this "belief" is in and of itself somewhat shaky. For mental state is only an "intervening variable" that we postulate. We say it acts as some sort of mediator between our language behavior and the language behavior of the other party. When, as often, we don't see a direct response to our verbal comments, we assume that the change must have been held in abeyance in some manner, and we refer to this manner as one's mental state. We could as easily call it the operative memory bank as mental state.

This process of "lifting out" is seen a little more clearly in apes than in normal children—because it happens more slowly, and because it does not always take a familiar form. Words, at first, are meaningless and evoke no change in the behavior of the ape. One can sit down in a nice pleasant location outdoors and comment on the flowers and the fruits that are all about, and the young ape merely wanders about noting only whether the intonation is soothing and pleasant or sharp. Nothing that is said alters the motion of the ape's exploration. However, as speech sounds become discriminated, attention begins to differentiate between utterances that are directed to the ape and utterances that are directed to others. This is apparent because utterances that are directed to the ape generally elicit fleeting eye contact toward the speaker, and those that are directed toward others often result in a brief visual fixation on the other party. The same sort of change can also be seen in young children and even perhaps in some pets.

After the initial orientation has permitted some words and/or phrases to be dissected from the speech stream, one begins to notice visual orientation toward an object when it is mentioned or shortly thereafter. For example, if Kanzi is walking near onions and he hears, "Oh look, there are some onions by Kanzi," he is likely to glance about himself, though he may not actually touch the onions. Once a word like "onions" can be pulled from the speech stream, the question arises as to how it is that Kanzi might even be able to realize that it could apply to onions, as opposed to all the other plants around him, the smell of the ground, the color of the sky, and so on.

The determination of the referent happens slowly across time, not on any one occasion. It happens because Kanzi hears a word that he can recognize in many different contexts. "Onion" is said many times, generally in a different physical setting and in a differential sentential context each time. Thus Kanzi could hear "Let's eat onions" (while someone else is eating an onion), "Put the onions in the backpack" (while someone holds a backpack open toward him after placing some onions in his hands), "Don't eat those onions" (after someone takes onions away from him that are for Panbanisha), "Let's look for onions" (while walking in the forest), and so on. Once the sound for onions is identified, then hearing it in many different contexts permits Kanzi to single out the common element of those different contexts, which happens to be the object onions. It is through this comparison and contrast across many different instances that some sort of "meaning apart from context" emerges. It can be said to be apart from the context, however, only in the sense that it is a common element of many contexts and, as such, comes to have its own "identity" different from the contexts in which it is encountered (Savage-Rumbaugh 1991).

This "identity" cannot be the same for each person, although for members of a common culture it will be similar. And for objects that are concrete, the overlap between individuals using the language will be high. Whenever the word is used in the future, it will be employed in a way that embodies some commonality that is a portion of the previous experience associated with that word. It is this process that is at the heart of metaphor and poetry as well. Thus a word like "fish" can become associated with the actual object as well as with the process of obtaining that object. The term "going fishing," once associated with that process, will come to mind whenever the behaviors that are linked to fishing come to mind. In part, the act of fishing implies an attempt to "catch" something, so it can convey this idea in a situation that is quite unlike that of fishing. Yet both the listener and the speaker of a common language will, at once, recognize this similarity, and the listener will perceive the intention of the speaker as he suggests "going fishing," even though this phrase has nothing to do with actual fish.

The same sort of process occurs when a word is learned that has no concrete external referent—such as "sorry." How does an ape come to feel contrition, and what makes him or her feel this way? Words like "sorry" occur in many different contexts as well; however, the utterances that contain them are generally of a more limited type than the utterances that contain a word like "fishing." One can hear utterances like " I am sorry," "He was sorry," "Are you sorry?" "You should be sorry," and even things like "It was a sorry sight," but one rarely hears sorry used as metaphor. Indeed, it is hard to use words that indicate any sort of internal state in a metaphorical way. Words that refer to internal physical states can never have a common referent in the sense that "fish" can have, since one person's internal state is not generally identical with anyone else's. Indeed, we have no way of knowing if it is ever like anyone else's nor is there any method of verifying that someone is actually in possession of such an internal state, other than by observing their external behavior. To use a word like "sorry" is to assume that the state that you are now experiencing is something like the state that others experienced when they used that word. Of course, whatever state it was that they experienced, you did not yourself experience, you only interpreted it. Thus, your use of the term could, in fact, be related to a quite different internal state. This is especially clear if the party claiming to be "sorry" happens to be an ape.

We are then forced to ask, can an ape really *be* sorry? But this question fools us, for it has no more meaning when applied to an ape than when applied to a human being. To *be* sorry is to equate some current state of one's own that is deserving of expression (the sorry state) with some state previously observed by another. To the degree that a speaker elects to make that equation (an equation, that is, between a current and past state)—she specifies the meaning of sorry for that individual. By social convention, certain behaviors that are different from those that occurred before the expression of the state of "sorry," may be required, before the acceptance of the expression of such a state as "sorry" is granted as valid by the recipient. The assumption is that because the execution of behaviors after uttering "sorry" differs from the behaviors emitted before, the change in behavior has been effected by some intervening mental state, expressed as "sorrow." The fact that we can never know that state on the part of another does not prevent us from learning when to use words like "sorry." We learn to utter them when we have behaved in a manner that is objected to by others. Saying "I am sorry" tends to reduce the likelihood that we will be the recipient of undesirable actions on the part of someone else, though this may not be our only goal in regretting our past actions.

Language, being what it is, can permit us to ask questions such as "Was he *really* sorry?" "Am I truly sorry?" "Why am I sorry?" Questions regarding the "real" mental state of self and others form the substance of clinical psychology. The difficulty with them is that such questions have "face validity." That is to say, given our understanding of words and grammar, such questions appear to us to be valid constructions, and if they are linguistically valid we often feel compelled to respond to them. Yet, except in a case where someone is intentionally misrepresenting the state of being sorry, there is clearly no more adequate means of determining if someone is "really sorry" than there is of determining whether they are "simply saying they are sorry."

Nonetheless, the fact that we can linguistically construct and contrast a state like "really sorry" with one like "just saying you're sorry" causes us to search for some means of verifying the one state as being different from the other. This state of affairs also has the unintended effect of implying that the state of being just "sorry" is not a "true" state. When the question is applied to one's self—that is, when one asks oneself "Am I truly sorry, or did I just think I was sorry"—the problem becomes multiplied and can extend one into the realm of inaction, since it can cause one to conclude that one is no longer able to monitor or evaluate one's own "mental state." Just as one can never experience the mental state of another, and thus can never know in a direct sense the state others express as "being sorry," one cannot make a judgement about one's own judgement of the existence of a state. To attempt to repeatedly do so leads one into a realm of self-doubt from which there is no clear return.

So how can an ape learn to be sorry? Certainly, a concept such as sorry entails the assumption that one is somehow aware of one's past actions, the effects of those actions on another, and the current desire to somehow absolve the effect by acting (or speaking) in a manner that brings that awareness to the behavioral foreground where it has implications for future actions. Apes are capable of forming such complex concepts and expressing them to one another through bodily postures and facial expressions. The former view of such expression has been that they are "innate" expressions, elicited by the actions of another, with no real cognizance of the "meaning" that is packed in a similar action or the utterance of a phrase such as "I'm sorry" by a person.

There seems to be some irony in the fact that when we attempt to determine if a person is really sorry, we try to look at her behavior, to see if she acts like she is sorry. If so, we are much more likely to credit her with such an internal state. In contrast, if a bonobo such as Kanzi behaves as though he is sorry, the inclination has been to label such behavior "instinctive." The use of such a label implies that Kanzi is not really aware of his past actions and thus can have no true desire to absolve himself of the effect that those actions entailed. Thus the very behavior that would define the actions of a human being as being "really sorry" (emotional facial expressions and postures) as opposed to simply claiming to be sorry, are, when seen in an ape, categorized as instinctive.

Slowly but surely, it is possible to begin to see that a great problem lies in our misleading use of terms such as "instinctive" and "innate." Whenever this term is applied to a behavior that exists in an ape, we can often find a nearly identical behavior in human beings that is not termed "innate." It is presumed that such actions are not "innate" in humans because they can be linguistically encoded and therefore cannot be simple responses to stimuli at hand. That is, a human can not only act sorry, he can say "I am sorry."

Consequently, there exist two completely different sets of terms for behaviors that are nearly identical in form and function between ourselves and apes. One set of terms (reserved for humans) presumes that awareness and intentionality underlie the behavior and that behavior is taken at face value as a validator of language expressions regarding the behavior. The other set of terms presumes that this not the case and these behaviors cannot be taken as equivalent to communication with awareness.

Yet we see that an ape such as Washoe or Kanzi can easily express a concept such as "I'm sorry" at both the behavioral and linguistic level. Should we then assume that they are aware of what they are doing when they say "I'm sorry" but not aware of what they are doing when they then proceed to act as though they are sorry? This makes little sense. Yet if they are aware of both the intent of the utterance and the intent of the action, and we can use their action to validate their utterance, just as is the case for human beings, what then is the case for apes who did not learn to utter "I'm sorry" but nevertheless express their sorrow by their actions? Must we continue to hold that they are only responding to an innate stimulus? To do so would seem odd, since it was, in part, through hearing his behavior characterized as "Kanzi is sorry" that Kanzi came to learn how it was that we employed the word "sorry." It was he who linked words to his actions and to what he was feeling, but to do so, he had to have experienced some awareness of what those past actions were and the nature of his present feeling. How can it be that it was language that permitted this to happen, since it is required to happen before the word "sorry" can be acquired?

The Achievement of Meaning Unbuttoned: The Emergence of the Social Contract

Certainly there is something extraordinarily incongruous in our rejection of the assignment of "semantic meaning" to the actions of wild apes with our own insistence on the exhibition of similar actions in other humans to verify meaning. We need to set aside this one-sided view of language and look at the behaviors of apes through the same lens through which we view ourselves. Is it possible to do so without committing the sin of "anthropomorphism?" Won't we see human thoughts, feelings, and mental states that are, in fact, not there? Of course we might. Certainly when we view the behaviors of other human beings, we sometimes see thoughts, feelings, and mental states that are not there. We do not always interpret the behaviors of others adequately, and there are vast differences among people in their skills of social interpretation.

We have devised scientific methods that reduce the probability that what is read in the behavior of others is indeed a product of our minds and not theirs. Such techniques include the use of multiple observers, repeated observations, and categorization of behaviors according to functional criteria. Yet even multiple observers and repeated observations cannot assure that what we record is completely free from "observer biasis." No technique is completely value free. The observer always has some effect on the data. But this is true in physics as well as in behavior.

When we adopt the alternative of studying animal behavior as though it cannot contain the same sorts of "mental state" variables as human behavior, we are, in essence, asserting that the very behaviors we depend on to validate our own "mental states" (facial expressions, postures, etc.) cannot possibly be taken as evidence of "mental states" in animals. Any such proposition lacks face validity at best and should require some proof. What evidence is there that an ape who behaves as though she is very sorry is not, in fact, experiencing the mental state of "being sorry"? Since we cannot directly know the mental state of another individual, there can be no such evidence.

It is true that PET scans can now depict a color picture of a "sad" thought, and some take this fact as direct evidence for the existence of the mental state of sadness. But one must recognize that a picture of the state of the brain during what we label "sadness" is no more revealing than a picture of the face during what we label "sadness." Each is a physical manifestation of an experienced state. Neither is uniquely closer to the actual "experience" than the other. The only difference is that others can "read" the face, while they do not normally have access to the brain patterns.

What would our science of animal behavior be like if we were to take the behavior of animals as intentionally communicative? How would it change the way we study them, and what we could we learn about them that we cannot learn otherwise? The first thing such an approach would offer is the seeking of a different sort of criterion for "explaining action." We would quickly find ourselves asking, "Why is it that a certain individual has elected to behave in a particular way?" Saying that it was the result of a "successful evolutionary strategy" would not seem entirely satisfactory, just as it does not seem an entirely satisfactory explanation of human behavior. For example, very different interpretations of bonobo social behavior may emerge from an "evolutionary strategy" explanation versus an "intentional stance" explanation, as follows.

Bonobos travel together from one feeding site to the next as a group. Fruit resources are generally scarce and widely dispersed. It is not possible to go on a random walk through the forest and find enough ripe food for a group of bonobos. They must have an extensive knowledge of the forest and its fruiting patterns. Once a decision is made to leave one fruiting resource and to travel to another, the entire group walks on the ground until they reach the new resource. If their judgment is bad and they have arrived before the fruit is ripe, they will have wasted much energy and may be far from another potential resource, as they often must travel for as long as two to three hours between fruiting areas. Bonobos rarely travel alone, and given the predators in their habitat, it is not likley that a single bonobo would long survive.

According to the conventional wisdom, bonobos are noted for having a social structure very unusual among apes. They are said to be the only ape species in which females are clearly dominant over males (Kano 1992). In fact, in the best-studied population, the dominant animal is said to be a female, who "rules" with the assistance of her son. Sons are said to stay near to their mothers and to support them for life, while daughters move to other groups. Because bonobo females engage in what has been called "G-G rubbing," or bouts of vigorous genito-genital contact, the bonobos are thought to be a rather divergent category of ape in which females have banded together, through sex, to wrest political control of the group from males (Wrangham in press). Evidence for the conclusion that females are indeed dominant over males is collected on the basis of determining who displaces whom at feeding sites and who it is that is first permitted to take sugar cane at feeding sites.

By asking questions such as "Who is the first individual to take sugar cane" and by pairing this information with the assumption that all individuals want sugar cane badly and that the animal who takes sugar cane first is politically the most powerful animal in the group, one arrives at a characterization of social structure such as that as just described. However, it is clear that if we were watching human beings enter a cafeteria, we could conclude very little regarding the structure of human groups by looking at who was the first one to take the food. There are all sorts of "social niceties" about offering food to others first. Any means of data collection that focused on "what happened" rather than "why it happened," from the perspective of the party who is producing the action, would come up with an inappropriate snapshot of human behavior.

So what if, instead of assuming that dominant animals will feed first, we were to ask questions like: Does a male move away when a female approaches? If so, does she do anything to scare him away? Does he want to eat sugar cane? Does she tell him that he cannot do so? Do males ever ask permission of females to take some sugar cane? Why do males stay with females and constantly display close and affectionate bonds if females displace them from food resources? Since bonobo males are larger than females, why do they permit females to be dominant? If G-G rubbing is used to establish female alliances that lead to female dominance, why don't males use homosexual behavior to a similar end to ensure male dominance? Male-male copulation without intromission occurs regularly; thus, it would seem that the males have a behavior pattern that ought to link them together just as do the females.

Questions about why something works one way and not another are rarely addressed by evolutionary biologists. Their goal is to determine why nature arranged things as she did, not why she could not have just as easily managed to arrange them in quite a different fashion. Whenever it is credible to state that a given behavior may increase "reproductive fitness," it is assumed that the behavior has been sufficiently explained. Such accounts of behavior stress that the unit of selection is the individual, and that each individual attempts, by maximizing his or her own fitness, to leave the maximum number of offspring. Because individuals are related and share a genetic heritage, assisting one's kin also increases an individual's inclusive fitness and thus an individual may in some cases benefit by ensuring the survival of his or her siblings. However, the idea that an individual may evolve strategies that act in the interests of his group is generally discredited on the basis of the fact that it is individuals, rather than groups, that reproduce. Thus, each indivdual is seen as existing in a state of rather constant competition with other group members. Mates, food, and other resources are viewed as contested items. Given this perspective, it seemed reasonable to assume that any individual in a bonobo group would attempt to gain preferential acess to a food resource if possible.

We might explain much of human behavior in the same manner, and some have tried. However, we also know that there are many solutions to the question of how to construct a society that is capable of producing and rearing babies. There are also many ways to describe the roles of given individuals within a society and many ways to determine who is "dominant." However, if you were to question most human beings about why they behaved in a particular manner on a particular occasion, their answer probably would have little to do with leaving the maximum number of offspring. It is also likely that they would not equate dominance with their ability to leave behind the maximum number of offspring.

Of course, evolutionary theory tells us that we do not have to understand the driving forces behind our actions in order to behave in a manner that is consistent with these forces. Such, we are often told, is the difference between distal and proximal causation. There need be no relationship between why a person thinks that he is engaging in a particular action and why he is "really" engaging in it. Of course, such an argument can be shown to have "face validity," in the sense that people often offer explanations of their own behavior that seem inconsistent at best. Thus, we accept the fact that it is legitimate to discount these explanations in our search for deeper and grander explanations, ones that are said to be based on a true understanding of the underlying variables, rather than those that "appear" to control a person's actions.

The trouble with accounts that emphasize the distinction between distal and proximal causes of behavior is that these two kinds of causes must, at some point, overlap. If not, then the distal causes cannot be said to actually operate. Distal and proximal causes may look very different because they operate on different time scales, one across generations and the other within a given life span. Still, since proximal decisions lead to the distal outcomes, there is no other option; so at some point proximal causes must act in a manner that permits the distal "effects" to manifest themselves. Thus, whatever an organism's proximal reason for behaving in a certain manner may be, that reason must produce the same outcome as would occur if distal causes were driving the behavior. For this reason the proximal causes are critical, and it becomes important to determine, from the perspective of the organism making proximal decisions, why those decision are made as they are.

To return to the example of the bonobos—why do females displace males at sugar cane feeding sites? If females are always the first to eat, what other explanation could there be? On what basis can we assume that the males would prefer to be the first to eat the sugar cane and that they would do so if they were not prevented by the females? Are there other behaviors exhibited by males that suggest that they are submissive to females? Do males keep their eye on the sugar cane while the females are eating? Do they ever start to eat but move away if a female comes over to them? Do they ever try to challenge younger females? Do they scream or appear to show some other sort of consternation if a female approaches while they are eating sugar cane?

Strangely enough, the answer to all of these questions appears to be no. By observing videotaped examples of what has been termed female displacement of males during sugar cane provisioning, the perspective of the male can be addressed more definitively. We do not have to limit ourselves to the simple fact that females take the sugar cane first. We can ask *how* they do this and *how* the males react to it.

During a typical provisioning session, the sugar cane is cut and laid out in sticks by trackers. Once the bonobos have arrived at the feeding site, they can observe the reprovisioning process while remaining from five to ten feet back as the trackers chop up and lay out the sugar cane. As soon as the trackers are done, the female bonobos rush in and begin gathering as many sticks as they can hold and carry away. When the females have all they can carry, they rush to the perimeter of the feeding area, or into the forest to consume the sugar cane at their leisure. The males may follow the females into the center within a few minutes, or they may wait and go in after the females have retreated to the periphery.

Analysis of thirty-one cases of filmed sugar cane provisioning indicated that females took sugar cane and left before males entered the provisioning area in 10 instances. In all remaining cases, females entered first and began taking sugar cane, but males entered shortly thereafter and took sugar cane side by side with the females. When females and males took sugar cane side by side, females did not threaten or displace males. Aggressive actions by males toward females was equally rare. In only two instances did an adult male charge an adult female. These two instances occurred after the females themselves engaged in a fight on entering the provisioning area, and the charges appeared to be designed to mildly discipline the females.

During the filmed bouts, there were as many as six adult females and their offspring and four adult males in the center of the clearing at once. All ten individuals picked up sugar cane sticks and tucked them under their arms as rapidly as possible. Since the sugar cane was left in an area of about fifteen square feet, all ten indivduals were close together and rushed about rapidly to grab as many choice sticks as they could. Not once was a conflict observed over who could take specific pieces of sugar cane. Their behavior was very well coordinated so that they almost never started to grab the same piece. Even when they did, one of the them simply let the other have it and grabbed a nearby piece without contest.

The only observed dominance contests were those which ocurred between females prior to entering the feeding area, or immediately after entering. Females and associated offspring always entered first, and there appeared to be some order regarding which female was permitted to be in the front of the group of females. Males entered later, with no obvious order among them. Males generally entered slowly, while the females raced in. Older juvenile and adolescent males always entered last and often not at all.

The males monitored the perimeter carefully while the females were busy taking sugar cane from the center of the site. If a human started to approach the site, males often displayed in his direction, apparently to keep him from getting too close to the females. On two occasions, males made clear hand gestures to the females waiting at the periphery of the clearing; the gestures seemed to signal that it was time for the females to enter. In response to these gestures, the females at once rushed to the center and began picking up sugar cane.

Males occasionally displayed toward females at the feeding site by dragging branches toward them and sometimes by flailing branches at them. However, these displays occurred after the sugar cane had been obtained. Such branch-dragging displays never caused females to run away or to stop eating their sugar cane. Generally females leaned over or moved a few feet away from a displaying male; most often they completely ignored him. The displays toward females seemed designed to get attention and were sometimes followed by copulation and sometimes followed by moving off into the forest after a male dragged branches into the forest. The only male branch-dragging display directed toward females during the procuring of sugar cane occurred after a dispute had erupted between females about the order of female entrance into the center clearing.

Oftentimes, prior to the approach of the females, the males would charge through the center of the clearing dragging large branches, particularly as the trackers who had chopped up the sugar cane began to move away. Vigorous branch-dragging by the males toward the trackers appeared to occur when the trackers were nearly finished cutting up sugar cane, as well as when all the sugar cane had been consumed and the trackers were nearby with additional sugar cane not yet chopped.

Thus it could be seen that it was possible for males to display at females in the feeding area; however, never when they did so did they then appear to be contesting acess to sugar cane. Instead, they focused their attention on the periphery of the feeding site, the trackers, or the forest beyond the feeding site. Sometimes they even repeatedly dragged branches to the edge of the feeding site and beyond into the forest. In such instances, all of which occurred after much sugar cane had been consumed, the male appeared to be attempting to get the females to travel to another location that lay in the direction that they had dragged their branches.

From these observations we can conclude that if females do indeed displace males, it must be on the basis of a prior understanding, that females *always* get to take sugar cane first if they so desire. It is *not* the case that males can be observed attempting to take sugar cane and are prevented from doing so by the females during provisioning. The second thing that we can conclude is that no male seems timid or hesitant around the females. Adult males do not flee when females approach, nor do they ever try to steal food at the sugar cane site when females are not looking. In short, males do not behave around females as though they are in submission and/or fearful.

Could these behavioral patterns simply reflect the "nature" of the bonobo male? This seems not to be the case, since adolescent males do behave in a submissive manner; they show overt deference to adult males. Adolescent males also tried to steal pieces of sugar cane when either females or males were not looking—something adult males never did. Moreover, adult males quickly and firmly disciplined adolescent males who tried to take sugar cane before the females had had their share. Such disciplinary action by adult males occured during one-third of the observed bouts. Thus, we are left with the puzzling observation that, in a society that is supposed to be dominated by females, males never appear to be frightened by females and, in addition, they act toward younger males in a manner which enforces the rule that females are the first to enter feeding sites.

Why should bonobo males discipline adolescent males who attempt to take food before the females had eaten? Is it possible that bonobos have a social rule about when the sexes eat? Could this be why females are never observed to threaten or remind males to stay away from the food? Could this be why males are never observed to steal food when females are not looking? Certainly, if there is a rule about when the sexes eat, it would be expected that more is going on than simply a female grabbing all the food for herself. If there is a rule regarding the order of eating, it should be the case that both sexes are aware of the rule, that both agree to it and abide by it, and that it is beneficial to both in some manner. One would also predict that if there is such a rule, then we should find that females, who are to eat first, leave some food for males, rather than take it all. If this were not the case, the rule would break down. Males would not follow the rule if they could not be assured of having food by waiting until the females had finished.

Of course, to propose that a nonhuman primate has a social rule is to raise many questions. How does such a rule arise, and how does it get communicated among the group? Do older individuals teach younger individuals the rule, as when the adult males disciplined the adolescent males for taking food before the females had eaten? And how can there be a rule without a language—without the rule ever being verbalized, how can it arise? And if there is a rule that is understood by all group members, how are transgressions of the rule handled? Can any member of the group punish any other member of the group for violating the rule, or does this task fall only to certain group members, and if so, how would such members know that this was their role? If not, what would stop the entire group from mobbing any individual who broke a rule? And how much punishment should an individual receive for breaking a rule? Should it fit the crime, so to speak—in degree, if not in kind?

In one case, when an older juvenile male tried to take food before the females had eaten, he was punished by a single adult male who proceeded to sit on him for several minutes before letting him up. Afterward the young male made profuse apologetic gestures, which were ignored by the adult male. The young male not only made these apologetic gestures toward the adult male, but toward other group members as well. It is noteworthy that the punished juvenile male was *not* trying to steal food from the adult male who punished him, but was only trying to enter the feeding area before the other males had begun to do so themselves.

It is equally intriguing that the young male apologized for his indiscretions to members of the group other than the male who had punished him. Why would a young male have been punished by an adult male when he was not trying to take food from that male? Why would the young male have made appeasing gestures to many other group members after having been punished for this action? Such actions make sense only in the context of the operation of social rules or principles. They do not make sense from a simple perspective of "dominance relations."

The analysis of the filmed provisioning bouts provided evidence supporting the existence of a societal rule that specifies when the sexes feed. Moreover, these observations suggested that all individuals in the social group were aware of this rule, and that they sought to behave in a manner that supported the rule and made over-enforcement a relatively infrequent event. Rather than being intimidated and/

or displaced by females, it appeared that the males were actually clearing the feeding site of people and making certain that it was safe for the females to enter. They were then monitoring the perimeter of the cleared feeding site while the females obtained their share of the food and carried it away. The males then helped themselves to the food that was always left behind.

Why should males cooperate to the benefit of females? Why should they behave in a manner that ensures that key group members have the greatest access to food? Rarely are bonobos found apart from their group; to be a bonobo is to exist within a group of bonobos. Consequently, behaviors that benefit the individual, at the expense of others in the group, decrease the integrity of the group and eventually put the survival of the individual at risk. Given the inevitable tension between the need to cooperate with other group members and the need to achieve access to resources for oneself, the emergence of social rules would seem to be an optimal solution. Social rules enable each individual to behave in tense social situations according to norms. As long as the norms that evolve ensure that each individual has access to prized resources in a manner that manages to preserve the integrity of the group, it is to an individual's advantage to learn and follow those social norms. Thus, in the bonobo, we apparently find rules about who enters feeding areas and when. We see rules about the roles of males and females during feeding. We see these rules being tested by adolescents and juveniles but not by adults. We find that these rules have specific requirements not about individual pieces of food but rather about the circumstances under which individuals are granted access to food resources.

Which interpretation of the behavior of male bonobos is accurate? Are they submissive to females, who have evolved a stategy of co-opting sexual behavior to give them dominance over males in the eternal battle of the sexes? Or are males cooperating to make certain that the most vulnerable and reproductively important members of the group (females and their young offspring) get priority access to food under protected conditions? Certainly more observations are warranted. What is important here is to recall that an alternative interpretation of behavior came about because of the raising of questions about "intentions." There was no evidence that females intended to keep males from taking sugar cane. There was evidence that the actual taking of sugar cane is a very coordinated affair, which may be guided by social norms agreed to by all parties.

The New Lens: Moving beyond Speciesism

This example serves to illustrate how a radically different level of complexity can emerge from studies of behavior if a few simple assumptions are made regarding the reasons for individual actions. When one determines, a priori, that all individual actions in animals are programmed by the ultimate distal cause of "leaving more offspring," all behavior is then forced through the narrow lens of the "individual reproductive competition hypothesis," and the acts of each individual are seen as being only in the service of its own immediate procreative interest. Each individual is viewed as a selfish creature or at best a creature whose only drive is to protect itself and closely related kin. Looking through this lens, one cannot conceive of questions regarding the kinds of social rules that might guide the behavior of groups.

Which account is closer to the truth, and how can we be certain? Of course, we can never enter the mind of an ape and ascertain whether apes have social rules that operate in the way that they appear to us to do. However, we also cannot enter the mind of a human being to ascertain that he or she perceives the rules of society in the same way that we do. The most we can do is to ask them—and to that end we must use language. Language itself provides us with an answer that can be seen as coming through a prism. For language usage—what you say, to whom you say it, and how you put it—are all facets of behavior that are themselves the function of social rules.

Language is a funny thing. We do not think of it as behavior, yet at heart that is all it really is—another form of behavior; a form that we use to characterize other parts of behavior, but a form that cannot be divorced from the rest of behavior.

Concepts that take on the garb of language seem to acquire a life of their own; thus we talk about ideas, we talk about concepts, we talk about trust, we talk about perception, we talk about learning, we talk about memory, we talk about declarative memory, we talk about procedural memory, and we talk about social rules, among many other things. But we often forget that these things are "talk." We forget that it is *we* who have labeled some behaviors memory, others learning, and others perception. We perceive some patterns of behavior that we can characterize as having common elements, and we give those patterns a name. Just as we call a boat the *Annabel Lee*, we call some patterns of behavior by a name (autism, procedural memory, etc.). We come to believe then that because these patterns have a name, they are more than behaviors. We often conclude they represent actual physical brain structures. Without these structures, we assume, we would be unable to generate the patterns of action to which we have assigned labels. Thus, if one lacked a Brocca's area, it was said, one would be incapable of articulate speech. It was then found that even children who lacked the complete left hemisphere could produce normal language. Such findings reveal that the structure we perceive in language cannot be located in the brain. It exists in the patterning of behavior, because we need it. We generate these structural speech patterns just as bonobos generate social rules or expected patterns of group behavior. There is nothing special about language, other than what it makes of itself.

Language is a funny thing. It permits us to think that we know things that indeed we do not know. It permits us to talk about things rather than to do them and to think we have actually done something by talking rather than by acting. It permits us to think that by talking in unison, we can come to act in unison—forgetting that the more feeble the link between word and deed the less likely words are to alter deeds. Should we wish to act in unison, it is far better that we sing than that we speak.

Language is a funny thing. It permits us to think that other species are not able to communicate the purposes or intentions of their actions to one another, nor to coordinate their behaviors, nor to plan their actions. It permits us to think this because it permits us to avoid hearing the kind of talking that other species are doing.

Language is a funny thing. It enables man to put himself above the "beasts" simply by the act of saying to himself, "God gave man dominion over all the creatures that walk the land and all the fish that swim in the sea."

What if we never said that to ourselves?

Notes

Chapter 1

1. Even the speech stream is perceived as whole because of the manner in which the mind elects to organize the waved input of sound. If a phonetician produces a spectrogram of a spoken utterance and separates it into the portions that correspond to consonants and vowels and then plays it back, no consonants can be heard, only clicks and hisses. We hear consonants in speech only because we are listening for the transition between the click and the frequency pattern of the vowel. This transition, in fact, exists not as a distinct measurable physical entity but only as a perceptual entity. Furthermore, the nature of the transition, as heard, is dependent on the information present, not just in the word, but in the entire sentence and in the situational context. Thus, if we are presented with a sentence such as "The—ares are about to foal," we hear the word "mares." But if we are presented with "The bartlett—ares are about to fall," we hear the word "pears." We construct the missing consonant without ever realizing that it was absent; and this construction is based on information that is not directly present in the sound input itself.

Chapter 2

1. The idea that the human body is a machine was itself revolutionary and was to have a large impact on the birth of the life sciences (see Shanker 1997a).

2. One finds yet another response—which Boas dubbed "theriophily"—in such works as the Earl of Rochester's "Satyr Against Mankind" or Swift's "The Beasts' Confession". This view is that, not only are animals intelligent: they are morally superior to man.

3. The *philosophes* laid great emphasis on the fact that apes have faces, arms, legs, and hands; that they walk almost upright; that they use sticks as weapons or as means to reaching objects; and that they love warmth and company (Hastings 1936, 111). All of these were seen as reasons for treating apes as a primitive species of man.

4. The discovery of beaver "societies" in North America had a dramatic effect on eighteenth-century attitudes toward animal cognition and communication. It was widely assumed that the formation of society was essential to the creation of language insofar as this resulted in the formation of more complex ideas, which demanded ever more complex means of communication, and which in turn would result in the creation of still more complex ideas (see Juliard 1970). Recall the famous quotation from *Leviathan* that in a state of nature there would be "No arts; no letters; no society; and which is worst of all, continual fear and danger of violent death; and the life of man, solitary, poor, nasty, brut-

ish, and short" (Hobbes 1651: I, 13). That is, without society man would sink to the level of the brutes: not simply because anarchy would reign, but because the formation of society is essential for the creation of language, and all the comforts which this affords.

5. The term "anthropomorphism" was originally coined to describe the attribution of human qualities or form to God. From around the middle of the nineteenth century it began to acquire its modern connotation, which, as Pamela Asquith defines it in Harré and Lamb's *Dictionary of Ethology and Animal Learning*, is "[t]he attribution to an animal of psychical capabilities like those of men and the supposition that it acts from similar motives. . . . It is generally thought to be erroenous and unscientific (i.e., anthropomorphic) to attribute human mental experiences to animals" (Asquith 1986: 8).

6. Compare Descartes's remark in his letter to More: "I am not disturbed by the astuteness and cunning of dogs and foxes, or all the things which animals do for the sake of food, sex, and fear; I claim that I can easily explain the origin of all of them from the constitution of their organs" (Descartes 1970: 243).

7. Compare Rousseau: "If men needed speech in order to learn to think, they needed still more to know how to think in order to discover the art of speech" (Rousseau 1755: 93).

8. Oxytocin, the so-called cuddle chemical, is stimulated in a nursing mother by the sound of a crying baby, or by the very act of nursing. The hormone is intimately connected with feelings of sexual arousal and pleasure. Phenylethylamine is an aphetamine-like chemical that is released by sexual attraction, which causes the neuropeptides to be transmitted at a much higher rate.

9. Although, interestingly enough, few seem able to describe the bonding experience.

10. That is, "In no case may we interpret an action as the outcome of a higher psychical faculty, if it can be interpreted as the outcome of one which stands lower in the psychological scale."

11. Innate releasing mechanisms are species-specific neurophysiological mechanisms corresponding to different behaviour patterns. There is an obvious and important parallel between IRMs and Turing Machine state-configurations. Both are said to mediate between stimulus and response; both to exclude cognition.

12. But even this way of presenting the issue is puzzling. Afer all, why does the adjective "human" occur at all in the definition of "anthropomorphism"? Why don't we simply speak of "the illicit attribution of mental experiences (or cognitive and linguistic abilities) to animals"?

13. *Language Comprehension in Ape and Child* documents Kanzi's comprehension skills under controlled conditions where (a) he could not see the experimenter at all, (b) where there was an array of objects and even duplicate objects differentially placed by location, and (c) where Kanzi was asked to do several different things with the items of each array, so that it could not be argued that he just did the obvious thing on each trial with new arrays of objects. Over 400 sentences were presented, and it was established that a two-and-a-half-year-old human child's performance was no better, and generally a little worse than Kanzi's. Kanzi's production skills, on the other hand, were more at the level of the one to one-and-a-half-year-old human child's level (see Savage-Rumbaugh et al. 1993).

14. Perhaps the most evocative displays of Kanzi's linguistic abilities are the ordinary routines that can be seen in the video *Kanzi: An Ape of Genius* for example, the scene in which one of the psychologists working at the LRC speaks to Kanzi on the telephone and promises to bring him a surprise when she comes to visit, and when Kanzi later sees her he immediately goes to the lexigram board and asks for his surprise. Or the scenes in which Kanzi is in the kitchen helping Savage-Rumbaugh prepare dinner, or in the woods

helping Savage-Rumbaugh on a cookout. In these scenes the verbal exchanges are an essential part of the activity in which Kanzi and Savage-Rumbaugh are engaged. The things that Savage-Rumbaugh asks him to do (e.g., "fill the pot with water," "turn off the tap," "get some sticks for the fire," "break this stick for me please") are *meaningful* in the context of this activity. This is an important point: something that those who insist that Kanzi should be exposed to arcane syntactic constructions designed to test his knowledge of 'subjectivity' or the binding principle tend to lose sight of. For, as Savage-Rumbaugh says at the beginning of *Language Comprehension in Ape and Child*: "The early emergence of complex language understanding is a phenomenon that is tightly linked to contextually specific real-world knowledge" (Savage-Rumbaugh et al., 1993: 1). When Kanzi is presented with meaningless constructions, that is "meaningless" in terms of the type of day-to-day activities in which he engages, he is indeed confused—as would be any young child if presented with the same anomalous constructions. Conversely, one must not be over-hasty in assuming that Kanzi has misundertood a request; sometimes his responses can make perfectly good sense, but are not in the least what was expected from him.

15. For example, Savage-Rumbaugh tells us in the opening chapter of the occasion when Kanzi said "kiwi ball," and then, when they arrived at Lookout, and after Kanzi had gone to the cooler where the kiwis were kept, he disappeared and reappeared shortly with his ball, which he had hidden in the bushes on the previous day.

16. This remarkable sequence can be seen on the NHK video *Kanzi: An Ape of Genius*.

17. Some psychoanalysts even claim that patients use gestures to communicate their thoughts before going on to do so verbally.

18. To be sure, there are signs of a species difference here, but they are more subtle than one might expect. For although Panzee does not understand sentences nearly as well as Panbanisha, and the words she uses are much more concrete, she outpaced Panbanisha in tool use, object manipulation, puzzles, and mazes.

Chapter 4

1. Related to this point is the fact that the female human pelvis opens further, and its roundedness permits the carrying of heavy offspring without falling over. The opening of the pubic area is also larger, which permits a larger head to pass through. The brain of the human infant is much larger relative to the size of the pubic opening than that of any other primate, making birth a more dangerous and difficult affair for humans than for other primates. Furthermore, the skull of the human infant closes much later, leaving the infant more vulnerable to injury for a longer period of time than is the case for other primate infants. All this suggests that if we did not possess the foresight and ability to take care of such "inadequate" babies with large soft heads and floppy necks, our species would not survive. This helplessness leads to a long dependency, during which there is time for observational learning, before the infant is skilled enough to begin to act on its own.

2. Indeed, it is because of this seeming paradox that some linguists are drawn to arguing that there *must* have been some catastrophe forty thousand years ago that, for reasons we shall never understand, resulted in a "monster mutation" from which emerged the mind of *Homo sapiens sapiens,* which was categorically different from any of the hominid minds that had preceded it (see Bickerton 1990).

3. The recent discovery of grinding stones in Australia suggests that we may have to push this figure back to thirty thousand years.

References

Aitcheson, Jean, and David Crystal. 1992. Language. In *The Oxford Companion to the English Language*, edited by Tom McArthur. Oxford: Oxford University Press.

Argyle, Michael. 1988. *Bodily Communication*. 2d ed. London: Routledge.

Asquith, Pamela J. 1986. Anthropomorphism. In *The Dictionary of Ethology and Animal Learning*, edited by Rom Harré and Roger Lamb. Cambridge: MIT Press.

Astington, Janet Wilde. 1993. *The Child's Discovery of the Mind*. Cambridge: Harvard University Press.

Bennett, J. 1991. How is cognitive ethology possible? In *Cognitive Ethology: The Minds of Other Animals*, *Essays in Honor of D. R. Griffin*, edited by C. A. Ristau. Hillsdale, N.J.: Lawrence Erlbaum.

Bickerton, D. 1984. The language bioprogram hypothesis. *Behavioral and Brain Sciences* 7: 173–221.

———. 1990. *Language and Species*. Chicago: University of Chicago Press.

Boesch, C., and H. Boesch. 1983. Sex differences in the use of natural hammers by wild chimpanzee: A preliminary report. *Journal of Human Evolution* 10: 585–93.

Bramblett, C. A. 1985. *Patterns of Primate Behavior*. Prospect Heights, Ill.: Waveland Press.

Brooks, L. R., and J. R. Vokey. 1991. Abstract analogies and abstracted grammars: Comments on Reber (1989) and Mathews et al. (1989). *Journal of Experimental Psychology: General* 120: 278–87.

Bruner, Jerome. 1983. *Child's Talk*. Oxford: Oxford University Press.

———. 1990 *Acts of Meaning*. Cambridge: Harvard University Press.

Button, Graham, Jeff Coulter, John R. E. Lee, and Wes Sharrock. 1995. *Computers, Minds and Conduct*. Oxford, England: Polity Press.

Byrne, R. 1995. *The Thinking Ape: Evolutionary Origins of Intelligence*. Oxford: Oxford University Press.

Byrne, R., and A. Whiten. 1990. Tactical Deception in Primates: The 1990 database. *Primate Report* 27: 1–101.

Canfield, John V. 1993. The Living Language: Wittgenstein and the empirical study of communication. *Language Sciences* 15, no. 1: 1–29.

———. 1995. The Rudiments of language. *Language & Communication* 15: 195–211.

Cheney, Dorothy L., and Robert M. Seyfarth. 1990. *How Monkeys See the World*. Chicago: University of Chicago Press.

Chevalier-Skolnikoff, S. and F. E. Poirier (ed.). 1977. *Primate Bio-Social Development: Biological, Social and Ecological Determinants*. New York, N.Y.: Garland Publishers.

Chomsky, Noam. 1980. *Rules and Representations*. New York: Columbia University Press.

———. 1957. *Syntactic Structures*. The Hague: Mouton.

Churchland, P. S. 1986. *Neurophilosophy: Toward a Unified Science of the Mind/Brain*. Cambridge: MIT Press.

Clarke-Stewart, K. 1989. Infant day care, maligned or malignant? *American Psychologist* 44: 266–273.

Condillac. 1798. *Oeuvres philosophiques de Condillac*. Edited by Georges le Roy. Paris: Presses Universitaires de France, 1947.

Cottingham, J., R. Stoothoff, and D. Murdoch, trans. 1986. *The Philosophical Writings of Descartes*. Vols. 1 and 2. Cambridge: Cambridge University Press.

Coulter, Jeff. 1989. *Mind in Action*. Oxford, England: Polity Press.

Crelin, E. S. 1987. *The Human Vocal Tract: Anatomy, Function, Development, and Evolution*. New York: Vantage Press.

Dennett, D. 1983. Intentional systems in cognitive ethology: The "Panglossian paradigm" defended. *Behavioral and Brain Sciences* 6: 343–90.

Descartes, R. 1637. Discourse on the Method. In *The Philosophical Writings of Descartes*, translated by J. Cottingham, R. Stoothoff, and D. Murdoch. Vol. 1. Cambridge: Cambridge University Press, 1986.

———. 1641. Meditations on First Philosophy. In *The Philosophical Writings of Descartes*, translated by J. Cottingham, R. Stoothoff, and D. Murdoch. Vol. 2. Cambridge: Cambridge University Press, 1986.

———. 1649. The Passions of the Soul. In *The Philosophical Writings of Descartes*, translated by J. Cottingham, R. Stoothoff, and D. Murdoch. Vol. 1. Cambridge: Cambridge University Press, 1986.

———. 1970. *Descartes: Philosophical Letters*. Translated by A. Kenny. Oxford: Clarendon Press.

Diamond, Cora. 1991. Eating meat and eating people. In *The Realistic Spirit: Wittgenstein, Philosophy, and the Mind*. Cambridge: MIT Press.

Dunn, Judy. 1991. Young children's understanding of other people: Evidence from observations within the family. In *Children's Theories of Mind*, edited by D. Frye and C. Moore. Hillsdale, N.J.: Lawrence Erlbaum.

Evans, E. P. 1906. *The Criminal Prosecution and Punishment of Animals*. London: Heinemann.

Everson, Stephen, ed. 1991. *Psychology*. Cambridge: Cambridge University Press.

Feder, K. L., and M. A. Park. 1989. *Human Antiquity: An introduction to Physical Anthropology and Archaeology*. Mountain View, Calif.: Mayfield.

Flavell, John. 1970. Concept Development. In *Carmichael's Manual of Child Psychology*, ed. P. H. Mussen. Vol. 1. New York: Wiley.

Frye, D., and C. Moore, eds. 1991. *Children's Theories of Mind*. Hillsdale, N.J.: Lawrence Erlbaum.

Gallistel, Charles R. 1990. *The Organization of Learning*. Cambridge: MIT Press.

Gardner, B. T., and Gardner, R. A. 1971. Two-way communication with an infant chimpanzee. In *Behavior of Nonhuman Primates*, edited by A. M. Schrier and F. Stollnitz. Vol. 4. New York: Academic Press.

Gardner, R. A., B. T. Gradner, and T. E. Van Contfort. 1989. *Teaching Sign Language to Chimpanzees*. Albany: State University of New York Press.

Garfinkel, Harold. 1967. *Studies in Ethnomethodology*. Englewood Cliffs, N.J.: Prentice Hall.

George, F. H. 1962. *The Brain as a Computer*. Oxford: Pergamon Press.

Goldfield, E. C. 1995. *Emergent Forms: Origins and Early Development of Human Action and Perception*. New York: Oxford University Press.

Greenfield, P. 1991. Language, tools, and brain: The ontogeny and phylogeny of hierarchically organized sequential behavior. *Behavioral and Brain Sciences* 14: 531–51.

————. Forthcoming. Culture as process: Empirical methodology for cultural psychology. In *Handbook of Cross-Cultural Psychology*, edited by J. W. Berry, Y. Poortinga, and J. Pandey. Vol. 1, *Theory and Method*. Boston: Allyn and Bacon.

Harris, Roy. 1983. Must Monkeys mean? In *The Meaning of Primate Signals*, edited by R. Harré and R. Reynolds. Cambridge: Cambridge Univesity Press.

————. 1990. On redefining linguistics. In *Redefining Linguistics*, edited by Hayley G. Davis and Talbot J. Taylor. London: Routledge.

————. 1995. *Signs of Writing*. London: Routledge.

Harris, Roy, and Talbot J. Taylor. 1989. *Landmarks in Linguistic Thought: The Western Tradition from Socrates to Saussure*. London: Routledge.

Hastings, Hester. 1936. *Man and Beast in French Thought of the Eighteenth Century*. Baltimore: Johns Hopkins University Press.

Heider, F. 1958. *The Psychology of Interpersonal Relations*. Hillsdale, N.J.: Lawrence Erlbaum.

Hinde, R. A. 1983. *Primate Social Relationships: An Integrated Approach*. Sunderland, Mass.: Sinauer.

Hobbes, Thomas. 1651. *Leviathan*. London.

Jones, S., R. Martin, and D. Pilbeam. 1992. *The Cambridge Encyclopedia of Human Evolution*. Cambrige: Cambridge University Press.

Juliard, Pierre. 1970. *Philosophies of Language in Eighteenth-century France*. The Hague: Mouton.

Kano, Takyoshi. 1992. *The Last Ape: Pygmy Chimpanzee Behavior and Ecology*. Stanford, Ca.: Stanford University Press.

King, B. 1994. *The Information Continuum: Evolution of Social Information Transfer in Monkeys, Apes, and Hominids*. Santa Fe: SAR Press.

Klein, R. G. 1989. *The Human Career: Human Biological and Cultural Origins*. Chicago: University of Chicago Press.

Kripke, Saul. 1982. *Wittgenstein on Rules and Private Language*. Oxford: Blackwell.

Kuhl, P. K. 1986. Infants' perception of speech. Precursors of Early Speech: proceedings of an international symposium held at the Wenner-Gren Center, Stockholm, September 19–22, 1984 / edited by Bjèorn Lindblom and Rolf Zetterstrèom. Wenner-Gren International Symposium Series, vol. 44. Southhampton, England: Camelot Press.

Lakoff, G. 1987. *Women, Fire and Dangerous Things: What Categories Reveal about the Mind*. Chicago: University of Chicago Press.

La Mettrie, Julien Offray de. 1748. *Man a Machine*. La Salle, Ill.: Open Court, 1912.

Langer, J. 1986. *The Origins of Logic: One to Two Years*. Orlando, Fl.: Academic Press.

————. 1993. Comparative cognitive development. In *Tools, Language and Cognition in Human Evolution*, edited by K. R. Gibson and T. Ingold. Cambridge: Cambridge University Press.

Leiber, J. 1984. The strange creature. In *The Meaning of Primate Signals*, edited by R. Harré and V. Reynolds. Cambridge: Cambridge University Press.

Liberman, A. M., F. S. Cooper, D. P. Shankweiler, and M. Studdert–Kennedy. 1967. Perception of the speech code. *Psychological Review* 74: 431–61.

Lieberman, P. 1975. *On the origins of language: An introduction to the evolution of speech*. New York: Macmillan.

————. 1984. *The Biology and Evolution of Language*. Cambridge: Harvard University Press.

————. 1991. *The Evolution of Uniquely Human Speech, Thought, and Behavior*. Cambridge: Harvard University Press.

Lock, A. 1980. *The Guided Reinvention of Language*. London: Academic Press.

Locke, John. 1690. *An Essay Concerning Human Understanding*. Edited by John Yolton. London: Dent, 1961.

Loeb, Jacques. 1900. *Comparative Physiology of the Brain and Comparative Psychology*. New York: Putnam.

———. 1912. The Significance of Tropisms for Psychology. In *The Mechanistic Conception of Life*, edited by Donald Fleming. Cambridge, Mass.: Belknap Press.

Malcolm, Norman. 1982. Wittgenstein: The relation of language to instinctive behaviour. *Philosophical Investigations* 5: 3–22.

Marcus, G. F. 1993. Negative evidence in language acquisition. *Cognition* 46: 53–85.

Markman, Ellen M. 1989. *Categorization and Naming in Children*. Cambridge: MIT Press.

McGrew, W. C. 1992. *Chimpanzee Material Culture: Implications for Human Evolution*. Cambridge: Cambridge University Press.

Mervis, C. B. 1987. Child-basic object categories and early lexical development. In *Concepts and conceptual development: Ecological and intellectual factors in categorization*, edited by U. Neisser. Cambridge: Cambridge University Press.

Nelson, K. 1985. *Making Sense: The Acquisition of Shared Meaning*. Orlando, Fl.: Academic Press.

Newmeyer, F. J. 1986. *Linguistic Theory in America*. San Diego: Academic Press.

Nisbett, R. E., and T. D. W. Wilson. 1977. Telling more than we can know: Verbal reports on mental processes. *Psychological Review* 84: 231–59.

Nishida, T., W. C. McGrew, P. Marler, M. Pickford, and F. de Waal. 1992. *Topics in Primatology. Vol. 1, Human Origins*. Tokyo: University of Tokyo Press.

Olson, D. R. 1994. *The World on Paper: The Conceptual and Cognitive Implications of Writing and Reading*. Cambridge: Cambridge University Press.

Pauly, P. J. 1981. The Loeb-Jennings Debate and the Science of Animal Behavior. *Journal of the History of the Behavioral Sciences* 17: 504–15.

Pavlov, I. P. 1927. *Conditioned Reflexes*. Translated and edited by B. V. Anrep. New York: Dover.

Peters, A. M. 1983. *The Units of Language Acquisition*. Cambridge Monographs and Texts in Applied Psycholinguistics. Cambridge: Cambridge University Press.

Piaget, Jean. 1965. *Insights and Illusions*. Translated by Wolfe Mays. London: Routledge and Kegan Paul.

Piggott, S. 1961. *The Dawn of Civilization*. New York: McGraw-Hill.

Pinker, Steven. 1994. *The Language Instinct*. New York: William Morrow.

Pinker. S. 1984. *Language Learnability and Language Development*. Cambridge: Harvard University Press.

Posner, M. I. 1989. *Foundations of Cognitive Science*. Cambridge: MIT Press.

Premack, D. 1986. *Gavagai!* Cambridge: MIT Press.

———. 1988. "Does the chimpanzee have a theory of mind?" revisited. In *Machiavellian Intelligence*, edited by R. Byrne and A. Whiten. Oxford: Oxford University Press.

Premack, D., and G. Woodruff. 1978. Does the chimpanzee have a theory of mind? *Behavioral and Brain Sciences* 4: 515–26.

Purves, P. D. 1994. *Neural Activity and the Growth of the Brain*. Cambridge: Cambridge University Press.

Quine, Willard Van Orman. 1960. *Word and Object*. Cambridge: MIT Press.

———. 1973. *The Roots of Reference*. La Salle, Ill.: Open Court.

Reber, A. S. 1989. Implicit learning and tacit knowledge. *Journal of Experimental Psycholgy: General* 118: 219–35.

Reynolds, V., and J. Reynolds. 1995. Riding on the backs of apes. In *Ape, Man, Apeman: Changing Views since 1600*, edited by R. Corbey and B. Theunissen. Leiden, Netherlands: Dept. of Prehistory.

Rosch, E. 1973. Natural categories. *Cognitive Psychology* 4: 328–50.

Rousseau, Jean Jacques. 1755. *The First and Second Discourses*. Translated by Roger D. and Judith R. Masters. New York: St. Martin's Press, 1964.

Saussure, F. de. 1916. *Cours de linguistique générale*. English translation by R. Harris. London: Duckworth, 1983.

Savage-Rumbaugh, E. S. 1984. Acquisition of functional symbol use in apes and children. In *Animal Congition*, edited by H. L. Roitblat, T. G. Bever, and H.S. Terrace. Hillsdale, N.J.: Erlbaum.

———. 1986. *Ape Language*. New York: Columbia University Press.

———. 1988. A new look at ape language: Comprehension of vocal speech and syntax. In *Comparative Perspectives in Modern Psychology*, edited by D. Leger. Nebraska Symposium on Motivation, vol. 35. Lincoln: University of Nebraska Press.

———. 1990. Language acquisition in a nonhuman species: Implications for the innateness debate. *Developmental Psychobiology* 23: 599–620.

———. 1991. Language learning in the bonobo: How and why they learn. In *Biological and Behavioral Determinants of Language Development*, edited by N. A. Krasnegor, D. M. Rumbaugh, R. L.Schiefelbushc, and M. Studdert–Kennedy. Hilldale N.J.: Erlbaum.

———. 1994. Hominid evolution: Looking to modern apes for clues. In *Hominid Culture in Primate Perspective*, edited by D. Quiatt and J. Itani. Boulder: University Press of Colorado.

Savage-Rumbaugh, E. S., and R. Lewin. 1994. *Kanzi: An Ape at the Brink of Human Mind*. New York: Wiley.

Savage-Rumbaugh, E. S., K. McDonald, R. A. Sevcik, W. D. Hopkins, and E. Rubert. 1986. Spontaneous symbol acquisition and communicative use by pygmy chimpanzees (*Pan paniscus*). *Journal of Experimental Psychology: General* 115: 211–35.

Savage-Rumbaugh, E. S., J. Murphy, R. Sevcik, K. E. Brakke, S. L. Williams, and D. M. Rumbaugh. 1993. Language comprehension in ape and child. *Monographs of the Society for Research in Child Development 58*, nos. 3–4.

Savage-Rumbaugh, E. S., R. Sevcik, D. M. Rumbaugh, and E. Rubert. 1985. The capacity of animals to acquire language: Do species differences have anything to say to us? In *Animal Intelligence: Proceedings of the Royal Society*, edited by L. Weiskrantz. Oxford: Clarendon Press.

Savage-Rumbaugh, E. S., D. M. Rumbaugh, and S. Boysen. 1980. Do apes use language? *American Scientist* 68: 49–61.

———. 1988. A new look at ape language: Comprehension of vocal speech and syntax. In *Comparative Perspectives in Modern Psychology*, edited by D. Leger. Nebraska Symposium on Motivation, vol. 35. Lincoln: University of Nebraska Press.

———. 1991. Language learning in the bonobo: How and why they learn. *In Biological and Behavioral Determinants of Language Development*, edited by In N.A. Krasnegor, D.M. Rumbaugh, R.L. Schiefelbusch, and M. Studdert–Kennedy. Hillsdale, N.J.: Erlbaum.

Savage-Rumbaugh, E. Sue, Jeannine Murphy, Rose A. Sevcik, Karen E. Brakke, Shelly L. Williams, and Duane M. Rumbaugh. 1993. *Language Comprehension in Ape and Child*. Monographs of the Society for Research in Child Development, serial no. 233, vol. 58, nos. 3–4.

Schick, K. D., and N. Toth. 1993. *Making Silent Stones Speak: Human Evolution and the Dawn of Technology*. New York: Simon and Schuster.

Schore, A. N. 1994. *Affect Regulation and Origin of the Self: The Neurobiology of Emotional Development*. Hillsdale, N.J.: Erlbaum.

Schultz, A. H. 1969. *The Life of Primates*. New York: Universe Books.

Sebeok, T. A., and R. Rosenthal. 1981. *The Clever Hans Phenomenon: Communication with Horses, Whales, Apes, and People. Annals of the New York Academy of Sciences* 364. New York, N.Y.

Service, E. R. 1962. *Primitive Social Organization: An Evolutionary Perspective*. New York: Random House.

Shanker, Stuart G. 1991. 'The Enduring Relevance of Wittgenstein's Remarks on Intentions. In *Investigating Psychology*, edited by John Hyman. London, Routledge.

———. 1992. In Search of Bruner. *Language & Communication* 12:

———. 1993. Locating Bruner. *Language & Communication* 13: 239–63.

———. 1995. Turing and the origins of AI: The mechanization of reason. *Philosophica Mathematica*, 3, series 3: 52–85.

———. 1997a. Descartes' legacy: The mechanist/vitalist debates. In *The Philosophy of Science, Logic and Mathematics in the Twentieth Century*. Vol. 9 of *The Routledge History of Philosophy*, edited by G. H. R. Parkinson and S. G. Shanker. London: Routledge.

———. 1997b. Wittgenstein versus Quine on the nature of language and cognition. In *Wittgenstein and Quine*, edited by R. L. Arrington and H. J. Glock. London: Routledge.

———. 1998. *Wittgenstein's Remarks on the Foundations of Artificial Intelligence*. London: Routledge.

Shanks, D. R. 1994. Human associative learning. In *Animal Learning and Cognition*, edited by N. J. Mackintosh. San Diego: Academic Press.

Shatz, Marilyn. 1994. *A Toddler's Life*. Oxford: Oxford University Press.

Shipley, T. 1995. *Intersensory Origin of Mind: A Revisit to Emergent Evolution*. London: Routledge.

Shotter, J. 1990. *Knowing of the Third Kind: Selected Writings on Psychology, Rhetoric, and the Culture of Everyday Social Life, Utrecht 1987–1990*. University of Utrecht.

———. 1993. *Conversational Realities: Constructing Life through Language*. London: Sage Publications.

Smith, Barbara H. 1988. *Contingencies of Value*. Cambridge: Harvard University Press.

Smith, Edward E. 1989. Concepts and Induction. In *Foundations of Cognitive Science*, edited by M. I. Posner. Cambridge: MIT Press.

Sorabji, Richard. 1993. *Animal Minds and Human Morals*. London: Duckworth.

Struhsaker, Thomas. 1967. Auditory communication among vervet monkeys (*Cercopithecus aethiops*). In *Social Communication among Primates*, edited by S. A. Altmann. Chicago: University of Chicago Press.

Taylor, Talbot J. 1984. Linguistic origins: Bruner and Condillac on learning how to talk. *Language & Communication* 4, no. 3: 209–24.

———. 1992. *Mutual Misunderstanding: Scepticism and the Theorizing of Language & Interpretation*. London: Routledge.

———. 1994. The Anthropomorphic and the Sceptical. *Language & Communication* 14: 115–27.

———. 1997. *Theorizing Language: Analysis, Normativity, Rhetoric, History*. Oxford: Pergamon Press.

Terrace, H. S. 1979. *Nim*. New York: Knopf.

————. 1984. Animal Cognition. In *Animal Cognition*, edited by H. L. Roitblat, T. G. Bever, and H. S. Terrace. Hillsdale, N.J.: Erlbaum.

————. 1985. Animal cognition: thinking without language. In *Animal Intelligence: Proceedings of the Royal Society*, edited by L. Weiskrantz. Oxford: Clarendon Press.

————. 1986. Preface to E. S. Savage-Rumbaugh, *Ape Language*. New York: Columbia University Press.

Tomasello, M. 1994. Can an ape understand a sentence? *Language & Communication* 14: 377–90.

Tomasello, M., A. C. Kruger, and H. H. Ratner. 1993. Cultural learning. *Behavioral and Brain Sciences* 16: 495–552.

Turing, Alan. 1950. Computing machinery and intelligence. In *Collected Works*, edited by D. C. Ince. Amsterdam: North-Holland, 1992.

Tuttle, R. H. 1986. *Apes of the World: Their Social Behavior, Communication, Mentality and Ecology*. Park Ridge, N.J.: Noyes Publications.

Vig, N. J., and M. E. Kraft. 1994. *Environmental Policies in the Nineties*. Washington, D.C.: Congressional Quarterly Press.

Vokey, J. R., and L. R. Brooks. 1992. Salience of item knowledge in learning artificial grammer. *Journal of Experimental Psychology: Learning, Memory and Cognition* 18: 328–44.

de Waal, F. 1989. *Chimpanzee Politics: Power and Sex among Apes*. Baltimore: Johns Hopkins University Press.

Waismann, Friedrich. 1965. *Principles of Linguistic Philosophy*. London: Macmillan.

Wallman, J. 1992. *Aping Language*. Cambridge: Cambridge University Press.

Wanner, E., and L. Gleitman. 1982. *Language Acquisition: The State of the Art*. New York: Cambridge University Press.

Wasow, T. 1989. Grammatical theory. In *Foundations of Cognitive Science*, edited by M. L. Posner. Cambridge: MIT Press.

Watson, John. 1907. Review of H. S. Jennings' *The Behaviour of the Lower Organisms*, *Psychological Bulletin* 4: 288–91.

————. 1913. Psychology as the behaviorist views it. *Psychological Review* 20: 158–77.

————. 1925. *Behaviorism*. New York: W. W. Norton Co.

Waxman, Sandra R. 1990. Contemporary approaches to concept development. *Cognitive Development* 6: 105–18.

Wellman, Henry. 1990. *The Child's Theory of Mind*. Cambridge: MIT Press.

Weyer, E., Jr. 1959. *Primitive Peoples Today*. Garden City, N.Y.: Dolphin Books.

Whiten, A., and R. Byrne. 1988. Tactical deception in primates. *Behavioral and Brain Sciences* 11: 233–44.

Wimmer, H., and J. Perner. 1983. Beliefs about beliefs: Representation and constraining function of wrong beliefs in young children's understanding of deception. *Cognition* 13: 103–28.

Wittgenstein, Ludwig. 1953. *Philosophical Investigations*. Translated by G. E. M. Anscombe. 3d ed. Oxford: Basil Blackwell, 1973.

————. 1960. *The Blue and Brown Books*. Oxford: Basil Blackwell.

————. 1980. *Remarks on the Philosophy of Psychology*. Edited by G. E. M. Anscombe and G. H. von Wright and translated by G. E. M. Anscombe. Oxford: Basil Blackwell.

Wrangham, R. W., and D. Peterson. 1997. *Demonic Males: Apes and the Origins of Human Violence*. Boston: Houghton Mifflin.

Wrangham, R. W., W. C. McGrew, F. B. M. de Waal, and P. G. Heltne. 1994. *Chimpanzee Cultures*. Cambridge: Harvard University Press.

Index